GIVE AND TAKE

Adam Grant is the youngest full professor and single highest-rated teacher at The Wharton School. His consulting and speaking clients include Google, the NFL, Goldman Sachs, Merck, Pixar, Facebook, the World Economic Forum, the United Nations, and the U.S. Army and Navy. He has been honored as one of *BusinessWeek*'s favorite professors, one of the world's top forty business professors under forty, and one of Malcolm Gladwell's favorite social science writers. He holds a PhD in organizational psychology from the University of Michigan and a BA from Harvard University, and is a former record-setting advertising director, junior Olympic springboard diver, and professional magician. Visit www.giveandtake.com

organizations to success. I can't think of another book with more powerful implications for both business *and* life."

—**Teresa Amabile**, author of *The Progress Principle*

"Adam Grant has written a landmark book that examines what makes some extraordinarily successful people so great. By introducing us to highly impressive individuals, he proves that, contrary to popular belief, the best way to climb to the top of the ladder is to take others up there with you. *Give and Take* presents the road to success for the twenty-first century."

—**Maria Eitel**, founding CEO and president, the Nike Foundation

"In an era of business literature that drones on with the same-old, over-used platitudes, Adam Grant forges into brilliant new territory. *Give and Take* helps readers understand how to maximize their effectiveness <u>and</u> help others simultaneously. It will serve as a new framework for both insight and achievement. A must read!"

—**Josh Linkner**, founder, ePrize, CEO, Detroit
Venture Partners, and author of *Disciplined Dreaming*

"What *The No *sshole Rule* did for corporate culture, *Give and Take* does for each of us as individuals. Grant presents an evidence-based case for the counterintuitive link between generosity and finishing first."

—**Douglas Stone and Sheila Heen**, coauthors of *Difficult Conversations*

"Adam Grant is a wunderkind. He has won every distinguished research award and teaching award in his field, and his work has changed the way that people see the world. If you want to be surprised—very pleasantly surprised—by what really drives success, then *Give and Take* is for you. If you want to make the world a better place, read this book. If you want to make your life better, read this book."

—**Tal Ben-Shahar**, author of *Happier*

"In one of the most engaging and insightful books I've read in years, Adam Grant makes a persuasive argument for a counterintuitive approach to success. *Give and Take* is an instant classic that should be read by anyone who wants to be more productive—and happier—in the office or at home."
                                                            —**Noah Goldstein**, author of *Yes!*

"*Give and Take* is sensational, with fascinating insights on page after page. I learned much that I intend to incorporate into my life immediately. The lessons will not only make you a better person, they will make you more capable of doing good for many people, including yourself."

                                            —**Rabbi Joseph Telushkin**, author of
                                            Jewish Literacy and *A Code of Jewish Ethics*

"Adam Grant is the first to define what has changed about relationships in a digital age—and he backs it up with empirical evidence. In *Give and Take*, he brilliantly demonstrates that in our deeply interconnected world, the roots of sustainable success lie in creating success for those around you. It's one of those rare books that is both enlightening immensely practical. You'll want to read and revisit it every year."

                                            —**Paul Saffo**, managing director, Foresight and member,
                                            World Economic Forum Council on Strategic Foresight

"Good guys finish first—and Adam Grant knows why. *Give and Take* is the smart surprise you can't afford to miss."

—**Daniel Gilbert**, author of *Stumbling on Happiness*

"*Give and Take* is an enlightening read for leaders who aspire to create meaningful and sustainable changes to their environments. Grant demonstrates how a generous orientation toward others can serve as a formula for producing successful leaders and organizational performance. His writing is as engaging and enjoyable as his style in the classroom."

—**Kenneth Frazier**, chairman, president, and CEO, Merck & Co., Inc.

"In this riveting and sparkling book, Adam Grant turns the conventional wisdom upside down about what it takes to win and get ahead. With page-turning stories and compelling studies, *Give and Take* reveals the surprising forces behind success and the steps we can take to enhance our own."

—**Laszlo Bock**, senior vice president of people operations, Google

"*Give and Take* dispels commonly held beliefs that equate givers with weakness and takers with strength. Grant shows us the importance of nurturing and encouraging prosocial behaviors."

—**Dan Ariely**, author of *Predictably Irrational*

"*Give and Take* defines a road to success marked by new ways of relating to colleagues and customers as well as new ways of growing a business."

—**Tony Hsieh**, CEO, Zappos.com and author of *Delivering Happiness*

"*Give and Take* will fundamentally change the way you think about success. Unfortunately in America, we have too often succumbed to the worldview that if everyone behaved in their own narrow self-interest, all would be fine. Adam Grant shows us with compelling research and fascinating stories there is a better way."

—**Lenny Mendonca**, director, McKinsey & Co.

"Adam Grant, a rising star of positive psychology, seamlessly weaves together science and stories of business success and failure, convincing us that giving is, in the long run, the recipe for success in the corporate world. En route you will find yourself reexamining your own life. Read it yourself, then give copies to the people you care most about in this world."

—**Martin Seligman**, author of *Learned Optimism* and *Flourish*

"*Give and Take* presents a groundbreaking new perspective on success. Adam Grant offers a captivating window into innovative principles that drive effectiveness at every level of an organization and can immediately be put into action. Along with being a fascinating read, this book holds the key to a more satisfied and productive workplace, better customer relationships, and higher profits." —**Chip Conley**, founder, Joie de Vivre Hotels and author of *Peak* and *Emotional Equations*

"*Give and Take* is a game changer. Reading Adam Grant's compelling book will change the way doctors doctor, managers manage, teachers teach, and bosses boss. It will create a society in which people do better by being better. Read the book and change the way you live and work."

—**Barry Schwartz**, author of *The Paradox of Choice* and *Practical Wisdom*

"*Give and Take* is a new behavioral benchmark for doing business for better, providing an inspiring new perspective on how to succeed to the benefit of all. Adam Grant provides great support for the new paradigm of creating a win win for people, planet, and profit with many fabulous insights and wonderful stories to get you fully hooked and infected with wanting to give more and take less."

—**Jochen Zeitz**, former CEO and chairman, PUMA

"*Give and Take* is a real gift. Adam Grant delivers a triple treat: stories as good as a well-written novel, surprising insights drawn from rigorous science, and advice on using those insights to catapult ourselves and our

GIVE AND TAKE

A Revolutionary Approach to Success

Adam Grant

PHOENIX

A PHOENIX PAPERBACK

First published in Great Britain in 2013
by Weidenfeld & Nicolson
This paperback edition published in 2014
by Phoenix,
an imprint of Orion Books Ltd,
Orion House, 5 Upper Saint Martin's Lane
London, WC2H 9EA

An Hachette UK company

1 3 5 7 9 10 8 6 4 2

A CIP catalogue record for this book
is available from the British Library.

ISBN: 978-1-7802-2472-5

Printed and bound by CPI Group (UK) Ltd, Croydon, CR0 4YY

The Orion Publishing Group's policy is to use papers
that are natural, renewable and recyclable and made
from wood grown in sustainable forests. The logging
and manufacturing processes are expected to conform to
environmental regulations of the country of origin.

www.orionbooks.co.uk

In memory of my friend

JEFF ZASLOW

who lived his life as a role model for the principles in this book.

CONTENTS

1
Good Returns

The Dangers and Rewards of Giving More Than You Get

The principle of give and take; that is diplomacy—give one and take ten.
—Mark Twain, author and humorist

On a sunny Saturday afternoon in Silicon Valley, two proud fathers stood on the sidelines of a soccer field. They were watching their young daughters play together, and it was only a matter of time before they struck up a conversation about work. The taller of the two men was Danny Shader, a serial entrepreneur who had spent time at Netscape, Motorola, and Amazon. Intense, dark-haired, and capable of talking about business forever, Shader was in his late thirties by the time he launched his first company, and he liked to call himself the "old man of the Internet." He loved building companies, and he was just getting his fourth start-up off the ground.

Shader had instantly taken a liking to the other father, a man named David Hornik who invests in companies for a living. At 5'4", with dark hair, glasses, and a goatee, Hornik is a man of eclectic interests: he collects *Alice in Wonderland* books, and in college he created his own major in computer music. He went on to earn a master's in criminology and a law degree, and after burning the midnight oil at a law firm, he accepted a job offer to join a venture capital firm, where he spent the next decade listening to pitches from entrepreneurs and deciding whether or not to fund them.

During a break between soccer games, Shader turned to Hornik and said, "I'm working on something—do you want to see a pitch?" Hornik specialized in Internet companies, so he seemed like an ideal investor to Shader. The interest was mutual. Most people who pitch ideas are first-time entrepreneurs, with no track record of success. In contrast, Shader was a blue-chip entrepreneur who had hit the jackpot not once, but twice. In 1999, his first start-up, Accept.com, was acquired by Amazon for $175 million. In 2007, his next company, Good Technology, was acquired by Motorola for $500 million. Given Shader's history, Hornik was eager to hear what he was up to next.

A few days after the soccer game, Shader drove to Hornik's office and pitched his newest idea. Nearly a quarter of Americans have trouble making online purchases because they don't have a bank account or credit card, and Shader was proposing an innovative solution to this problem. Hornik was one of the first venture capitalists to hear the pitch, and right off the bat, he loved it. Within a week, he put Shader in front of his partners and offered him a term sheet: he wanted to fund Shader's company.

Although Hornik had moved fast, Shader was in a strong position. Given Shader's reputation, and the quality of his idea, Hornik knew plenty of investors would be clamoring to work with Shader. "You're rarely the only investor giving an entrepreneur a term sheet," Hornik explains. "You're competing with the best venture capital firms in the country, and trying to convince the entrepreneur to take your money instead of theirs."

The best way for Hornik to land the investment was to set a deadline for Shader to make his decision. If Hornik made a compelling offer with a short fuse, Shader might sign it before he had the chance to pitch to other investors. This is what many venture capitalists do to stack the odds in their favor.

But Hornik didn't give Shader a deadline. In fact, he practically invited Shader to shop his offer around to other investors. Hornik believed that entrepreneurs need time to evaluate their options, so as a matter of principle, he refused to present exploding offers. "Take as much time as you need to make the right decision," he said. Although Hornik hoped Shader would conclude that the right decision was to sign with him, he put Shader's best interests ahead of his own, giving Shader space to explore other options.

Shader did just that: he spent the next few weeks pitching his idea to other investors. In the meantime, Hornik wanted to make sure he was still a strong contender, so he sent Shader his most valuable resource: a list of forty references who could attest to Hornik's caliber as an investor. Hornik knew that entrepreneurs look for the same attributes in investors that we all seek in financial advisers: competence and trustworthiness. When entrepreneurs sign with an investor, the investor joins their board of directors and provides expert advice. Hornik's list of references reflected the blood, sweat, and tears that he had devoted to entrepreneurs over the course of more than a decade in the venture business. He knew they would vouch for his skill and his character.

A few weeks later, Hornik's phone rang. It was Shader, ready to announce his decision.

"I'm sorry," Shader said, "but I'm signing with another investor."

The financial terms of the offer from Hornik and the other investor were virtually identical, so Hornik's list of forty references should have given him an advantage. And after speaking with the references, it was clear to Shader that Hornik was a great guy.

But it was this very same spirit of generosity that doomed Hornik's case. Shader worried that Hornik would spend more time encouraging him than challenging him. Hornik might not be tough enough to help Shader start a successful business, and the other investor had a reputation for being a brilliant adviser who questioned and pushed entrepreneurs. Shader walked away thinking, "I should probably add somebody to the board who will challenge me more. Hornik is so affable that I don't know what he'll be like in the board-room." When he called Hornik, he explained, "My heart said to go with you, but my head said to go with them. I decided to go with my head instead of my heart."

Hornik was devastated, and he began to second-guess himself. "Am I a dope? If I had applied pressure to take the term sheet, maybe he would have taken it. But I've spent a decade building my reputation so this wouldn't happen. How did this happen?"

David Hornik learned his lesson the hard way: good guys finish last.

Or do they?

★ ★ ★

According to conventional wisdom, highly successful people have three things in common: motivation, ability, and opportunity. If we want to succeed, we need a combination of hard work, talent, and luck. The story of Danny Shader and David Hornik highlights a fourth ingredient, one that's critical but often neglected: success depends heavily on how we approach our interactions with other people. Every time we interact with another person at work, we have a choice to make: do we try to claim as much value as we can, or contribute value without worrying about what we receive in return?

As an organizational psychologist and Wharton professor, I've dedicated more than ten years of my professional life to studying these choices at organizations ranging from Google to the U.S. Air Force, and it turns out that they have staggering consequences for success. Over the past three decades, in a series of groundbreaking studies, social scientists have discovered that people differ dramatically in their preferences for reciprocity—their desired mix of taking and giving. To shed some light on these preferences, let me introduce you to two kinds of people who fall at opposite ends of the reciprocity spectrum at work. I call them takers and givers.

Takers have a distinctive signature: they like to get more than they give. They tilt reciprocity in their own favor, putting their own interests ahead of others' needs. Takers believe that the world is a competitive, dog-eat-dog place. They feel that to succeed, they need to be better than others. To prove their competence, they self-promote and make sure they get plenty of credit for their efforts. Garden-variety takers aren't cruel or cutthroat; they're just cautious and self-protective. "If I don't look out for myself first," takers think, "no one will." Had David Hornik been more of a taker, he would have given Danny Shader a deadline, putting his goal of landing the investment ahead of Shader's desire for a flexible timeline.

But Hornik is the opposite of a taker; he's a *giver*. In the workplace, givers are a relatively rare breed. They tilt reciprocity in the other direction, preferring to give more than they get. Whereas takers tend to be self-focused, evaluating what other people can offer them, givers are other-focused, paying more attention to what other people need from them. These preferences aren't about money: givers and takers aren't distinguished by how much they donate to charity or the compensation that they command from their employers. Rather, givers and takers differ in their attitudes and actions toward other people. If you're a taker, you help others strategically, when the benefits to *you* outweigh the personal costs. If you're a giver, you might use a different cost-benefit analysis: you help whenever the benefits to *others* exceed the personal costs. Alternatively, you might not think about the personal costs at all, helping others without expecting anything in return. If you're a giver at work, you simply strive to be generous in sharing your time, energy, knowledge, skills, ideas, and connections with other people who can benefit from them.

It's tempting to reserve the giver label for larger-than-life heroes such as Mother Teresa or Mahatma Gandhi, but being a giver doesn't require extraordinary acts of sacrifice. It just involves a focus on acting in the interests of others, such as by giving help, providing mentoring, sharing credit, or making connections for others. Outside the workplace, this type of behavior is quite common. According to research led by Yale psychologist Margaret Clark, most people act like givers in close relationships. In marriages and friendships, we contribute whenever we can without keeping score.

But in the workplace, give and take becomes more complicated. Professionally, few of us act purely like givers or takers, adopting a third style instead. We become *matchers*, striving to preserve an equal balance of giving and getting. Matchers operate on the principle of fairness: when they help others, they protect themselves by seeking reciprocity. If you're a matcher, you believe in tit for tat, and your relationships are governed by even exchanges of favors.

Giving, taking, and matching are three fundamental styles of social interaction, but the lines between them aren't hard and fast. You might find that you shift from one reciprocity style to another as you travel across different work roles and relationships.* It wouldn't be surprising if you act like a taker when negotiating your salary, a giver when mentoring someone with less experience than you, and a matcher when sharing expertise with a colleague. But evidence shows that at work, the vast majority of people develop a primary reciprocity style, which captures how they approach most of the people most of the time. And this primary style can play as

---

*Alan Fiske, an anthropologist at UCLA, finds that people engage in a mix of giving, taking, and matching in every human culture—from North to South America, Europe to Africa, and Australia to Asia. While living with a West African tribal group in Burkina Faso called the Mossi, Fiske found people switching between giving, taking, and matching. When it comes to land, the Mossi are givers. If you want to move into their village, they will automatically grant you land without expecting anything in return. But in the marketplace, the Mossi are more inclined toward taking, haggling aggressively for the best prices. And when it comes to cultivating food, the Mossi are likely to be matchers: everyone is expected to make an equal contribution, and meals are divided into even shares.

much of a role in our success as hard work, talent, and luck.

In fact, the patterns of success based on reciprocity styles are remarkably clear. If I asked you to guess who's the most likely to end up at the bottom of the success ladder, what would you say—takers, givers, or matchers?

Professionally, all three reciprocity styles have their own benefits and drawbacks. But there's one style that proves more costly than the other two. Based on David Hornik's story, you might predict that givers achieve the worst results—and you'd be right. Research demonstrates that givers sink to the bottom of the success ladder. Across a wide range of important occupations, givers are at a disadvantage: they make others better off but sacrifice their own success in the process.

In the world of engineering, the least productive and effective engineers are givers. In one study, when more than 160 professional engineers in California rated one another on help given and received, the least successful engineers were those who gave more than they received. These givers had the worst objective scores in their firm for the number of tasks, technical reports, and drawings completed—not to mention errors made, deadlines missed, and money wasted. Going out of their way to help others prevented them from getting their own work done.

The same pattern emerges in medical school. In a study of more than six hundred medical students in Belgium, the students with the lowest grades had unusually high scores on giver statements like "I love to help others" and "I anticipate the needs of others." The givers went out of their way to help their peers study, sharing what they already knew at the expense of filling gaps in their own knowledge, and it gave their peers a leg up at test time. Salespeople are no different. In a study I led of salespeople in North Carolina, compared with takers and matchers, givers brought in two and a half times less annual sales revenue. They were so concerned about what was best for their customers that they weren't willing to sell aggressively.

Across occupations, it appears that givers are just too caring, too trusting, and too willing to sacrifice their own interests for the benefit of others. There's even evidence that compared with takers, on average, givers earn 14 percent less money, have twice the risk of becoming victims of crimes, and are judged as 22 percent less powerful and dominant.

So if givers are most likely to land at the bottom of the success ladder, who's at the top—takers or matchers?

Neither. When I took another look at the data, I discovered a surprising pattern: *It's the givers again.*

As we've seen, the engineers with the lowest productivity are mostly givers. But when we look at the engineers with the highest productivity, the evidence shows that they're givers too. The California engineers with the best objective scores for quantity and quality of results are those who consistently give more to their colleagues than they get. The worst performers and the best performers are givers; takers and matchers are more likely to land in the middle.

This pattern holds up across the board. The Belgian medical students with the lowest grades have unusually high giver scores, but so do the students with the *highest* grades. Over the course of medical school, being a giver accounts for 11 percent higher grades. Even in sales, I found that the least productive salespeople had 25 percent higher giver scores than average performers—but so did the most productive salespeople. The top performers were givers, and they averaged 50 percent more annual revenue than the takers and matchers. Givers dominate the bottom *and* the top of the success ladder. Across occupations, if you examine the link between reciprocity styles and success, the givers are more likely to become champs—not only chumps.

Guess which one David Hornik turns out to be?

★   ★   ★

After Danny Shader signed with the other investor, he had a gnawing feeling. "We just closed a big round. We should be celebrating. Why am I not happier? I was excited about my investor, who's exceptionally bright and talented, but I was missing the opportunity to work with Hornik." Shader wanted to find a way to engage Hornik, but there was a catch. To involve him, Shader and his lead investor would have to sell more of the company, diluting their ownership.

Shader decided it was worth the cost to him personally. Before the financing closed, he invited Hornik to invest in his company. Hornik accepted the offer and made an investment, earning some ownership of the company. He began coming to board meetings, and Shader was impressed with Hornik's ability to push him to consider new directions. "I got to see the other side of him," Shader says. "It had just been overshadowed by how affable he is." Thanks in part to Hornik's advice, Shader's start-up has taken off. It's called PayNearMe, and it enables Americans who don't have a bank account or a credit card to make online purchases with a barcode or a card, and then pay cash for them at participating establishments. Shader landed major partnerships with 7-Eleven and Greyhound to provide these services, and in the first year and a half since launching, PayNearMe has been growing at more than 30 percent per month. As an investor, Hornik has a small share in this growth.

Hornik has also added Shader to his list of references, which is probably even more valuable than the deal itself. When entrepreneurs call to ask about Hornik, Shader tells them, "You may be thinking he's just a nice guy, but he's a lot more than that. He's phenomenal: super-hardworking and very courageous. He can be both challenging and supportive at the same time. And he's incredibly responsive, which is one of the best characteristics you can have in an investor. He'll get back to you any hour—day or night—quickly, on anything that matters."

The payoff for Hornik was not limited to this single deal on PayNearMe. After seeing Hornik in action, Shader came to admire Hornik's commitment to acting in the best interests of entrepreneurs, and he began to set Hornik up with other investment opportunities. In one case, after meeting the CEO of a company called Rocket Lawyer, Shader recommended Hornik as an investor. Although the CEO already had a term sheet from another investor, Hornik ended up winning the investment.

Although he recognizes the downsides, David Hornik believes that operating like a giver has been a driving force behind his success in venture capital. Hornik estimates that when most venture capitalists offer term sheets to entrepreneurs, they have a signing rate near 50 percent: "If you get half of the deals you offer, you're doing pretty well." Yet in eleven years as a venture capitalist, Hornik has offered twenty-eight term sheets to entrepreneurs, and twenty-five have accepted. Shader is one of just three people who have ever turned down an investment from Hornik. The other 89 percent of the time entrepreneurs have taken Hornik's money. Thanks to his funding and expert advice, these entrepreneurs have gone on to build a number of successful start-ups—one was valued at more than $3 billion on its first day of trading in 2012, and others have been acquired by Google, Oracle, Ticketmaster, and Monster.

Hornik's hard work and talent, not to mention his luck at being on the right sideline at his daughter's soccer game, played a big part in lining up the deal with Danny Shader. But it was his reciprocity style that ended up winning the day for him. Even better, he wasn't the only winner. Shader won too, as did the companies to which Shader later recommended Hornik. By operating as a giver, Hornik created value for himself while maximizing opportunities for value to flow outward for the benefit of others.

* * *

In this book, I want to persuade you that we underestimate the success of givers like David Hornik. Although we often stereotype givers as chumps and doormats, they turn out to be surprisingly successful. To figure out why givers dominate the top of the success ladder, we'll examine startling studies and stories that illuminate how giving can be more powerful—and less dangerous—than most people believe. Along the way, I'll introduce you to successful givers from many different walks of life, including consultants, lawyers, doctors, engineers, salespeople, writers, entrepreneurs, accountants, teachers, financial advisers, and sports executives. These givers reverse the popular plan of succeeding first and giving back later, raising the possibility that those who give first are often best positioned for success later.

But we can't forget about those engineers and salespeople at the bottom of the ladder. Some givers do become pushovers and doormats, and I want to explore what separates the champs from the chumps. The answer is less about raw talent or aptitude, and more about the strategies givers use and the choices they make. To explain how givers avoid the bottom of the success ladder, I'm going to debunk two common myths about givers by showing you that they're not necessarily nice, and they're not necessarily altruistic. Successful givers recognise that there's a big difference between taking and receiving. Taking is using other people solely for one's own gain. Receiving is accepting help from others while maintaining a willingness to pay it back and forward. We all have goals for our own individual achievments, and it turns out that the givers who excel are willing to ask for help when they need it. Successful givers are every bit as ambitious as takers and matchers. They simply have a different way of pursuing their goals.

This brings us to my third aim, which is to reveal what's unique about the success of givers. Let me be clear that givers, takers, and matchers all can—and do—achieve success. But there's something distinctive that happens when givers succeed: it spreads and cascades. When takers win, there's usually someone else who loses. Research shows that people tend to envy successful takers and look for ways to knock them down a notch. In contrast, when givers like David Hornik win, people are rooting for them and supporting them, rather than gunning for them. Givers succeed in a way that creates a ripple effect, enhancing the success of people around them. You'll see that the difference lies in how giver success creates value, instead of just claiming it. As the venture capitalist Randy Komisar remarks, "It's easier to win if everybody wants you to win. If you don't make enemies out there, it's easier to succeed."

But in some arenas, it seems that the costs of giving clearly outweigh the benefits. In politics, for example, Mark Twain's opening quote suggests that diplomacy involves taking ten times as much as giving. "Politics," writes former president Bill Clinton, "is a 'getting' business. You have to get support, contributions, and votes, over and over again." Takers should have an edge in lobbying and outmaneuvering their opponents in competitive elections, and matchers may be well suited to the constant trading of favors that politics demands. What happens to givers in the world of politics?

Consider the political struggles of a hick who went by the name Sampson. He said his goal was to be the "Clinton of Illinois," and he set his sights on winning a seat in the Senate. Sampson was an unlikely candidate for political office, having spent his early years working on a farm. But Sampson had great ambition; he made his first run for a seat in the state legislature when he was just twenty-three years old. There were thirteen candidates, and only the top four won seats. Sampson made a lackluster showing, finishing eighth.

After losing that race, Sampson turned his eye to business, taking out a loan to start a small shop with a friend. The business failed, and Sampson was unable to repay the loan, so his possessions were seized by local authorities. Shortly thereafter, his business partner died without assets, and Sampson took on the debt. Sampson jokingly called his liability "the national debt": he owed fifteen times his annual income. It would take him years, but he eventually paid back every cent.

After his business failed, Sampson made a second run for the state legislature. Although he was only twenty-five years old, he finished second, landing a seat. For his first legislative session, he had to borrow the money to buy his first suit. For the next eight years, Sampson served in the state legislature, earning a law degree along the way. Eventually, at age forty-five, he was ready to pursue influence on the national stage. He made a bid for the Senate.

Sampson knew he was fighting an uphill battle. He had two primary opponents: James Shields and Lyman Trumbull. Both had been state Supreme Court justices, coming from backgrounds far more privileged than Sampson's. Shields, the incumbent running for reelection, was the nephew of a congressman. Trumbull was the grandson of an eminent Yale-educated historian. By comparison, Sampson had little experience or political clout.

In the first poll, Sampson was a surprise front-runner, with 44 percent support. Shields was close behind at 41 percent, and Trumbull was a distant third at 5 percent. In the next poll, Sampson gained ground, climbing to 47 percent support. But the tide began to turn when a new candidate entered the race: the state's current governor, Joel Matteson. Matteson was popular, and he had the potential to draw votes from both Sampson and Trumbull. When Shields withdrew from the race, Matteson quickly took the lead. Matteson had 44 percent, Sampson was down to 38 percent, and Trumbull was at just 9 percent. But hours later, Trumbull won the election with 51 percent, narrowly edging out Matteson's 47 percent.

Why did Sampson plummet, and how did Trumbull rise so quickly? The sudden reversal of their positions was due to a choice made by Sampson, who seemed plagued by pathological giving. When Matteson entered the race, Sampson began to doubt his own ability to garner enough support to win. He knew that Trumbull had a small but loyal following who would not give up on him. Most people in Sampson's shoes would have lobbied Trumbull's followers to jump ship. After all, with just 9 percent support, Trumbull was a long shot.

But Sampson's primary concern wasn't getting elected. It was to prevent Matteson from winning. Sampson believed that Matteson was engaging in questionable practices. Some onlookers had accused Matteson of trying to bribe influential voters. At minimum, Sampson had reliable information that some of his own key supporters had been approached by Matteson. If it appeared that Sampson would not stand a chance, Matteson argued, the voters should shift their loyalties and support him.

Sampson's concerns about Matteson's methods and motives proved prescient. A year later, when Matteson was finishing his term as governor, he redeemed old government checks that were outdated or had been previously redeemed, but were never canceled. Matteson took home several hundred thousand dollars and was indicted for fraud.

In addition to harboring suspicions about Matteson, Sampson believed in Trumbull, as they had something in common when it came to the issues. For several years, Sampson had campaigned passionately for a major shift in social and economic policy. He believed it was vital to the future of his state, and in this he and Trumbull were united. So instead of trying to convert Trumbull's loyal followers, Sampson decided to fall on his own sword. He told his floor manager, Stephen Logan, that he would withdraw from the race and ask his supporters to vote for Trumbull. Logan was incredulous: why should the man with a larger following hand over the election to an adversary with a smaller following? Logan broke down into tears, but Sampson would not yield. He withdrew and asked his supporters to vote for Trumbull. It was enough to propel Trumbull to victory, at Sampson's expense.

That was not the first time Sampson put the interests of others ahead of his own. Before he helped Trumbull win the Senate race, despite earning acclaim for his work as a lawyer, Sampson's success was stifled by a crushing liability. He could not bring himself to defend clients if he felt they were guilty. According to a colleague, Sampson's clients knew "they would win their case—if it was fair; if not, that it was a waste of time to take it to him." In one case, a client was accused of theft, and Sampson approached the judge. "If you can say anything for the man, do it—I can't. If I attempt it, the jury will see I think he is guilty, and convict him." In another case, during a criminal trial, Sampson leaned over and said to an associate, "This man is guilty; you defend him, I can't." Sampson handed the case over to the associate, walking away from a sizable fee. These decisions earned him respect, but they raised questions about whether he was tenacious enough to make tough political decisions.

Sampson "comes very near being a perfect man," said one of his political rivals. "He lacks but one thing." The rival explained that Sampson was unfit to be trusted with power, because his judgment was too easily clouded by concern for others. In politics, operating like a giver put Sampson at a disadvantage. His reluctance to put himself first cost him the Senate election, and left onlookers wondering whether he was strong enough for the unforgiving world of politics. Trumbull was a fierce debater; Sampson was a pushover. "I regret my defeat," Sampson admitted, but he maintained that Trumbull's election would help to advance the causes they shared. After the election, a local reporter wrote that in comparison with Sampson, Trumbull was "a man of more real talent and power."

But Sampson wasn't ready to step aside forever. Four years after helping Lyman Trumbull win the seat, Sampson ran for the Senate again. He lost again. But in the weeks leading up to the vote, one of the most outspoken supporters of Sampson's was none other than Lyman Trumbull. Sampson's sacrifice had earned goodwill, and Trumbull was not the only adversary who became an advocate in response to Sampson's giving. In the first Senate race, when Sampson had 47 percent of the vote and seemed to be on the brink of victory, a Chicago lawyer and politician named Norman Judd led a strong 5 percent who would not waver in their loyalty to Trumbull. During Sampson's second Senate bid, Judd became a strong supporter.

Two years later, after two failed Senate races, Sampson finally won his first election at the national level. According to one commentator, Judd never forgot Sampson's "generous behavior" and did "more than anyone else" to secure Sampson's nomination.

In 1999, C-SPAN, the cable TV network that covers politics, polled more than a thousand knowledgeable viewers. They rated the effectiveness of Sampson and three dozen other politicians who vied for similar offices. Sampson came out at the very top of the poll, receiving the highest evaluations. Despite his losses, he was more popular than any other politician on the list. You see, Sampson's Ghost was a pen name that the hick used in letters.

His real name was Abraham Lincoln.

In the 1830s, Lincoln was striving to be the DeWitt Clinton of Illinois, referencing a U.S. senator and New York governor who spearheaded the construction of the Erie Canal. When Lincoln withdrew from his first Senate race to help Lyman Trumbull win the seat, they shared a commitment to abolishing slavery. From emancipating slaves, to sacrificing his own political opportunities for the cause, to refusing to defend clients who appeared to be guilty, Lincoln consistently acted for the greater good. When experts in history, political science, and psychology rated the presidents, they identified Lincoln as a clear giver. "Even if it was inconvenient, Lincoln went out of his way to help others," wrote two experts, demonstrating "obvious concern for the well-being of individual citizens." It is noteworthy that Lincoln is seen as one of the least self-centered, egotistical, boastful presidents ever. In independent ratings of presidential biographies, Lincoln scored in the top three—along with Washington and

Fillmore—in giving credit to others and acting in the best interests of others. In the words of a military general who worked with Lincoln, "he seemed to possess more of the elements of greatness, combined with goodness, than any other."

In the Oval Office, Lincoln was determined to put the good of the nation above his own ego. When he won the presidency in 1860, he invited the three candidates whom he defeated for the Republican nomination to become his secretary of state, secretary of the treasury, and attorney general. In *Team of Rivals,* the historian Doris Kearns Goodwin documents how unusual Lincoln's cabinet was. "Every member of the administration was better known, better educated, and more experienced in public life than Lincoln. Their presence in the cabinet might have threatened to eclipse the obscure prairie lawyer."

In Lincoln's position, a taker might have preferred to protect his ego and power by inviting "yes men" to join him. A matcher might have offered appointments to allies who had supported him. Yet Lincoln invited his bitter competitors instead. "We needed the strongest men of the party in the Cabinet," Lincoln told an incredulous reporter. "I had no right to deprive the country of their services." Some of these rivals despised Lincoln, and others viewed him as incompetent, but he managed to win them all over. According to Kearns Goodwin, Lincoln's "success in dealing with the strong egos of the men in his cabinet suggests that in the hands of a truly great politician the qualities we generally associate with decency and morality—kindness, sensitivity, compassion, honesty, and empathy—can also be impressive political resources."

If politics can be fertile ground for givers, it's possible that givers can succeed in any job. Whether giving is effective, though, depends on the particular kind of exchange in which it's employed. This is one important feature of giving to keep in mind as we move through the ideas in this book: on any particular morning, giving may well be incompatible with success. In purely zero-sum situations and win-lose interactions, giving rarely pays off. This is a lesson that Abraham Lincoln learned each time he chose to give to others at his own expense. "If I have one vice," Lincoln said, "and I can call it nothing else—it is not to be able to say no!"

But most of life isn't zero-sum, and on balance, people who choose giving as their primary reciprocity style end up reaping rewards. For Lincoln, like David Hornik, seemingly self-sacrificing decisions ultimately worked to his advantage. When we initially concluded that Lincoln and Hornik lost, we hadn't stretched the time horizons out far enough. It takes time for givers to build goodwill and trust, but eventually, they establish reputations and relationships that enhance their success. In fact, you'll see that in sales and medical school, the giver advantage grows over time. In the long run, giving can be every bit as powerful as it is dangerous. As Chip Conley, the renowned entrepreneur who founded Joie de Vivre Hotels, explains, "Being a giver is not good for a 100-yard dash, but it's valuable in a marathon."

In Lincoln's era, the marathon took a long time to run. Without telephones, the Internet, and high-speed transportation, building relationships and reputations was a slow process. "In the old world, you could send a letter, and no one knew," Conley says. Conley believes that in today's connected world, where relationships and reputations are more visible, givers can accelerate their pace. "You no longer have to choose," says Bobbi Silten, the former president of Dockers, who now runs global social and environmental responsibility for Gap Inc. "You can be a giver *and* be successful."

The fact that the long run is getting shorter isn't the only force that makes giving more professionally productive today. We live in an era when massive changes in the structure of work—and the technology that shapes it—have further amplified the advantages of being a giver. Today, more than half of American and European companies regularly use teams to get work done. We rely on teams to build cars and houses, perform surgeries, fly planes, fight wars, play symphonies, produce news reports, audit companies, and provide consulting services. Teams depend on givers to share information, volunteer for unpopular tasks, and provide help.

When Lincoln invited his rivals to join his cabinet, they had the chance to see firsthand how much he was willing to contribute for the sake of other people and his country. Several years before Lincoln became president, one of his rivals, Edwin Stanton, had rejected him as a cocounsel in a trial, calling him a "gawky, long-armed ape." Yet after working with Lincoln, Stanton described him as "the most perfect ruler of men the world has ever seen." As we organize more people into teams, givers have more opportunities to demonstrate their value, as Lincoln did.

Even if you don't work in a team, odds are that you hold a service job. Most of our grandparents worked in independent jobs producing goods. They didn't always need to collaborate with other people, so it was fairly inefficient to be a giver. But now, a high percentage of people work in interconnected jobs providing services to others. In the 1980s, the service sector made up about half of the world's gross domestic product (GDP). By 1995, the service sector was responsible for nearly two thirds of world GDP. Today, more than 80 percent of Americans work in service jobs.

As the service sector continues to expand, more and more people are placing a premium on providers who have established relationships and reputations as givers. Whether your reciprocity style is primarily giver, taker, or matcher, I'm willing to bet that you want your key service providers to be givers. You hope your doctor, lawyer, teacher, dentist, plumber, and real estate agent will focus on contributing value to you, not on claiming value from you. This is why David Hornik has an 89 percent success rate: entrepreneurs know that when he offers to invest in their companies, he has their best interests at heart. Whereas many venture capitalists don't consider unsolicited pitches, preferring to spend their scarce time on people and ideas that have already shown promise, Hornik responds personally to e-mails from complete strangers. "I'm happy to be as helpful as I can independent of whether I have some economic interest," he says. According to Hornik, a successful venture capitalist is "a service provider. Entrepreneurs are not here to serve venture capitalists. We are here to serve entrepreneurs."

The rise of the service economy sheds light on why givers have the worst grades and the best grades in medical school. In the study of Belgian medical students, the givers earned significantly lower grades in their first year of medical school. The givers were at a disadvantage—and the negative correlation between giver scores and grades was stronger than the effect of smoking on the odds of getting lung cancer.

But that was the only year of medical school in which the givers underperformed. By their second year, the givers had made up the gap: they were now slightly outperforming their peers. By the sixth year, the givers earned substantially higher grades than their peers. A giver style, measured *six years earlier*, was a better predictor of medical school grades than the effect of smoking on lung cancer rates (and the effect of using nicotine patches on quitting smoking). By the seventh year of medical school, when the givers became doctors, they had climbed still further ahead. The effect of giving on final medical school performance was stronger than the smoking effects above; it was even greater than the effect of drinking alcohol on aggressive behavior.

Why did the giver disadvantage reverse, becoming such a strong advantage?

Nothing about the givers changed, but their program did. As students progress through medical school, they move from independent classes into clinical rotations, internships, and patient care. The further they advance, the more their success depends on teamwork and service. Whereas takers sometimes win in independent roles where performance is only about individual results, givers thrive in interdependent roles where collaboration matters. As the structure of class work shifts in medical school, the givers benefit from their natural tendencies to collaborate effectively with other medical professionals and express concern to patients.

This giver advantage in service roles is hardly limited to medicine. Steve Jones, the award-winning former CEO of one of the largest banks in Australia, wanted to know what made financial advisers successful. His team studied key factors such as financial expertise and effort. But "the single most influential factor," Jones told me, "was whether a financial adviser had the client's best interests at heart, above the company's and even his own. It was one of my three top priorities to get that value instilled, and demonstrate that it's in everybody's best interests to treat clients that way."

One financial adviser who exemplifies this giver style is Peter Audet, a broad-shouldered Aussie who once wore a mullet and has an affinity for Bon Jovi. He began his career as a customer service representative answering phones for a large insurance company. The first year after he was hired, Peter won the Personality of the Year award, beating out hundreds of other employees based on his passion for helping customers, and became the youngest department supervisor in the whole company. Years later, when Peter joined a group of fifteen executives for a give-and-take exercise, the average executive offered help to three colleagues. Peter offered help to all fifteen of them. He is such a giver that he even tries to help the job applicants he doesn't hire, spending hours making connections for them to find other opportunities.

In 2011, when Peter was working as a financial adviser, he received a call from an Australian client. The client wanted to make changes to a small superannuation fund valued at $70,000. A staff member was assigned to the client, but looked him up and saw that he was a scrap metal worker. Thinking like a matcher, the staff member declined to make the visit: it was a waste of his time. It certainly wasn't worth Peter's time. He specialized in high net worth clients, whose funds were worth a thousand times more money, and his largest client had more than $100 million. If you calculated the dollar value of Peter's time, the scrap metal worker's fund was not even worth the amount of time it would take to drive out to his house. "He was the tiniest client, and no one wanted to see him; it was beneath everybody," Peter reflects. "But you can't just ignore someone because you don't think they're important enough."

Peter scheduled an appointment to drive out to see the scrap metal worker and help him with the plan changes. When he pulled up to the house, his jaw dropped. The front door was covered in cobwebs and had not been opened in months. He drove around to the back, where a thirty-four-year-old man opened the door. The living room was full of bugs, and he could see straight through to the roof: the entire ceiling had been ripped out. The client made a feeble gesture to some folding chairs, and Peter began working through the client's plan changes. Feeling sympathy for the client, who seemed like an earnest, hardworking blue-collar man, Peter made a generous offer. "While I'm here, why don't you tell me a bit about yourself and I'll see if there's anything else I can help you with."

The client mentioned a love of cars, and walked him around back to a dingy shed. Peter braced himself for another depressing display of poverty, envisioning a pile of rusted metal. When Peter stepped inside the shed, he gasped. Spread out before him in immaculate condition were a first-generation Chevy Camaro, built in 1966; two vintage Australian Valiant cars with 1,000-horsepower engines for drag racing; a souped-up coupe utility car; and a Ford coupe from the movie *Mad Max*. The client was not a scrap metal worker; he owned a lucrative scrap metal business. He had just bought the house to fix it up; it was on eleven acres, and it cost $1.4 million. Peter spent the next year reengineering the client's business, improving his tax position, and helping him renovate the house. "All I did was start out by doing a kindness," Peter notes. "When I got to work the next day, I had to laugh at my colleague who wasn't prepared to give a bit by driving out to visit the client." Peter went on to develop a strong relationship with the client, whose fees multiplied by a factor of a hundred the following year, and expects to continue working with him for decades.

Over the course of his career, giving has enabled Peter Audet to access opportunities that takers and matchers routinely miss, but it has also cost him dearly. As you'll see in chapter 7, he was exploited by two takers who nearly put him out of business. Yet Peter managed to climb from the bottom to the top of the success ladder, becoming one of the more productive financial advisers in Australia. The key, he believes, was learning to harness the benefits of giving while minimizing the costs. As a managing director at Genesys Wealth Advisers, he managed to rescue his firm from the brink of bankruptcy and turn it into an industry leader, and he chalks his success up to being a giver. "There's no doubt that I've succeeded in business because I give to other people. It's my weapon of choice," Peter says. "When I'm head-to-head with another adviser to try and win business, people tell me this is why I win."

Although technological and organizational changes have made giving more advantageous, there's one feature of giving that's more timeless: when we reflect on our guiding principles in life, many of us are intuitively drawn to giving. Over the past three decades, the esteemed psychologist Shalom Schwartz has studied the values and guiding principles that matter to people in different cultures around the world. One of his studies surveyed reasonably representative samples of thousands of adults in Australia, Chile, Finland, France, Germany, Israel, Malaysia, the Netherlands, South Africa, Spain,

Sweden, and the United States. He translated his survey into a dozen languages, and asked respondents to rate the importance of different values. Here are a few examples:

List 1

- Wealth (money, material possessions)
- Power (dominance, control over others)
- Pleasure (enjoying life)
- Winning (doing better than others)

List 2

- Helpfulness (working for the well-being of others)
- Responsibility (being dependable)
- Social justice (caring for the disadvantaged)
- Compassion (responding to the needs of others)

Takers favor the values in List 1, whereas givers prioritize the values in List 2. Schwartz wanted to know where most people would endorse giver values. Take a look back at the twelve countries above. Where do the majority of people endorse giver values above taker values?

All of them. In all twelve countries, most people rate giving as their single most important value. They report caring more about giving than about power, achievement, excitement, freedom, tradition, conformity, security, and pleasure. In fact, this was true in more than seventy different countries around the world. Giver values are the number-one guiding principle in life to most people in most countries—from Argentina to Armenia, Belgium to Brazil, and Slovakia to Singapore. In the majority of the world's cultures, including that of the United States, the majority of people endorse giving as their single most important guiding principle.

On some level, this comes as no surprise. As parents, we read our children books like *The Giving Tree* and emphasize the importance of sharing and caring. But we tend to compartmentalize giving, reserving a different set of values for the sphere of work. We may love Shel Silverstein for our kids, but the popularity of books like Robert Greene's *The 48 Laws of Power*—not to mention the fascination of many business gurus with Sun Tzu's *The Art of War*—suggests that we don't see much room for giver values in our professional lives.

As a result, even people who operate like givers at work are often afraid to admit it. In the summer of 2011, I met a woman named Sherryann Plesse, an executive at a prestigious financial services firm. Sherryann was clearly a giver: she spent countless hours mentoring junior colleagues and volunteered to head up a women's leadership initiative and a major charitable fund-raising initiative at her firm. "My default is to give," she says. "I'm not looking for quid pro quo; I'm looking to make a difference and have an impact, and I focus on the people who can benefit from my help the most."

To enrich her business acumen, Sherryann left her job for six weeks, enrolling in a leadership program with sixty executives from companies around the world. To identify her strengths, she underwent a comprehensive psychological assessment. Sherryann was shocked to learn that her top professional strengths were kindness and compassion. Fearing that the results would jeopardize her reputation as a tough and successful leader, Sherryann decided not to tell anyone. "I didn't want to sound like a flake. I was afraid people would perceive me differently, perhaps as a less serious executive," Sherryann confided. "I was conditioned to leave my human feelings at the door, and win. I want my primary skills to be seen as hardworking and results-oriented, not kindness and compassion. In business, sometimes you have to wear different masks."

The fear of being judged as weak or naïve prevents many people from operating like givers at work. Many people who hold giver values in life choose matching as their primary reciprocity style at work, seeking an even balance of give and take. In one study, people completed a survey about whether their default approach to work relationships was to give, take, or match. Only 8 percent described themselves as givers; the other 92 percent were not willing to contribute more than they received at work. In another study, I found that in the office, more than three times as many people prefer to be matchers than givers.

People who prefer to give or match often feel pressured to lean in the taker direction when they perceive a workplace as zero-sum. Whether it's a company with forced ranking systems, a group of firms vying to win the same clients, or a school with required grading curves and more demand than supply for desirable jobs, it's only natural to assume that peers will lean more toward taking than giving. "When they anticipate self-interested behavior from others," explains the Stanford psychologist Dale Miller, people fear that they'll be exploited if they operate like givers, so they conclude that "pursuing a competitive orientation is the rational and appropriate thing to do." There's even evidence that just putting on a business suit and analyzing a Harvard Business School case is enough to significantly reduce the attention that people pay to relationships and the interests of others. The fear of exploitation by takers is so pervasive, writes the Cornell economist Robert Frank, that "by encouraging us to expect the worst in others it brings out the worst in us: dreading the role of the chump, we are often loath to heed our nobler instincts."

Giving is especially risky when dealing with takers, and David Hornik believes that many of the world's most successful venture capitalists operate like takers—they insist on disproportionately large shares of entrepreneurs' start-ups and claim undue credit when their investments prove successful. Hornik is determined to change these norms. When a financial planner asked him what he wanted to achieve in life, Hornik said that "above all, I want to demonstrate that success doesn't have to come at someone else's expense."

In an attempt to prove it, Hornik has broken two of the most sacred rules in the venture business. In 2004, he became the first venture capitalist to start a blog. Venture capital was a black box, so Hornik invited entrepreneurs inside. He began to share information openly online, helping entrepreneurs to improve their pitches by gaining a deeper understanding of how venture capitalists think. Hornik's partners, and his firm's general counsel, discouraged him from doing it. Why would he want to give away trade secrets? If other investors read his blog, they could steal ideas without sharing any in return. "The idea of a venture capitalist talking about what he was doing was considered insane," Hornik reflects. "But I really wanted to engage in a conversation with a broad set of entrepreneurs, and be helpful to them." His critics were right: "Lots of venture capitalists ended up reading it. When I talked about specific companies I was excited about, getting deals became more competitive." But that was a price that Hornik was willing to pay. "My focus was entirely on creating value for entrepreneurs," he says, and he has maintained the blog for the past eight years.

Hornik's second unconventional move was ignited by his frustration with dull speakers at conferences. Back in college, he had teamed up with a professor to run a speakers' bureau so he could invite interesting people to campus. The lineup included the inventor of the game Dungeons & Dragons, the world yo-yo champion, and the animator who created the Wile E. Coyote and Road Runner cartoon characters for Warner Bros. By comparison, speakers at venture capital and technology conferences weren't measuring up. "I discovered that I stopped going in to hear the speakers, and I would spend all my time chatting with people in the lobby about what they're working on. The real value of these events was the conversations and relationships that were created between people. What if a conference was about conversations and relationships, not content?"

In 2007, Hornik planned his first annual conference. It was called The Lobby, and the goal was to bring entrepreneurs together to share ideas about new media. Hornik was putting about $400,000 on the line, and people tried to talk him out of it. "You could destroy your firm's reputation," they warned, hinting that if the conference failed, Hornik's own career might be ruined. But he pressed forward, and when it was time to send out invitations, Hornik did the unthinkable. He invited venture capitalists at rival firms to attend the conference.

Several colleagues thought he was out of his mind. "Why in the world would you let other venture capitalists come to the conference?" they asked. If Hornik met an entrepreneur with a hot new idea at The Lobby, he would have a leg up on landing the investment. Why would he want to give away his advantage and help his competitors find opportunities? Once again, Hornik ignored the naysayers. "I want to create an experience to benefit everyone, not just me." One of the rival venture capitalists who attended liked the format so much that he created his own Lobby-style conference, but he didn't invite Hornik—or any other venture capitalists. His partners wouldn't let him. Nevertheless, Hornik kept inviting venture capitalists to The Lobby.

David Hornik recognizes the costs of operating like a giver. "Some people think I'm delusional. They believe the way you achieve is by being a taker," he says. If he were more of a taker, he probably wouldn't accept unsolicited pitches, respond personally to e-mails, share information with competitors on his blog, or invite his rivals to benefit from The Lobby conference. He would protect his time, guard his knowledge, and leverage his connections more carefully. And if he were more of a matcher, he would have asked for quid pro quo with the venture capitalist who attended The Lobby but didn't invite Hornik to his own conference. But Hornik pays more attention to what other people need than to what he gets from them.

Hornik has been extremely successful as a venture capitalist while living by his values, and he's widely respected for his generosity. "It's a win-win," Hornik reflects. "I get to create an environment where other people can get deals and build relationships, and I live in the world I want to live in." His experience reinforces that giving not only is professionally risky; it can also be professionally rewarding.

Understanding what makes giving both powerful and dangerous is the focus of *Give and Take*. The first section unveils the principles of giver success, illuminating how and why givers rise to the top. I'll show you how successful givers have unique approaches to interactions in four key domains: networking, collaborating, evaluating, and influencing. A close look at networking highlights fresh approaches for developing connections with new contacts and strengthening ties with old contacts. Examining collaboration reveals what it takes to work productively with colleagues and earn their respect. Exploring how we evaluate others offers counterintuitive techniques for judging and developing talent to get the best results out of others. And an analysis of influence sheds light on novel strategies for presenting, selling, persuading, and negotiating, all in the spirit of convincing others to support our ideas and interests. Across these four domains, you'll see what successful givers do differently—and what takers and matchers can learn from their approach. Along the way, you'll find out how America's best networker developed his connections, why the genius behind one of the most successful shows in television history toiled for years in anonymity, how a basketball executive responsible for some of the worst draft busts in history turned things around, whether a lawyer who stumbles on his words can beat a lawyer who speaks with confidence, and how you can spot a taker just from looking at a Facebook profile.

In the second part of the book, the focus shifts from the benefits of giving to the costs, and how they can be managed. I'll examine how givers protect themselves against burnout and avoid becoming pushovers and doormats. You'll discover how a teacher reduced her burnout by giving more rather than less, how a billionaire made money by giving it away, and the ideal number of hours to volunteer if you want to become happier and live longer. You'll see why giving slowed one consultant's path to partner but accelerated another's, why we misjudge who's a giver and who's a taker, and how givers protect themselves at the bargaining table. You'll also gain knowledge about how givers avoid the bottom of the success ladder and rise to the top by nudging other people away from taking and toward giving. You'll learn about a ninety-minute activity that unleashes giving in remarkable ways, and you'll figure out why people give things away for free that they could easily sell for a profit on Craigslist, why some radiologists get better but others get worse, why thinking about Superman makes people less likely to volunteer, and why people named Dennis are unusually likely to become dentists.

By the time you finish reading this book, you may be reconsidering some of your fundamental assumptions about success. If you're a self-sacrificing giver, you'll find plenty of insights for ascending from the bottom to the top of the success ladder. If you endorse giver values but act like a matcher at work, you may be pleasantly surprised by the wealth of opportunities to express your values and find meaning in helping others without compromising your own success. Instead of aiming to succeed first and give back later, you might decide that giving first is a promising path to succeeding later. And if you currently lean toward taking, you may just be tempted to shift in the giver direction, seeking to master the skills of this growing breed of people who achieve success by contributing to others.

But if you do it only to succeed, it probably won't work.

2

The Peacock and the Panda

How Givers, Takers, and Matchers Build Networks

Every man must decide whether he will walk in the light of creative altruism
or in the darkness of destructive selfishness.

—Martin Luther King Jr., civil rights leader and Nobel Peace Prize winner

Several decades ago, a man who started his life in poverty lived the American Dream. He came from humble beginnings, growing up in Missouri farm towns without indoor plumbing. To help support his family, the young man worked long hours on farms and paper routes. He put himself through college at the University of Missouri, graduated Phi Beta Kappa, and completed a master's degree and then a doctorate in economics. He pursued a life of public service, enlisting in the Navy and then serving in several important roles in the U.S. government, earning the Navy Commendation Medal and National Defense Service Medal. From there, he built his own company, where he was chairman and CEO for fifteen years. By the time he stepped down, his company was worth $110 billion, with more than twenty thousand employees in forty countries around the world. For five consecutive years, *Fortune* named his company "America's Most Innovative Company" and one of the twenty-five best places to work in the country. When asked about his success, he acknowledged the importance of "Respect . . . the golden rule . . . Absolute integrity . . .

Everyone knows that I personally have a very strict code of personal conduct that I live by." He set up a charitable family foundation, giving over $2.5 million to more than 250 organizations, and donated 1 percent of his company's annual profits to charity. His giving attracted the attention of former president George W. Bush, who commended him as a "good guy" and a "generous person."

Then he was indicted.

His name was Kenneth Lay, and he is best remembered as a primary villain in the Enron scandal. Enron was an energy, commodities, and securities firm headquartered in Houston. In October 2001, Enron lost $1.2 billion in shareholder equity after reporting third-quarter losses of $618 million, the biggest earnings restatement in U.S. history. In December, Enron went bankrupt, leaving twenty thousand employees jobless, many watching their life savings practically erased by the company's fall. Investigators found that Enron had deceived investors by reporting false profits and hiding debts of more than $1 billion, manipulated energy and power markets in California and Texas, and won international contracts by giving illegal bribes to foreign governments. Lay was convicted on six counts of conspiracy and fraud.

We can debate about how much Lay truly knew about Enron's illegal activities, but it's difficult to deny that he was a taker. Although Lay may have looked like a giver to many observers, he was a faker: a taker in disguise. Lay felt entitled to use Enron's resources for personal gain. As Bethany McLean and Peter Elkind describe in *The Smartest Guys in the Room*, Lay took exorbitant loans from the company and had his staff put his sandwiches on silver platters and fine china. A secretary once tried to reserve an Enron plane for an executive to do business, only to learn that the Lay family was currently using three Enron planes for personal travel. From 1997 to 1998, $4.5 million in Enron commissions went to a travel agency owned by Lay's sister. According to accusations, he sold more than $70 million in stock just before Enron went bankrupt, taking the treasure from a sinking ship. This behavior was foreshadowed in the 1970s when Lay worked at Exxon. A boss wrote a reference recommending Lay highly, but warned that he was "Maybe too ambitious." Observers now believe that as early as 1987, at Enron Oil, Lay approved and helped to conceal the activities of two traders who set up fake companies and stole $3.8 million while allowing Enron to avoid massive trading losses. When the losses were discovered, Enron Oil had to report an $85 million hit, and Lay denied knowledge and responsibility: "If anyone could say that I knew, let them stand up." According to McLean and Elkind, one trader started to stand up but was physically restrained by two colleagues.

How did a taker end up becoming so successful? He knew somebody. In fact, he knew a whole lot of somebodies. Ken Lay profited greatly from claiming his company's financial resources as his own, but much of his success in growing that company came the old-fashioned way: he built a network of influential contacts and leveraged them for his own benefit. Lay was a master networker from the start. In college, he impressed an economics professor named Pinkney Walker and started his ascent on the shoulders of Walker's connections. Walker helped Lay land an assignment as an economist at the Pentagon, and then a position as a chief assistant in the White House in the Nixon administration.

By the mid-1980s, Lay became the head of Enron after engineering the company's move to Houston following a merger. As he consolidated his power, he began to hobnob with political power brokers who could support Enron's interests. He put Pinkney Walker's brother Charles on Enron's board and developed a relationship with George H. W. Bush, who was running for president. In 1990, Lay cochaired an important Summit of Industrialized Nations meeting for Bush in Houston, putting on a dazzling show and charming the crowd, which included British prime minister Margaret Thatcher,

German chancellor Helmut Kohl, and French president François Mitterrand. After Bush lost his reelection bid to Bill Clinton, Lay wasted no time in reaching out to a friend who was a key aide to the president-elect—the friend had gone to kindergarten with Clinton. Soon, Lay was playing golf with the new president. Several years later, as George W. Bush gained power, Lay used his connections to lobby for energy deregulation and get his supporters in important government positions in Texas and the White House, influencing policies in Enron's favor. At nearly every stage in his career, Lay was able to dramatically improve his company's prospects—or his own—by making use of well-placed contacts in his network.

For centuries, we have recognized the importance of networking. According to Brian Uzzi, a management professor at Northwestern University, networks come with three major advantages: private information, diverse skills, and power. By developing a strong network, people can gain invaluable access to knowledge, expertise, and influence. Extensive research demonstrates that people with rich networks achieve higher performance ratings, get promoted faster, and earn more money. And because networks are based on interactions and relationships, they serve as a powerful prism for understanding the impact of reciprocity styles on success. How do people relate to others in their networks, and what do they see as the purpose of networking?

On the one hand, the very notion of networking often has negative connotations. When we meet a new person who expresses enthusiasm about connecting, we frequently wonder whether he's acting friendly because he's genuinely interested in a relationship that will benefit both of us, or because he wants something from us. At some point in your life, you've probably experienced the frustration of dealing with slick schmoozers who are nice to your face when they want a favor, but end up stabbing you in the back—or simply ignoring you—after they get what they want. This faker style of networking casts the entire enterprise as Machiavellian, a self-serving activity in which people make connections for the sole purpose of advancing their own interests. On the other hand, givers and matchers often see networking as an appealing way to connect with new people and ideas. We meet many people throughout our professional and personal lives, and since we all have different knowledge and resources, it makes sense to turn to these people to exchange help, advice, and introductions. This raises a fundamental question: Can people build up networks that have breadth and depth using different reciprocity styles? Or does one style consistently create a richer network?

In this chapter, I want to examine how givers, takers, and matchers develop fundamentally distinct networks, and why their interactions within these networks have different characters and consequences. You'll see how givers and takers build and manage their networks differently, and learn about some clues that they leak along the way—including how we could have recognized the takers at Enron four years before the company collapsed. Ultimately, I want to argue that while givers and takers may have equally large networks, givers are able to produce far more lasting value through their networks, and in ways that might not seem obvious.

In 2011, *Fortune* conducted extensive research to identify the best networker in the United States. The goal was to use online social networks to figure out who had the most connections to America's most powerful people. The staff compiled a list of the *Fortune* 500 CEOs, as well as *Fortune*'s lists of the 50 smartest people in technology, the 50 most powerful women, and the 40 hottest rising stars in business under age forty. Then, they cross-referenced this list of 640 powerful people against LinkedIn's entire database of more than ninety million members.

The winning networker was connected on LinkedIn to more of *Fortune*'s 640 movers and shakers than anyone else on earth. The winner had more than 3,000 LinkedIn connections, including

Netscape cofounder Marc Andreessen, Twitter cofounder Evan Williams, Flickr cofounder Caterina Fake, Facebook cofounder Dustin Moskovitz, Napster cofounder Sean Parker, and Half.com founder Josh Kopelman—not to mention the former chef of the Grateful Dead. As you'll see later, this networker extraordinaire is a giver. "It seems counterintuitive, but the more altruistic your attitude, the more benefits you will gain from the relationship," writes LinkedIn founder Reid Hoffman. "If you set out to help others," he explains, "you will rapidly reinforce your own reputation and expand your universe of possibilities." Part of this, I'll argue, has to do with the way networks themselves have changed and are still evolving. At the heart of my inquiry, though, lies an exploration of how the motives with which we approach networking shape the strength and reach of those networks, as well as the way that energy flows through them.

Spotting the Taker in a Giver's Clothes

If you've ever put your guard up when meeting a new colleague, it's probably because you thought you picked up on the scent of self-serving motives. When we see a taker coming, we protect ourselves by closing the door to our networks, withholding our trust and help. To avoid getting shut out, many takers become good fakers, acting generously so that they can waltz into our networks disguised as givers or matchers. For the better part of two decades, this worked for Ken Lay, whose favors and charitable contributions enabled people to see him in a positive light, opening the door to new ties and sources of help.

But it can be difficult for takers to keep up the façade in all of their interactions. Ken Lay was charming when mingling with powerful people in Washington, but many of his peers and subordinates saw through him. Looking back, one former Enron employee said, "If you wanted to get Lay to attend a meeting, you needed to invite someone important." There's a Dutch phrase that captures this duality beautifully: "kissing up, kicking down." Although takers tend to be dominant and controlling with subordinates, they're surprisingly submissive and deferential toward superiors. When takers deal with powerful people, they become convincing fakers. Takers want to be admired by influential superiors, so they go out of their way to charm and flatter. As a result, powerful people tend to form glowing first impressions of takers. A trio of German psychologists found that when strangers first encountered people, the ones they liked most were those "with a sense of entitlement and a tendency to manipulate and exploit others."

When kissing up, takers are often good fakers. In 1998, when Wall Street analysts visited Enron, Lay recruited seventy employees to pretend to be busy traders, hoping to wow the analysts with the image of a productive energy trading business. Lay led the analysts through the charade, where the employees were asked to bring personal photos to a different floor of the building so it looked like they worked there, and put on a show. They made imaginary phone calls, creating a ruse that they were busy buying and selling energy and gas. This is another sign that Lay was a taker: he was obsessed with making a good impression upward, but worried less about how he was seen by those below him. As Samuel Johnson purportedly wrote, "The true measure of a man is how he treats someone who can do him absolutely no good."

Takers may rise by kissing up, but they often fall by kicking down. When Lay sought to impress the Wall Street analysts, he did so by exploiting his own employees, asking them to compromise their integrity to construct a façade that would deceive the analysts. Research shows that as people gain power, they feel large and in charge: less constrained and freer to express their natural tendencies. As takers gain power, they pay less attention to how they're perceived by those below and next to them; they feel entitled to pursue self-serving goals and claim as much value as they can. Over time, treating peers and subordinates poorly jeopardizes their relationships and reputations. After all, most people are matchers: their core values emphasize fairness, equality, and reciprocity. When takers violate these principles, matchers in their networks believe in an eye for an eye, so they want to see justice served.

To illustrate, imagine that you're participating in a famous study led by Daniel Kahneman, the Nobel Prize–winning psychologist at Princeton. You're playing what's known as the ultimatum game, and you sit down across the table from a stranger who has just been given $10. His task is to present you with a proposal about how the money will be divided between the two of you. It's an ultimatum: you can either accept the proposal as it stands and split the money as proposed, or you can reject it, and both of you will get nothing. You might never see each other again, so he acts like a taker, keeping $8 and offering you only $2. What do you do?

In terms of pure profit, it's rational for you to accept the offer. After all, $2 is better than nothing. But if you're like most people, you reject it. You're willing to sacrifice the money to punish the taker for being unfair, walking away with nothing just to keep him from earning $8. Evidence shows that the vast majority of people in this position reject proposals that are imbalanced to the tune of 80 percent or more for the divider.*

Why do we punish takers for being unfair? It's not spite. We're not getting revenge on takers for trying to take advantage of us. It's about justice. If you're a matcher, you'll also punish takers for acting unfairly toward *other* people. Gretchen Rubin calls matchers the "karma police." In another study spearheaded by Kahneman, people had a choice between splitting $12 evenly with a taker who had made

---

*Interestingly, in ultimatum games, it's rare for the divider to propose anything that's so lopsided. More than three quarters of dividers propose a perfectly even split, acting like matchers.

an unfair proposal in the past or splitting $10 evenly with a matcher who had made a fair proposal in the past. More than 80 percent of the people preferred to split $10 evenly with the matcher, accepting $5 rather than $6 to prevent the taker from getting $6.

In networks, new research shows that when people get burned by takers, they punish them by sharing reputational information. "Gossip represents a widespread, efficient, and low-cost form of punishment," write the social scientists Matthew Feinberg, Joey Cheng, and Robb Willer. When reputational information suggests that someone has taker tendencies, we can withhold trust and avoid being exploited. Over time, as their reputations spread, takers end up cutting existing ties and burning bridges with potential new ties. When Lay's taking was revealed, many of his former supporters—including the Bush family—distanced themselves from him. As Wayne Baker, a University of Michigan sociologist and networking expert, explains, "If we create networks with the sole intention of *getting something*, we won't succeed. We can't *pursue* the benefits of networks; the benefits ensue from investments in meaningful activities and relationships."

Before we make the leap of investing in relationships, though, we need to be able to recognize takers in our everyday interactions. For many of us, a challenge of networking lies in trying to guess the motives or intentions of a new contact, especially since we've seen that takers can be quite adept at posing as givers when there's a potential return. Is the next person you meet interested in a genuine connection or merely seeking personal gains—and is there a good way to tell the difference?

Luckily, research shows that takers leak clues. Well, more precisely, takers *lek* clues.

In the animal kingdom, *lekking* refers to a ritual in which males show off their desirability as mates. When it's time to breed, they gather in a common place and take their established positions. They put on extravagant displays to impress and court female audiences.

Some do mating dances. Some sing alluring songs. Some even do acrobatics. The most striking display of lekking occurs among male peacocks. Each mating season, the males assume their positions and begin parading their plumage. They strut. They spread their feathers. They spin around to flaunt their tails.

In the CEO kingdom, takers do a dance that looks remarkably similar.

In a landmark study, strategy professors Arijit Chatterjee and Donald Hambrick studied more than a hundred CEOs in computer hardware and software companies. They analyzed each company's annual reports over more than a decade, looking for signs of lekking. What they found would forever change the face of leadership.

It turns out that we could have anticipated the collapse of Enron as early as 1997, without ever meeting Ken Lay or looking at a single number. The warning signs of Enron's demise are visible in a single image, captured four years before the company unraveled. Take a look at the two pictures of CEOs below, reproduced from their companies' annual reports. Both men started their lives in poverty, worked in the Nixon administration, founded their own companies, became rich CEOs, and donated substantial sums of money to charity. Can you tell from their faces—or their clothes—which one was a taker?

The man on the left is Jon Huntsman Sr., a giver whom we'll meet in chapter 6, from his company's 2006 annual report. The photo on the right depicts Ken Lay. Thousands of experts have analyzed Enron's financial statements, but they've missed an important fact: a picture really is worth a thousand words. Had we looked more carefully at the Enron reports, we might have recognized the telltale signs of takers lekking at the helm.

But these signs aren't where I expected to find them—they're not in the faces or attire of the CEOs. In their study of CEOs in the computer industry, Chatterjee and Hambrick had a hunch that takers would see themselves as the suns in their companies' solar systems. They found several clues of takers lekking at the top. One signal appeared in CEO interviews. Since takers tend to be self-absorbed, they're more likely to use first-person singular pronouns like *I, me, mine, my,* and *myself*—versus first-person plural pronouns like *we, us, our, ours,* and *ourselves*. In the computer industry, when talking about the company, on average, 21 percent of CEOs' first-person pronouns were in the singular. For the extreme takers, 39 percent of their first-person pronouns were in the singular. Of every ten words that the taker CEOs uttered referencing themselves, four were about themselves alone and no one else.

Another signal was compensation: the taker CEOs earned far more money than other senior executives in their companies. The takers saw themselves as superior, so they felt entitled to substantial pay discrepancies in their own favor. In the computer industry, a typical taker CEO took home more than triple the annual salary and bonus of anyone else in the company. By contrast, the average across the industry was for CEOs to earn just over one and a half times the next highest paid. The taker CEOs also commanded stock options and other noncash compensation of seven times higher than the next highest paid, compared with the industry average of two and a half times higher.*

But the most interesting clue was in the annual reports that the companies produced for shareholders each year. Below are the pictures of Ken Lay and Jon Huntsman Sr. that I showed you before, but now they're in context.

The photo on the left appeared in Huntsman's 2006 annual report. His image is tiny, taking up less than 10 percent of the page. The photo on the right appeared in Enron's 1997 annual report. The image of Lay takes up an entire page.

When Chatterjee and Hambrick looked at the annual reports from the computer companies, they noticed dramatic differences in the prominence of the CEO's image. In some annual reports, the

---

* In the computer industry study, when taker CEOs were at the helm, firms had more fluctuating, extreme performance, as measured by total shareholder returns and return on assets. They had bigger wins, but bigger losses. The takers were supremely confident in their bets, so they swung for the fences. They made bold, grandiose moves, which included more and larger acquisitions, as well as major upheavals to company strategy. Sometimes these moves paid off, but in the long run, the takers often put their companies in jeopardy. By contrast, new evidence shows that technology firms led by givers have higher returns on assets. Firms perform better when CEOs care more about the company's success than their own and emphasise the importance of giving back.

CEO wasn't pictured at all. In other reports, there was a full-page photo of the CEO alone. Guess which one is the taker?

For the taker CEOs, it was all about *me*. A big photo is self-glorifying, sending a clear message: "I am the central figure in this company." But is this really a signal of being a taker? To find out, Chatterjee and Hambrick invited security analysts who specialized in the information technology sector to rate the CEOs. The analysts rated whether each CEO had an "inflated sense of self that is reflected in feelings of superiority, entitlement, and a constant need for attention and admiration . . . enjoying being the center of attention, insisting upon being shown a great deal of respect, exhibitionism, and arrogance." The analysts' ratings correlated almost perfectly with the size of the CEOs' photos.

At Enron, in that prescient 1997 report, the spotlight was on Ken Lay. Of the first nine pages, two were dominated by giant full-page images of Lay and then-COO Jeff Skilling. The pattern continued in 1998 and 1999, with full-page photos of Lay and Skilling. By 2000, Lay and Skilling had moved up to pages four and five, albeit with smaller images. There were four different photos of each of them, like a film-strip—only they were better fit for a cartoon. Three of the photos of Lay were virtually identical, revealing the subtle, smug smile of an executive who knew he was special. A fairy-tale ending was not in the cards for Lay, who died of a heart attack before sentencing.

So far, we've looked at two different ways to recognize takers. First, when we have access to reputational information, we can see how people have treated others in their networks. Second, when we have a chance to observe the actions and imprints of takers, we can look for signs of lekking. Self-glorifying images, self-absorbed conversations, and sizable pay gaps can send accurate, reliable signals that someone is a taker. Thanks to some dramatic changes in the world since 2001, these signals are easier to spot today than ever before. Networks have become more transparent, providing us with new windows through which we can view other people's reputations and lekking.

The Transparent Network

In 2002, just months after Enron fell apart, a computer scientist by the name of Jonathan Abrams founded Friendster, creating the world's first online social network. Friendster made it possible for people to post their profiles online and broadcast their connections to the world. In the following two years, entrepreneurs launched LinkedIn, Myspace, and Facebook. Strangers now had access to one another's relationships and reputations. By 2012, the world population reached seven billion. At the same time, Facebook's active users approached a billion, meaning that more than 10 percent of the people in the world are connected on Facebook. "Social networks have always existed," write psychologists Benjamin Crosier, Gregory Webster, and Haley Dillon. "It is only recently that the Internet has provided a venue for their electronic explosion. . . . From mundane communication to meeting the love of one's life to inciting political revolutions, network ties are the conduits by which information and resources are spread."

These online connections have simulated a defining feature of the old world. Before technological revolutions helped us communicate by phone and e-mail, and travel by car and plane, people had relatively manageable numbers of social ties in tightly connected, transparent circles. Within these insulated networks, people could easily gather reputational information and observe lekking. As communication and transportation became easier, and the sheer size of the population grew, interactions became more dispersed and anonymous. Reputations and lekking became less visible. This is why Ken Lay was able to keep much of his taking hidden. As he moved from one position and organization to another, his contacts didn't always have easy access to one another, and the new people who entered his network didn't gain a great deal of information about his reputation. Inside Enron, his impromptu actions couldn't be documented on YouTube, broadcast on Twitter, easily indexed in a Google search, or posted anonymously on internal blogs or the company intranet.

Now, it's much harder for takers to get away with being fakers, fooling people into thinking they're givers. On the Internet, we can now track down reputational information about our contacts by accessing public databases and discovering shared connections. And we no longer need a company's annual report to catch a taker, because lekking in its many sizes and forms abounds in social network profiles. Tiny cues like words and photos can reveal profound clues about us, and research suggests that ordinary people can identify takers just by looking at their Facebook profiles. In one study, psychologists asked people to fill out a survey measuring whether they were takers. Then, the psychologists sent strangers to visit their Facebook pages. The strangers were able to detect the takers with astonishing accuracy.

The takers posted information that was rated as more self-promoting, self-absorbed, and self-important. They featured quotes that were evaluated as boastful and arrogant. The takers also had significantly more Facebook friends, racking up superficial connections so they could advertise their accomplishments and stay in touch to get favors, and posted vainer, more flattering pictures of themselves.

Howard Lee, the former head of South China at Groupon, is one of a growing number of people who use social media to catch takers. When Lee hired salespeople, many of the strong candidates were aggressive, making it difficult to distinguish the takers from the candidates who are simply gregarious and driven. Lee was enamored with one candidate who had an outstanding résumé, aced his interview, and had glowing references. But the candidate could have been faking: "talking to someone for an hour only gives you a glimpse, the tip of the iceberg," Lee thought, "and the references were self-selected." A taker could easily find some superiors to sing his praises.

So Lee searched through his LinkedIn and Facebook networks and identified a mutual connection, who shared some disconcerting information about the candidate. "He seemed to be a taker, and it carried a lot of weight. If he's been ruthless in one company, do I want to work with him?" Lee feels that online social networks have revolutionized Groupon's hiring process. "Nowadays, I don't need to call in to a company to find out about someone's reputation. Everyone is incredibly connected. Once they make it past the technical rounds, I check their LinkedIn or Facebook. Sometimes we have mutual friends, or went to the same school, or the people on my team will have a link to them," Lee explains. "You can understand someone's reputation at a peer level pretty quickly." When your relationships and reputations are visible to the world, it's harder to achieve sustainable success as a taker.

In Silicon Valley, a quiet man who looks like a panda bear is taking transparent networks to the next level. His name is Adam Forrest Rifkin, and he has been called the giant panda of programming. He describes himself as a shy, introverted computer nerd who has two favorite languages: JavaScript, the computer programming language, and Klingon, the language spoken by the aliens on *Star Trek*.* Rifkin is an "anagramaniac": he has spent countless hours rearranging the letters in his name to find the one that captures him best, generating candidates such as *Offer Radiant Smirk* and *Feminist Radar Fork*. Rifkin has two master's degrees in computer science, owns a patent, and has developed supercomputer applications for NASA and Internet systems for Microsoft. As the new millennium

---

* This is a nod to a "Weird Al" Yankovic song about nerds, which includes the line, "I'm fluent in JavaScript as well as Klingon." For the record, Rifkin worries about the amount of time that he has wasted in his life typing two spaces after a period, instead of one.

approached, Rifkin cofounded KnowNow, a software start-up with Rohit Khare, helping companies manage information more efficiently and profitably. KnowNow achieved a decade of success after bringing in more than $50 million in venture funding. By 2009, while still in his thirties, Rifkin announced his retirement.

I came across Rifkin while scrolling through the LinkedIn connections of David Hornik, the venture capitalist whom you met in the previous chapter. When I clicked on Rifkin's profile, I saw that he was coming out of retirement to launch a start-up called PandaWhale, with the goal of creating a public, permanent record of the information that people exchange. Since Rifkin is clearly a staunch advocate of transparency in networks, I was curious to see what his own network looks like. So I did what's only natural in a connected world: I went to Google and typed "Adam Rifkin." As I scrolled through the search results, the sixteenth link caught my eye. It said that Adam Rifkin was *Fortune*'s best networker.

What Goes Around Comes Around

In 2011, Adam Rifkin had more LinkedIn connections to the 640 powerful people on *Fortune*'s lists than any human being on the planet. He beat out luminaries like Michael Dell, the billionaire founder of the Dell computer company, and Jeff Weiner, the CEO of LinkedIn.* I was stunned that a shy, *Star Trek*–loving, anagram-obsessing software geek managed to build a network that includes the founders of Facebook, Netscape, Napster, Twitter, Flickr, and Half.com.

Adam Rifkin built his network by operating as a bona fide giver. "My network developed little by little, in fact a little every day

* Technically, since LinkedIn employees have a host of advantages in connecting with people on LinkedIn, insiders were excluded from the *Fortune* analysis. Unofficially, it is noteworthy that Rifkin topped every LinkedIn employee except two: founder Reid Hoffman and board member and investor David Sze.

through small gestures and acts of kindness, over the course of many years," Rifkin explains, "with a desire to make better the lives of the people I'm connected to." Since 1994, Rifkin has served as a leader and watchdog in a wide range of online communities, working diligently to strengthen relationships and help people resolve online conflicts. As the cofounder of Renkoo, a start-up with Joyce Park, Rifkin created applications that were used more than 500 million times by more than 36 million people on Facebook and Myspace. Despite their popularity, Rifkin wasn't satisfied. "If you're going to get tens of millions of people using your software, you really should do something meaningful, something that changes the world," he says. "Frankly, I would like to see more people helping other people." He decided to shut down Renkoo and become a full-time giver, offering extensive guidance to start-ups and working to connect engineers and entrepreneurs with businesspeople in larger companies.

To this end, in 2005, Rifkin and Joyce Park founded 106 Miles, a professional network with the social mission of educating entrepreneurial engineers through dialogue. This network has brought together more than five thousand entrepreneurs who meet twice every month to help one another learn and succeed. "I get roped into giving free advice to other entrepreneurs, which is usually worth less than they pay for it," he muses, but "helping others is my favorite thing to do."

This approach has led to great things—not just for Rifkin, but also for those he's shepherded along the way. In 2001, Rifkin was a big fan of Blogger, an early blog publishing service. Blogger had run out of funding, so Rifkin offered a contract to Blogger's founder to do some work for his own first start-up, KnowNow. "We decided to hire him because we wanted to see Blogger survive," Rifkin says. "We gave him a contract to build something for our company so we could use it as a demo and he could keep Blogger going." The money from the contract helped the founder keep Blogger afloat, and he went on to cofound a company called Twitter. "There were several other people who also contracted with Evan Williams so he could keep his company going," Rifkin reflects. "You never know where somebody's going to end up. It's not just about building your reputation; it really is about being there for other people."

In the search for *Fortune*'s best networker, when Rifkin popped up as the winner, the reporter on the story, Jessica Shambora, laughed out loud. "Not surprisingly, I had already met him! Someone had referred me to him for a story I was researching on virtual goods and social networks." Shambora, who now works at Facebook, says that Rifkin is "the consummate networker, and he didn't get that way by being some sort of climber, or calculated. People go to Adam because they know his heart is in the right place." When he first moved up to Silicon Valley, Rifkin felt that giving was a natural way to come out of his shell. "As a very shy, sheltered computer guy, the concept of the network was my north star," he says. "When you have nothing, what's the first thing you try to do? You try to make a connection and have a relationship that gives you an opportunity to do something for someone else."

On Rifkin's LinkedIn page, his motto is "I want to improve the world, and I want to smell good while doing it." As of September 2012, on LinkedIn, 49 people have written recommendations for Rifkin, and no attribute is mentioned more frequently than his giving. A matcher would write recommendations back for the same 49 people, and perhaps sprinkle in a few unsolicited recommendations for key contacts, in the hopes that they'll reciprocate. But Rifkin gives more than five times as much as he gets: on LinkedIn, he has written detailed recommendations for 265 different people. "Adam is off the charts in how much he helps," says the entrepreneur Raymond Rouf. "He gives a lot more than he receives. It's part of his mantra to be helpful."

Rifkin's networking style, which exemplifies how givers tend to approach networks, stands in stark contrast to the way that takers and matchers tend to build and extract value from their connections. The fact that Rifkin gives a lot more than he receives is a key point: takers and matchers also give in the context of networks, but they tend to give strategically, with an expected personal return that exceeds or equals their contributions. When takers and matchers network, they tend to focus on who can help them in the near future, and this dictates what, where, and how they give. Their actions tend to exploit a common practice in nearly all societies around the world, in which people typically subscribe to a norm of reciprocity: you scratch my back, I'll scratch yours. If you help me, I'm indebted to you, and I feel obligated to repay. According to the psychologist Robert Cialdini, people can capitalize on this norm of reciprocity by giving what they want to receive. Instead of just reactively doing favors for the people who have already helped them, takers and matchers often proactively offer favors to people whose help they want in the future.* As networking guru Keith Ferrazzi summarizes in *Never Eat Alone*, "It's better to give before you receive."

Ken Lay lived by this principle: he had a knack for doing unrequested favors so that important people would feel compelled to respond in kind. When he was kissing up, he went out of his way to rack up credits with powerful people who he could call in later. In 1994, George W. Bush was running for governor of Texas. Bush was an underdog, but just in case, Lay made a donation of $12,500, as did his wife. Once Bush was elected governor, Lay supported one of Bush's literacy initiatives and ended up writing him two dozen lobbying letters. According to one citizen watchdog leader, Lay commanded "quid pro quo," helping Bush so that Bush would

---

* Of course, when takers and matchers give to receive, they do so with different aims. Takers are usually looking to get as much as possible, whereas matchers are motivated to maintain equal exchanges.

support utility deregulation. In one letter, Lay subtly hinted at his willingness to continue reciprocating if Bush helped to advance his goals: "let me know what Enron can do to be helpful in not only passing electricity restructuring legislation but also in pursuing the rest of your legislative agenda."

Reciprocity is a powerful norm, but it comes with two downsides, both of which contribute to the cautiousness with which many of us approach networking. The first downside is that people on the receiving end often feel like they're being manipulated. Dan Weinstein, a former Olympic speed skater and current marketing consultant at Resource Systems Group, notes that "some of the bigger management consulting firms own box seats at major sporting events. When these firms offer Red Sox tickets to their clients, the clients know that they're doing so, at least in part, with the hopes of getting something in return." When favors come with strings attached or implied, the interaction can leave a bad taste, feeling more like a transaction than part of a meaningful relationship. Do you really care about helping me, or are you just trying to create quid pro quo so that you can ask for a favor?

Apparently, Ken Lay made such an impression on George W. Bush. When Bush was running for governor, he asked Lay to chair one of his finance campaigns. At the time, Lay didn't think Bush had a chance, so he declined, stating that he was already serving on a business council for the Democratic incumbent, Ann Richards. As a consolation prize, he made his $12,500 donation. Then, toward the end of the campaign, when it looked like Bush had a good chance of winning, Lay quickly made another donation of $12,500. Even though Lay ended up donating more money to Bush than to Richards, his decision to give only when it was strategic left an indelible dent in the relationship. This decision "relegated him forever to the periphery of George W. Bush's inner circle," wrote one journalist, citing a dozen insiders who confided that Lay created "a distance between them that was never really bridged." Bush never invited Lay to stay in the White House, as his father had. When the Enron scandal broke, Lay reached out to a number of political officials for help, but Bush wasn't one of them—the relationship wasn't strong enough.

There's a second downside of reciprocity, and it's one to which matchers are especially vulnerable. Matchers tend to build smaller networks than either givers, who seek actively to help a wider range of people, or takers, who often find themselves expanding their networks to compensate for bridges burned in previous transactions. Many matchers operate based on the attitude of "I'll do something for you, if you'll do something for me," writes LinkedIn founder Reid Hoffman, so they "limit themselves to deals in which their immediate benefit is at least as great as the benefits for others . . . If you insist on a quid pro quo every time you help others, you will have a much narrower network." When matchers give with the expectation of receiving, they direct their giving toward people who they think can help them. After all, if you don't benefit from having your favors reciprocated, what's the value of being a matcher?

As these disadvantages of strict reciprocity accrue over time, they can limit both the quantity and quality of the networks that takers and matchers develop. Both disadvantages ultimately arise out of a shortsightedness about networks, in that takers and matchers make hard-and-fast assumptions about just who will be able to provide the most benefit in exchange. At its core, the giver approach extends a broader reach, and in doing so enlarges the range of potential payoffs, even though those payoffs are not the motivating engine. "When you meet people," says former Apple evangelist and Silicon Valley legend Guy Kawasaki, regardless of who they are, "you should be asking yourself, 'How can I help the other person?'" This may strike some as a way to overinvest in others, but as Adam Rifkin once learned to great effect, we can't always predict who can help us.

Waking the Sleeping Giants

In 1993, a college student named Graham Spencer teamed up with five friends to build an Internet start-up. Spencer was a shy, introverted computer engineer with a receding hairline, huge glasses, and an obsession with comic books. Looking back, he says Superman taught him justice and virtue, the X-Men kindled concern for oppressed groups, and Spider-Man gave him hope: "even superheroes could have a rough time in school."

Spencer and his friends cofounded Excite, an early Web portal and search engine that quickly became one of the most popular sites on the Internet. In 1998, Excite was purchased for $6.7 billion, and Spencer was flying high as its largest shareholder and chief technology officer. In 1999, shortly after selling Excite, Spencer received an e-mail out of the blue from Adam Rifkin, who was asking for advice on a start-up. They had never met, but Spencer volunteered to sit down with Rifkin anyway. After they met, Spencer connected Rifkin with a venture capitalist who ended up funding his start-up. How did Rifkin get access to Spencer? And why did Spencer go out of his way to help Rifkin?

Early in 1994, five years before seeking Spencer's help, Rifkin became enamored with an emerging band. He wanted to help the band gain popularity, so he put his computer prowess into action and created a fan website, hosted on the Caltech server. "It was an authentic expression of being a fan of music. I loved the music." The page took off: hundreds of thousands of people found it as the band skyrocketed from anonymity into stardom.

The band was called Green Day.

Rifkin's fan site was so popular in the burgeoning days of the commercial Internet that in 1995, Green Day's managers contacted him to ask if they could take it over and make it the band's official page. "I said, 'Great, it's all yours'," Rifkin recalls. "I just gave it to them." The previous summer, in 1994, millions of people had visited Rifkin's site. One of the visitors, a serious punk rock fan, felt that Green Day was really pop music. He had e-mailed Rifkin to educate him about "real" punk rock.

The fan was none other than Graham Spencer. Spencer suggested that when people searched for punk rock on the Internet, they should find more than Green Day. When Rifkin read the e-mail, he imagined Spencer as a stereotypical punk rock fan with a green Mohawk. Rifkin had no idea that Spencer would ever be able to help him—it would only come out much later that Spencer had just started Excite. A taker or matcher might have ignored the e-mail from Spencer. But as a giver, Rifkin's natural inclination was to help Spencer spread the word about punk rock and help struggling bands build up a fan base. So Rifkin set up a separate page on the Green Day fan site with links to the punk rock bands that Spencer suggested.

There's an elegance to Adam Rifkin's experience with Graham Spencer, a satisfying sense of good deeds rewarded. But if we take a closer look, we find an example of just what makes giver networks so powerful, and it has as much to do with the five years that passed after Rifkin's generosity as with the generosity itself. Rifkin's experiences foreshadow how givers have the advantage of accessing the full breadth of their networks.

One of Rifkin's maxims is "I believe in the strength of weak ties." It's in homage to a classic study by the Stanford sociologist Mark Granovetter. Strong ties are our close friends and colleagues, the people we really trust. Weak ties are our acquaintances, the people we know casually. Testing the common assumption that we get the most help from our strong ties, Granovetter surveyed people in professional, technical, and managerial professions who had recently changed jobs. Nearly 17 percent heard about the job from a strong tie. Their friends and trusted colleagues gave them plenty of leads.

But surprisingly, people were significantly more likely to benefit from weak ties. Almost 28 percent heard about the job from a weak tie. Strong ties provide bonds, but weak ties serve as bridges: they provide more efficient access to new information. Our strong ties tend to travel in the same social circles and know about the same opportunities as we do. Weak ties are more likely to open up access to a different network, facilitating the discovery of original leads.

Here's the wrinkle: it's tough to ask weak ties for help. Although they're the faster route to new leads, we don't always feel comfortable reaching out to them. The lack of mutual trust between acquaintances creates a psychological barrier. But givers like Adam Rifkin have discovered a loophole. It's possible to get the best of both worlds: the trust of strong ties coupled with the novel information of weak ties.

The key is reconnecting, and it's a major reason why givers succeed in the long run.

After Rifkin created the punk rock links on the Green Day site for Spencer in 1994, Excite took off, and Rifkin went back to graduate school. They lost touch for five years. When Rifkin was moving to Silicon Valley, he dug up the old e-mail chain and drafted a note to Spencer. "You may not remember me from five years ago; I'm the guy who made the change to the Green Day website," Rifkin wrote. "I'm starting a company and moving to Silicon Valley, and I don't know a lot of people. Would you be willing to meet with me and offer advice?"

Rifkin wasn't being a matcher. When he originally helped Spencer, he did it with no strings attached, never intending to call in a favor. But five years later, when he needed help, he reached out with a genuine request. Spencer was glad to help, and they met up for coffee. "I still pictured him as this huge guy with a Mohawk," Rifkin says. "When I met him in person, he hardly said any words at all. He was even more introverted than I am." By the second meeting, Spencer was introducing Rifkin to a venture capitalist. "A completely random set of events that happened in 1994 led to reengaging with him over e-mail in 1999, which led to my company getting founded in 2000," Rifkin recalls. "Givers get lucky."

Yet there's reason to believe that part of what Rifkin calls luck is in fact a predictable, patterned response that most people have to givers. Thirty years ago, the sociologist Fred Goldner wrote about what it means to experience the opposite of paranoia: *pronoia*. According to the distinguished psychologist Brian Little, pronoia is "the delusional belief that other people are plotting your well-being, or saying nice things about you behind your back."

If you're a giver, this belief may be a reality, not a delusion. What if other people are actually plotting the success of givers like Adam Rifkin?

In 2005, when Rifkin was starting Renkoo with Joyce Park, they didn't have any office space, so they were working out of Rifkin's kitchen. A colleague went out of his way to introduce Rifkin to Reid Hoffman, who had recently founded LinkedIn, which had fewer than fifty employees at the time. Hoffman met up with Rifkin and Park on a Sunday and offered them free desks at LinkedIn, putting Rifkin in the heart of Silicon Valley. "In the summer of 2005, one of the companies right next to us was YouTube, and we got to meet them in their infancy before they really took off," Rifkin says.

Rifkin's experience sheds new light on the old saying that what goes around comes around. These karmic moments can often be traced to the fact that matchers are on a mission to make them happen. Just as matchers will sacrifice their own interests to punish takers who act selfishly toward others, they'll go out of their way to reward givers who act generously toward others. When Adam Rifkin helped people in his network, the matchers felt it was only fair to plot his well-being. True to form, he used his newfound access at LinkedIn to plot the well-being of other people in his network, referring engineers for jobs at LinkedIn.

On a Wednesday evening in May, I got to see the panda in his natural habitat. At a bar for a 106 Miles meeting in Redwood City, Rifkin walked in with a huge grin, wearing a San Francisco Giants jersey. He was immediately swarmed by a group of tech entrepreneurs—some smooth, others endearingly awkward. As dozens of entrepreneurs piled into the bar, Rifkin was able to tell me each of their stories, which was no small feat for someone who receives more than eight hundred e-mails in a typical day.

His secret was deceptively simple: he asked thoughtful questions and listened with remarkable patience. Early in the evening, Rifkin asked one budding entrepreneur how his company was doing. The entrepreneur talked for fourteen minutes without interruption. Although the monologue might have exhausted even the most curious of tech geeks, Rifkin never lost interest. "Where do you need help?" he asked, and the entrepreneur mentioned a need for a programmer specializing in an obscure computer language. Rifkin started scrolling through his mental Rolodex and recommended candidates to contact. Later in the evening, one of those candidates arrived in person, and Rifkin made the introduction. As the crowd grew, Rifkin still took the time to have a personal conversation with everyone there. When new members approached him, he typically spent fifteen or twenty minutes getting to know them, asking what motivated them and how he could help them. Many of those people were complete strangers, but just as he had helped Graham Spencer eighteen years earlier without thinking twice, he took it upon himself to find them jobs, connect them to potential cofounders, and offer advice for solving problems in their companies. Each time he gave, he created a new connection. But is it really possible to keep up with all of these contacts?

Dormant Ties

Because he maintains such a large network, Adam Rifkin has a growing number of dormant ties—people he used to see often or know well, but with whom he has since fallen out of contact. According to management professors Daniel Levin, Jorge Walter, and Keith Murnighan, "adults accumulate thousands of relationships over their lifetimes, but, prior to the Internet, they actively maintained no more than 100 or 200 at any given time." For the past few years, these professors have been asking executives to do something that they dread: reactivate their dormant ties. When one executive learned of the assignment, "I groaned. If there are dormant contacts, they are dormant for a reason, right? Why would I want to contact them?"

But the evidence tells a different story. In one study, Levin and colleagues asked more than two hundred executives to reactivate ties that had been dormant for a minimum of three years. Each executive reached out to two former colleagues and sought advice on an ongoing work project. After receiving the advice, they rated its value: to what extent did it help them solve problems and gain useful referrals? They also rated the advice that they received from two current contacts on the same project. Surprisingly, the executives rated the advice from the dormant ties as contributing more value than the advice from the current ties. Why?

The dormant ties provided more novel information than the current contacts. Over the past few years, while they were out of touch, they had been exposed to new ideas and perspectives. The current contacts were more likely to share the knowledge base and viewpoint that the executives already possessed. One executive commented that "before contacting them I thought that they would not have too much to provide beyond what I had already thought, but I was proved wrong. I was very surprised by the fresh ideas."

Dormant ties offer the access to novel information that weak ties afford, but without the discomfort. As Levin and colleagues explain, "reconnecting a dormant relationship is not like starting a relationship from scratch. When people reconnect, they still have *feelings of trust*." An executive divulged that "I feel comfortable . . . I didn't need to guess what his intentions were . . . there was mutual trust that we built years ago that made our conversation today smoother." Reactivating a dormant tie actually required a shorter conversation, since there was already some common ground. The executives didn't need to invest in building a relationship from the start with their dormant ties, as they would with weak ties.

Levin and colleagues asked another group of more than one hundred executives to identify ten dormant ties and rank them in order of the likely value they would provide. The executives then reactivated all ten dormant ties and rated the value of the conversations. All ten dormant ties provided high value, and there were no differences by rank: the executives got just as much value from their tenth choice as from their first choice. When we need new information, we may run out of weak ties quickly, but we have a large pool of dormant ties that prove to be helpful. And the older we get, the more dormant ties we have, and the more valuable they become. Levin and colleagues found that people in their forties and fifties received more value from reactivating dormant ties than people in their thirties, who in turn benefited more than people in their twenties. The executive who groaned about reconnecting admitted that it "has been eye-opening for me . . . it has shown me how much potential I have in my Rolodex."

Dormant ties are the neglected value in our networks, and givers have a distinctive edge over takers and matchers in unlocking this value. For takers, reactivating dormant ties is a challenge. If the dormant ties are fellow takers, they'll be suspicious and self-protective, withholding novel information. If the dormant ties are matchers, they may be motivated to punish takers, as we saw in the ultimatum game. If the dormant ties are smart givers, as you'll see later in this book, they won't be so willing to help takers. And of course, if a taker's self-serving actions were what caused a tie to become dormant in the first place, it may be impossible to revive the relationship at all.

Matchers have a much easier time reconnecting, but they're often uncomfortable reaching out for help because of their fidelity to the norm of reciprocity. When they ask for a favor, they feel that they'll owe one back. If they're already indebted to the dormant tie and haven't yet evened the score, it's doubly difficult to ask. And for many matchers, dormant ties haven't built up a deep reservoir of trust, since they've been more like transactional exchanges than meaningful relationships.

According to networking experts, reconnecting is a totally different experience for givers, especially in a wired world. Givers have a track record of generously sharing their knowledge, teaching us their skills, and helping us find jobs without worrying about what's in it for them, so we're glad to help them when they get back in touch with us. Today, Adam Rifkin spends less time networking with new people than he did earlier in his career, focusing instead on a growing number of dormant ties. "Now my time is spent going back to people who I haven't talked to in a while." When he reactivates one of his many dormant ties, the contact is usually thrilled to hear from him. His generosity and kindness have earned their trust. They're grateful for his help, and they know it didn't come with strings attached; he's always willing to share his knowledge, offer advice, or make an introduction. In 2006, Rifkin was looking for a dynamite speaker for a 106 Miles meeting. He reconnected with Evan Williams, and although Williams had become famous and was extremely busy with the launch of Twitter, he agreed. "Five years later, when we asked him to speak to the group, he never forgot," Rifkin says.

The type of goodwill that givers like Rifkin build is the subject of fascinating research. Traditionally, social network researchers map information exchange: the flows of knowledge from person to person. But when Wayne Baker collaborated with University of Virginia professor Rob Cross and IBM's Andrew Parker, he realized that it was also possible to track the flows of energy through networks. In a range of organizations, employees rated their interactions with one another on a scale from strongly de-energizing to strongly energizing. The researchers created an energy network map, which looked like a model of a galaxy.

The takers were black holes. They sucked the energy from those around them. The givers were suns: they injected light around the organization. Givers created opportunities for their colleagues to contribute, rather than imposing their ideas and hogging credit for achievements. When they disagreed with suggestions, givers showed respect for the people who spoke up, rather than belittling them.

If you mapped energy in Adam Rifkin's network, you'd find that he looks like the sun in many different solar systems. Several years ago at a holiday party, Rifkin met a struggling entrepreneur named Raymond Rouf. They started chatting, and Rifkin gave him some feedback. Six months later, Rouf was working on a new start-up and reached out to Rifkin for advice. Rifkin replied the same day and set up a breakfast for the next morning, where he spent two hours giving more feedback to Rouf. A few months later, they crossed paths again. Rouf had gone two years without an income, and the plumbing in his house wasn't working, so he bought a gym membership just to shower there. He ran into Rifkin, who asked how the start-up was going and offered some invaluable insights about how to reposition his company. Rifkin then proceeded to introduce Rouf to a venture capitalist, who ended up funding his company and becoming a board member. "The two of them would have meetings about me, to discuss how they could help me," Rouf says. Rouf's company, Graph-Science, has become one of the top Facebook analytics companies in the world—and he says it never would have happened without Rifkin's help.

Rifkin has even managed to light up projects for a Hollywood writer/director. As you'll see in chapter 8, they met because Rifkin shared his contact information openly on the Internet. In a casual conversation, the Hollywood director mentioned that he had just finished production on a Showtime series and asked Rifkin for help. "Although he is quite successful in his chosen field, I didn't put too much credence in his skill as a Hollywood publicist," says the director. "Boy was I wrong!" Within twenty-four hours, Rifkin set up meetings and private screenings of the show with top-ranking executives at Twitter and YouTube. The Hollywood contact explains:

> It's important to emphasize: Adam had absolutely no stake in my show's success. Sink or swim, he wouldn't benefit or suffer either way. But true to his genuine joy of giving, he went out of his way to introduce us to countless media opportunities. When the dust had settled, he was singlehandedly responsible for positive and glowing articles in countless national media outlets as well as incredible social media publicity. In the end, his generosity was more far reaching and far more effective than our show's highly paid Hollywood publicist. As a result, the show enjoyed the highest ratings ever received in its time slot in Showtime's history! Showtime, so impressed with our modest show's numbers, has already given the green light to another series. His generosity is responsible for the show being a hit and Showtime saying yes to my current series.

For someone who gives off these vibes and inspires such goodwill, reconnecting is an energizing experience. Think back to the 265 people for whom Rifkin has written LinkedIn recommendations, or the hundreds of entrepreneurs he helps in 106 Miles. It's not a stretch to imagine that every one of them will be enthusiastic about reconnecting with Rifkin, and helping him out, if they happen to lose touch.

But Adam Rifkin isn't after their help—at least not for himself. Rifkin's real aim is to change our fundamental ideas about how we build our networks and who should benefit from them. He believes that we should see networks as a vehicle for creating value for everyone, not just claiming it for ourselves. And he is convinced that this giver approach to networking can uproot the traditional norm of reciprocity in a manner that's highly productive for all involved.

The Five-Minute Favor

In 2012, a LinkedIn recruiter named Stephanie was asked to list the three people who had the most influence on her career. Adam Rifkin was shocked to learn that he appeared on her list, because they had met only once, months earlier. Stephanie was searching for a job and met Rifkin through a friend of a friend. He gave her advice, primarily by text message, and helped her find job leads. She e-mailed him to express her gratitude and offered to reciprocate: "I know we only met in person once and we talk only occasionally, but you have helped me more than you know . . . I really would like to do something to help give back to you."

But Stephanie wasn't just looking to help Adam Rifkin. Instead, she volunteered to attend a 106 Miles meeting of Silicon Valley entrepreneurs so she could help Rifkin help them. At the meeting, Stephanie would give entrepreneurs feedback on their ideas, offer to test their product prototypes, and facilitate connections with potential collaborators and investors. The same thing has happened with many other people whom Rifkin helps. Raymond Rouf often drops by 106 Miles meetings to assist other entrepreneurs. So does an engineer named Bob, who met Rifkin in a bar in 2009. They struck up a conversation, and Rifkin learned that Bob was out of work, so he made some introductions that landed Bob a position. The company went out of business, and Rifkin made more connections that resulted in a job for Bob at a start-up, which was acquired six months later by Google. Today, Bob is a successful Google engineer, and he's paying the help he received forward across the 106 Miles network.

This is a new spin on reciprocity. In traditional old-school reciprocity, people operated like matchers, trading value back and forth with one another. We helped the people who helped us, and we gave to the people from whom we wanted something in return. But today, givers like Adam Rifkin are able to spark a more powerful form of reciprocity. Instead of trading value, Rifkin aims to add value. His giving is governed by a simple rule: the five-minute favor. "You should be willing to do something that will take you five minutes or less *for anybody*."

Rifkin doesn't think about what any of the people he helps will contribute back to him. Whereas takers accumulate large networks to look important and gain access to powerful people, and matchers do it to get favors, Rifkin does it to create more opportunities for giving. In the words of Harvard political scientist Robert Putnam, "I'll do this for you without expecting anything specific back from you, in the confident expectation that someone else will do something for me down the road." When people feel grateful for Rifkin's help, like Stephanie, they're more likely to pay it forward. "I have always been a very genuine and kind-hearted person," Stephanie says, "but I had tried to hide it and be more competitive so that I could get ahead. The important lesson I learned from Adam is that you can be a genuinely kind-hearted person and still get ahead in the world." Every time Rifkin generously shares his expertise or connections, he's investing in encouraging the people in his network to act like givers. When Rifkin does ask people for help, he's usually asking for assistance in helping someone else. This increases the odds that the people in his vast network will seek to add value rather than trade value, opening the door for him and others to gain benefits from people they've never helped—or even met. By creating a norm of adding value, Rifkin transforms giving from a zero-sum loss to a win-win gain.

When takers build networks, they try to claim as much value as possible for themselves from a fixed pie. When givers like Rifkin build networks, they expand the pie so that everyone can get a larger slice. Nick Sullivan, an entrepreneur who has benefited from Rifkin's help, says that "Adam has the same effect on all of us: getting us to help people." Rouf elaborates: "Adam always wants to make sure that whoever he's giving to is also giving to somebody else. If people benefit from his advice, he makes sure they help other people he gives advice to—it's creating a network, and making sure that everybody in his network is helping each other, paying it forward."

Cutting-edge research shows how Rifkin motivates other people to give. Giving, especially when it's distinctive and consistent, establishes a pattern that shifts other people's reciprocity styles within a group. It turns out that giving can be contagious. In one study, contagion experts James Fowler and Nicholas Christakis found that giving spreads rapidly and widely across social networks. When one person made the choice to contribute to a group at a personal cost over a series of rounds, other group members were more likely to contribute in future rounds, even when interacting with people who weren't present for the original act. "This influence persists for multiple periods and spreads up to three degrees of separation (from person to person to person to person)," Fowler and Christakis find, such that "each additional contribution a subject makes . . . in the first period is tripled over the course of the experiment by other subjects who are directly or indirectly influenced to contribute more as a consequence."

When people walk into a new situation, they look to others for clues about appropriate behavior. When giving starts to occur, it becomes the norm, and people carry it forward in interactions with other people. To illustrate, imagine that you're assigned to a group of four. The other three people are strangers, and you'll each make anonymous decisions, with no opportunity to communicate, during six rounds. In each round, each of you will receive $3 and decide whether to take it for yourselves or give it to the group. If you take it, you get the full $3. If you give it to the group, every group member gets $2, including you. At the end of each round, you'll find out what everyone decided. The group is better off if everyone gives—each member would end up receiving $8 per round, for a maximum total over six rounds of $48. But if you give and no one else does, you only get $12. This creates an incentive to take, which will guarantee you $18.

Since you can't communicate with one another, giving is a risky strategy. But in the actual study, 15 percent of the participants were consistent givers: they contributed to the group in all six rounds, making a personal sacrifice for the benefit of the group. And it wasn't as costly as you'd expect. Surprisingly, the consistent givers still ended up doing well: they walked away with an average of 26 percent more money than participants from groups without a single consistent giver. How could they give more and get more?

When the groups included one consistent giver, the other members contributed more. The presence of a single giver was enough to establish a norm of giving. By giving, participants were able to make their group members better off and managed to get more in the process. Even though they earned 50 percent less from each contribution, because they inspired others to give, they made a larger total sum available to all participants. The givers raised the bar and expanded the pie for the whole group.

In this experiment, the consistent givers were doing the equivalent of a five-minute favor when they contributed their money every round. They were making small sacrifices to benefit each member of the group, and it inspired the group members to do the same.

Through the five-minute favor, Rifkin is expanding the pie for his whole network. In 106 Miles, the norm is for all five thousand entrepreneurs to help one another. Rifkin explains that "you're not doing somebody a favor because you're getting something in return. The goal of the group is to instill the value of giving: you don't have to be transactional about it, you don't have to trade it. If you do something for somebody in the group, then when you need it, someone in the group will do something for you."

For takers and matchers, this type of relentless giving still seems a bit risky. Can givers like Adam Rifkin maintain their productivity, especially when there are no guarantees that their help will come back around to benefit them directly? To shed light on this question, Stanford professor Frank Flynn studied professional engineers at a large telecommunications firm in the Bay Area. He asked the engineers to rate themselves and one another on how much they gave and received help from one another, which allowed him to identify which engineers were givers, takers, and matchers. He also asked each engineer to rate the status of ten other engineers: how much respect did they have?

The takers had the lowest status. They burned bridges by constantly asking for favors but rarely reciprocating. Their colleagues saw them as selfish and punished them with a lack of respect. The givers had the highest status, outdoing the matchers and takers. The more generous they were, the more respect and prestige they earned from their colleagues. Through giving more than they got, givers signaled their unique skills, demonstrated their value, and displayed their good intentions.

Despite being held in the highest esteem, the givers faced a problem: they paid a productivity price. For three months, Flynn measured the quantity and quality of work completed by each engineer. The givers were more productive than the takers: they worked harder and got more done. But the matchers had the highest productivity, beating out the givers. The time that the givers devoted to helping their colleagues apparently detracted from their ability to finish jobs, reports, and drawings. The matchers were more likely to call in favors and receive help, and it appeared to keep them on track. On the face of it, this seems like a stumbling block to the giver style of networking. If givers sacrifice their productivity by helping others, how can it be worth it?

Yet Adam Rifkin has managed to be a giver and stay highly productive as the cofounder of several successful companies. How does he avoid the tradeoff between giving and productivity? He gives more.

In the study of engineers, the givers didn't always pay a productivity price. Flynn measured whether the engineers were givers, matchers, or takers by asking their colleagues to rate whether they gave more, the same, or less than they received. This meant that some engineers could score as givers even if they didn't help others very often, as long as they asked for less in return. When Flynn examined the data based on how often the engineers gave and received help, the givers only took a productivity dive when they gave infrequently. Of all engineers, the most productive were those who gave often—and gave more than they received. These were the true givers, and they had the highest productivity and the highest status: they were revered by their peers. By giving often, engineers built up more trust and attracted more valuable help from across their work groups—not just from the people they helped.

This is exactly what has happened to Adam Rifkin with his five-minute favors. In the days before social media, Rifkin might have toiled in anonymity. Thanks to the connected world, his reputation as a giver has traveled faster than the speed of sound. "It takes him no time to raise funding for his start-ups," Rouf says with a trace of astonishment. "He has such a great reputation; people know he's a good guy. That's a dividend that gets paid because of who he is."

Rifkin's experience illustrates how givers are able to develop and leverage extraordinarily rich networks. By virtue of the way they interact with other people in their networks, givers create norms that favor adding rather than claiming or trading value, expanding the pie for all involved. When they truly need help, givers can reconnect with dormant ties, receiving novel assistance from near-forgotten but trusted sources. "I'll sum up the key to success in one word: generosity," writes Keith Ferrazzi. "If your interactions are ruled by generosity, your rewards will follow suit." Perhaps it's not a coincidence that Ivan Misner, the founder and chairman of BNI, the world's largest business networking organization, needs just two words to describe his guiding philosophy: "Givers gain."

After years of rearranging the letters in his name, Adam Rifkin has settled on the perfect anagram: *I Find Karma*.

3

The Ripple Effect

*Collaboration and the Dynamics of
Giving and Taking Credit*

---

*It is well to remember that the entire universe, with one trifling exception,
is composed of others.*

—John Andrew Holmes, former U.S. representative and senator

You probably don't recognize George Meyer's name, but you're definitely familiar with his work. In fact, odds are that someone close to you is a big fan of his ideas, which have captivated an entire generation of people around the world. Although I didn't know it belonged to him until recently, I've admired his work since I was nine years old. Meyer is a tall, angular man in his mid-fifties who sports long, stringy hair and a goatee. If you ran into him on the street, you wouldn't be able to place his face, but you might have a hunch that he's a Grateful Dead fan. You'd be right: in the last five years of Jerry Garcia's life, Meyer attended at least seventy different Grateful Dead concerts.

Meyer attended college at Harvard, where he was nearly suspended after he sold a refrigerator to a freshman and accepted payment, but never delivered it. He was almost suspended again when he used an electric guitar to shatter a window of a dorm room. A rare bright spot in his college career was being elected president of the

Harvard Lampoon, the famous comedy magazine, but it was quickly tarnished by an attempted coup. According to journalist David Owen, Meyer's peers "tried to overthrow him in a bitter and vituperative internal battle, because they thought he wasn't responsible enough."

After graduating from college in 1978, Meyer moved back home and looked for ways to earn quick cash. He spent much of his time in college gambling on dog races at a greyhound track, so he thought he might be able to make a career out of it. He parked himself at a public library and began analyzing scientific strategies for beating the system. It didn't work: after two weeks, he ran out of money.

Three decades later, George Meyer is one of the most successful people in show business. He has been a major contributor to a movie that grossed more than $527 million. He has won seven Emmy Awards and invented several words that have entered English dictionaries—one of which was uttered every day by my college roommate for four years. But he is most celebrated for his role in a television phenomenon that has changed the world. Insiders maintain that as much as any other person, he is responsible for the success of the show that *Time* magazine named the single best television series of the twentieth century.

In 1981, at the recommendation of two friends, Meyer sent a few writing samples to a new NBC show called *Late Night with David Letterman*. "Everything in his submission, down to the last little detail, was so beautifully honed," Letterman gushed to Owen. "I haven't run across anybody quite like that since." During the first season, Meyer invented what was to become one of Letterman's signature routines: using a steam roller to crush ordinary objects, like pieces of fruit. After two years with Letterman, Meyer left to work on *The New Show* with Lorne Michaels and then joined *Saturday Night Live*, departing in 1987 to write a script for a Letterman movie that was ultimately shelved.

When Meyer's two friends recommended him to Letterman, they called him "the funniest man in America." This wasn't a statement to be taken lightly—the two went on to become an Emmy-winning pair of comedy writers on shows like *Seinfeld*, *The Wonder Years*, and *Monk*. And if you look at what George Meyer has accomplished since he finished the Letterman movie script, you might be inclined to agree with them.

George Meyer is the mastermind of much of the humor on *The Simpsons*, the longest-running sitcom and animated program in America.

The Simpsons has won twenty-seven prime-time Emmy Awards, six of which went to Meyer, and changed the face of animated comedy. Although Meyer didn't launch *The Simpsons*—it was created by Matt Groening and developed with James L. Brooks and Sam Simon—there is widespread consensus that Meyer was the most important force behind the show's success. Meyer was hired to write for *The Simpsons* before it premiered in 1989, and he was a major contributor for sixteen seasons as a writer and executive producer. Meyer "has so thoroughly shaped the program that by now the comedic sensibility of *The Simpsons* could be viewed as mostly his," writes Owen. According to humor writer Mike Sacks, "Meyer is largely considered among the writing staff to be its behind-the-scenes genius among geniuses," the man "responsible for the best lines and jokes." Jon Vitti, one of the original *Simpsons* writers who authored many of the early episodes and later served as a producer on *The Office*, elaborated that Meyer is "the one in the room who writes more of the show than anyone else—his fingerprints are on nearly every script. He exerts as much influence on the show as anyone can without being one of the creators."

How does a man like George Meyer become so successful in collaborative work? Reciprocity styles offer a powerful lens for explaining why some people flourish in teams while others fail. In

Multipliers, former Oracle executive Liz Wiseman distinguishes between geniuses and genius makers. Geniuses tend to be takers: to promote their own interests, they "drain intelligence, energy, and capability" from others. Genius makers tend to be givers: they use their "intelligence to amplify the smarts and capabilities" of other people, Wiseman writes, such that "lightbulbs go off over people's heads, ideas flow, and problems get solved." My goal in this chapter is to explore how these differences between givers and takers affect individual and group success.

Collaboration and Creative Character

When we consider what it takes to attain George Meyer's level of comedic impact, there's little question that creativity is a big part of the equation. Carolyn Omine, a longtime *Simpsons* writer and producer, says that Meyer "has a distinct way of looking at the world. It's completely unique." Executive producer and show-runner Mike Scully once commented that when he first joined *The Simpsons*, Meyer "just blew me away. I had done a lot of sitcom work before, but George's stuff was so different and so original that for a while I wondered if I wasn't in over my head."

To unlock the mystery of how people become highly creative, back in 1958, a Berkeley psychologist named Donald MacKinnon launched a path-breaking study. He wanted to identify the unique characteristics of highly creative people in art, science, and business, so he studied a group of people whose work involves all three fields: architects. To start, MacKinnon and his colleagues asked five independent architecture experts to submit a list of the forty most creative architects in the United States. Although they never spoke to one another, the experts achieved remarkably high consensus. They could have nominated up to two hundred architects in total, but after accounting for overlap, their lists featured just eighty-six. More than half of those architects were nominated by more than one expert, more than a third by the majority of the experts, and 15 percent by all five experts.

From there, forty of the country's most creative architects agreed to be dissected psychologically. MacKinnon's team compared them with eighty-four other architects who were successful but not highly creative, matching the creative and "ordinary" architects on age and geographic location. All of the architects traveled to Berkeley, where they spent three full days opening up their minds to MacKinnon's team, and to science. They filled out a battery of personality questionnaires, experienced stressful social situations, took difficult problem-solving tests, and answered exhaustive interview questions about their entire life histories. MacKinnon's team pored over mountains of data, using pseudonyms for each architect so they would remain blind to who was highly creative and who was not.

One group of architects emerged as significantly more "responsible, sincere, reliable, dependable," with more "good character" and "sympathetic concern for others" than the other. The karma principle suggests that it should be the creative architects, but it wasn't. It was the ordinary architects. MacKinnon found that the creative architects stood out as substantially more "demanding, aggressive, and self-centered" than the comparison group. The creative architects had whopping egos and responded aggressively and defensively to criticism. In later studies, the same patterns emerged from comparisons of creative and less creative scientists: the creative scientists scored significantly higher in dominance, hostility, and psychopathic deviance. Highly creative scientists were rated by observers as creating and exploiting dependency in others. Even the highly creative scientists themselves agreed with statements like "I tend to slight the contribution of others and take undue credit for myself" and "I tend to be sarcastic and disparaging in describing the worth of other researchers."

Takers have a knack for generating creative ideas and

championing them in the face of opposition. Because they have supreme confidence in their own opinions, they feel free of the shackles of social approval that constrict the imaginations of many people. This is a distinctive signature of George Meyer's comedy. In 2002, he wrote, directed, and starred in a small play called *Up Your Giggy*. In his monologues, he called God "a ridiculous superstition, invented by frightened cavemen" and referred to marriage as "a stagnant cauldron of fermented resentments, scared and judgmental conformity, exaggerated concern for the children . . . and the secret dredging-up of erotic images from past lovers in a desperate and heartbreaking attempt to make spousal sex even possible."

The secret to creativity: be a taker?

Not so fast. Meyer may harbor a cynical sense of humor, deep-seated suspicion about time-honored traditions, and a few past indiscretions, but in a Hollywood universe dominated by takers, he has spent much of his career in giver style. It started early in life: growing up, he was an Eagle Scout and an altar boy. At Harvard, Meyer majored in biochemistry and was accepted to medical school, but decided not to attend. He was turned off by the hypercompetitive premed students he met in college, who would regularly "sabotage each other's experiments—so lame." After being elected president of the *Lampoon*, when peers attempted to depose him, Owen notes that "Meyer not only survived that coup but also, characteristically, became a close friend of his principal rival." After graduating and failing at the dog track, Meyer worked in a cancer research lab and as a substitute teacher. When I asked Meyer what drew him to comedy, he said, "I love to make people laugh, entertain people, and try to make the world a little better."

Meyer has used his comedic talent to promote social and environmental responsibility. In 1992, an early *Simpsons* episode that Meyer wrote, "Mr. Lisa Goes to Washington," was nominated for an Environmental Media Award, granted to the best episodic comedy on television with a pro-environmental message. During his tenure, *The Simpsons* won six of these awards. In 1995, *The Simpsons* won a Genesis Award from the Humane Society for raising public awareness of animal issues. Meyer is a vegetarian who practices yoga, and in 2005 he cowrote *Earth to America*, a TBS special that utilized comedy as a vehicle for raising awareness about global warming and related environmental issues. He has done extensive work for Conservation International, producing humorous PowerPoint lectures to promote biodiversity. In 2007, when scientists discovered a new species of moss frogs in Sri Lanka, they named it after Meyer's daughter, honoring his contributions to the Global Amphibian Assessment to protect frogs.

Even more impressive than Meyer's work on behalf of the planet is how he works with other people. His big break came when he was working on the Letterman movie script in 1988. To provide some variety in his workday, he wrote and self-published a humor magazine called *Army Man*. "There were very few publications that were just trying to be funny," Meyer told humorist Eric Spitznagel, "so I tried to make something that had no agenda other than to make you laugh." The first issue of *Army Man* was only eight pages long. Meyer typed it himself, arranged it on his bed, and started making photocopies. Then he gave away his best comedy, sending copies to about two hundred friends for free.

Readers found *Army Man* hilarious and started passing it along to their friends. The magazine quickly attracted a cult following, and it made *Rolling Stone* magazine's Hot List of the year's best in entertainment. Soon, Meyer's friends began sending him submissions to feature in future issues. By the second issue, there was enough demand for Meyer to circulate about a thousand copies. He shut it down after the third issue, in part because he couldn't publish all of his friends' submissions but couldn't bear to turn them down.

The first issue of *Army Man* debuted when *The Simpsons* was getting off the ground, and it made its way into the hands of executive producer Sam Simon, who was just about to recruit a writing team. Simon hired Meyer and a few of the other contributors to *Army Man*, and they went on to make *The Simpsons* a hit together. In the writers' room, George Meyer established himself as a giver. Tim Long, a *Simpsons* writer and five-time Emmy winner, told me that "George has the best reputation of anyone I know. He's incredibly generous in giving and helping other people." Similarly, Carolyn Omine marvels, "Everybody who knows George knows he is a truly good person. He has a code of honor, and he lives by this code, with a supernatural amount of integrity."

George Meyer's success highlights that givers can be every bit as creative as takers. By studying his habits in collaboration, we can gain a rich appreciation of how givers work in ways that contribute to their own success—and the success of those around them. But to develop a complete understanding of what givers do effectively in collaboration, it's important to compare them with takers. The research on creative architects suggests that takers often have the confidence to generate original ideas that buck traditions and fight uphill battles to champion these ideas. But does this independence come at a price?

Flying Solo

In the twentieth century, perhaps no person was more emblematic of eminent creativity than Frank Lloyd Wright. In 1991, Wright was recognized as the greatest American architect of all time by the American Institute of Architects. He had an extraordinarily productive career, designing the famous Fallingwater house near Pittsburgh, the Guggenheim Museum, and more than a thousand other structures—roughly half of which were built. In a career that spanned seven decades, he completed an average of more than 140 designs and 70 structures per decade.

Although Wright was prolific throughout the first quarter of the twentieth century, beginning in 1924, he took a nine-year nosedive. As of 1925, "Wright's career had dwindled to a few houses in Los Angeles," write sociologist Roger Friedland and architect Harold Zellman. After studying Wright's career, the psychologist Ed de St. Aubin concluded that the lowest Wright "ever sank architecturally occurred in the years between 1924 and 1933 when he completed only two projects." Over those nine years, Wright was about thirty-five times less productive than usual. During one two-year period, he didn't earn a single commission, and he was "floundering profession-ally," notes architecture critic Christopher Hawthorne. By 1932, "the world-famous Frank Lloyd Wright" was "all but unemployed," wrote biographer Brendan Gill. "His last major executed commission had been a house for his cousin" in 1929, and "he was continuously in debt," to the point of struggling "to find the wherewithal to buy groceries." What caused America's greatest architect to languish?

Wright was one of the architects invited to participate in MacKin-non's study of creativity. Although he declined the invitation, the portrait of the creative architect that emerged from MacKinnon's analysis was the spitting image of Wright. In his designs, Frank Lloyd Wright appeared to be a humanitarian. He introduced the concept of organic architecture, striving to foster harmony between people and the environments in which they lived. But in his interactions with other people, he operated like a taker. Experts believe that as an apprentice, Wright designed at least nine bootleg houses, violating the terms of his contract that prohibited independent work. To hide the illegal work, Wright reportedly persuaded one of his fellow draftsmen to sign off on several of the houses. At one point, Wright promised his son John a salary for working as an assistant on several projects. When John asked him to be paid, Wright sent him a bill itemizing the total amount of money that John had cost over the course of his life, from birth to the present.

When designing the famous Fallingwater house, Wright stalled for months. When the client, Edgar Kaufmann, finally called Wright to announce that he was driving 140 miles to see his progress, Wright claimed the house was finished. But when Kaufmann arrived, Wright had not even completed a drawing, let alone the house. In the span of a few hours, before Kaufmann's eyes, Wright sketched out a detailed design. Kaufmann had commissioned a weekend cottage at one of his family's favorite picnic spots, where they could see a waterfall. Wright had a radically different idea in mind: he drew the house on a rock on top of the waterfall, which would be out of sight from the house. He convinced Kaufmann to accept it, and eventually charged him $125,000 for it, more than triple the $35,000 specified in the contract. It's unlikely that a giver would have ever been comfortable deviating so far from a client's expectations, let alone convincing him to endorse it enthusiastically and charging extra for it. It was a taker's mind-set, it seems, that gave Wright the gall to develop a truly original vision and sell it to a client.

But the very same taker tendencies that served Wright well in Fallingwater also precipitated his nine-year slump. For two decades, until 1911, Wright made his name as an architect living in Chicago and Oak Park, Illinois, where he benefited from the assistance of craftspeople and sculptors. In 1911, he designed Taliesin, an estate in a remote Wisconsin valley. Believing he could excel alone, he moved out there. But as time passed, Wright spun his wheels during "long years of enforced idleness," Gill wrote. At Taliesin, Wright lacked access to talented apprentices. "The isolation he chose by creating Taliesin," de St. Aubin observes, "left him without the elements that had become essential to his life: architectural commissions and skillful workers to help him complete his building designs."

Frank Lloyd Wright's drought lasted until he gave up on independence and began to work interdependently again with talented collaborators. It wasn't his own idea: his wife Olgivanna convinced him to start a fellowship for apprentices to help him with his work. When apprentices joined him in 1932, his productivity soared, and he was soon working on the Fallingwater house, which would be seen by many as the greatest work of architecture in modern history. Wright ran his fellowship program for a quarter century, but even then, he struggled to appreciate how much he depended on apprentices. He refused to pay apprentices, requiring them to do cooking, cleaning, and fieldwork. Wright "was a great architect," explained his former apprentice Edgar Tafel, who worked on Fallingwater, "but he needed people like myself to make his designs work—although you couldn't tell him that."

Wright's story exposes the gap between our natural tendencies to attribute creative success to individuals and the collaborative reality that underpins much truly great work. This gap isn't limited to strictly creative fields. Even in seemingly independent jobs that rely on raw brainpower, our success depends more on others than we realize. For the past decade, several Harvard professors have studied cardiac surgeons in hospitals and security analysts in investment banks. Both groups specialize in knowledge work: they need serious smarts to rewire patients' hearts and organize complex information for stock recommendations. According to management guru Peter Drucker, these "knowledge workers, unlike manual workers in manufacturing, own the means of production: they carry that knowledge in their heads and can therefore take it with them." But carrying knowledge isn't actually so easy.

In one study, professors Robert Huckman and Gary Pisano wanted to know whether surgeons get better with practice. Since surgeons are in high demand, they perform procedures at multiple hospitals. Over a two-year period, Huckman and Pisano tracked 38,577 procedures performed by 203 cardiac surgeons at forty-three different hospitals. They focused on coronary artery bypass grafts, where surgeons open a patient's chest and attach a vein from a leg or a section of chest artery to bypass a blockage in an artery to the heart. On average, 3 percent of patients died during these procedures.

When Huckman and Pisano examined the data, they discovered a remarkable pattern. Overall, the surgeons didn't get better with practice. They only got better at the *specific hospital* where they practiced. For every procedure they handled at a given hospital, the risk of patient mortality dropped by 1 percent. But the risk of mortality stayed the same at other hospitals. The surgeons couldn't take their performance with them. They weren't getting better at performing coronary artery bypass grafts. They were becoming more familiar with particular nurses and anesthesiologists, learning about their strengths and weaknesses, habits, and styles. This familiarity helped them avoid patient deaths, but it didn't carry over to other hospitals. To reduce the risk of patient mortality, the surgeons needed relationships with specific surgical team members.

While Huckman and Pisano were collecting their hospital data, down the hall at Harvard, a similar study was under way in the financial sector. In investment banks, security analysts conduct research to produce earnings forecasts and make recommendations to money management firms about whether to buy or sell a company's stock. Star analysts carry superior knowledge and expertise that they should be able to use regardless of who their colleagues are. As investment research executive Fred Fraenkel explains: "Analysts are one of the most mobile Wall Street professions because their expertise is portable. I mean, you've got it when you're here and you've got it when you're there. The client base doesn't change. You need your Rolodex and your files, and you're in business."

To test this assumption, Boris Groysberg studied more than a thousand equity and fixed-income security analysts over a nine-year period at seventy-eight different firms. The analysts were ranked in effectiveness by thousands of clients at investment management institutions based on the quality of their earnings estimates, industry knowledge, written reports, service, stock selection, and accessibility and responsiveness. The top three analysts in each of eighty industry sectors were ranked as stars, earning between $2 million and $5 million. Groysberg and his colleagues tracked what happened when the analysts switched firms. Over the nine-year period, 366 analysts— 9 percent—moved, so it was possible to see whether the stars maintained their success in new firms.

Even though they were supposed to be individual stars, their performance wasn't portable. When star analysts moved to a different firm, their performance dropped, and it stayed lower for at least five years. In the first year after the move, the star analysts were 5 percent less likely to be ranked first, 6 percent less likely to be ranked second, 1 percent less likely to be ranked third, and 6 percent more likely to be unranked. Even five years after the move, the stars were 5 percent less likely to be ranked first and 8 percent more likely to be unranked. On average, firms lost about $24 million by hiring star analysts. Contrary to the beliefs of Fraenkel and other industry insiders, Groysberg and his colleagues conclude that "hiring stars is advantageous neither to stars themselves, in terms of their performance, nor to hiring companies in terms of their market value."

But some of the star analysts did maintain their success. If they moved with their teams, the stars showed no decline at all in performance. The star analysts who moved solo had a 5 percent probability of being ranked first, while the star analysts who moved with teammates had a 10 percent probability of being ranked first—the same as those who didn't move at all. In another study, Groysberg and his colleagues found that analysts were more likely to maintain their star performance if they worked with high-quality colleagues in their teams and departments. The star analysts relied on knowledgeable colleagues for information and new ideas.

The star investment analysts and the cardiac surgeons depended heavily on collaborators who knew them well or had strong skills of their own. If Frank Lloyd Wright had been more of a giver than a taker, could he have avoided the nine years in which his income and reputation plummeted? George Meyer thinks so.

I Wish I Could Hate You

After Meyer left *Saturday Night Live* in 1987, he hightailed it out of New York City and moved to Boulder, Colorado, to work on the Letterman movie script alone. Just like Frank Lloyd Wright, Meyer had isolated himself from his collaborators. But in stark contrast to Wright, Meyer recognized that he needed other people to succeed. He knew his performance was interdependent, not independent: his ability to make people laugh was due in part to collaborating with fellow comedy writers. So he reached out to people who had worked with him at the *Lampoon* and on his past shows, inviting them to contribute to *Army Man*. "I believe that collaboration is such a beautiful thing, especially in comedy," Meyer told me. "In a community of funny people, you can get that rare synergy, jokes you never could have come up with on your own." Four colleagues ended up helping Meyer with the inaugural issue. One of those colleagues was Jack Handey, who contributed an early installment of "Deep Thoughts," which went on to become a wildly popular series of jokes. Meyer published "Deep Thoughts" three years before they became famous on *Saturday Night Live*, and they contributed to the success of *Army Man*.

The juxtaposition of George Meyer with Frank Lloyd Wright reveals how givers and takers think differently about success. Wright thought he could take his architectural genius from Chicago, where he worked with a team of experts, to a remote part of Wisconsin, where he was largely alone. Wright's family motto was "truth against the world," and it's a familiar theme in Western culture. We tend to privilege the lone genius who generates ideas that enthrall us, or change our world. According to research by a trio of Stanford psychologists, Americans see independence as a symbol of strength, viewing interdependence as a sign of weakness. This is particularly true of takers, who tend to see themselves as superior to and separate from others. If they depend too much on others, takers believe, they'll be vulnerable to being outdone. Like Wright, the star analysts who left their investment banks without their successful teams—or without considering the quality of the new teams they were joining—fell into this trap.

Givers reject the notion that interdependence is weak. Givers are more likely to see interdependence as a source of strength, a way to harness the skills of multiple people for a greater good. This appreciation of interdependence heavily influenced the way that Meyer collaborated. He recognized that if he could contribute effectively to the group, everyone would be better off, so he went out of his way to support his colleagues. When Meyer wrote for *Saturday Night Live* in the mid-1980s as a virtual unknown, he was almost always in the office, making himself available to give feedback. He ended up helping famous comedians like Jon Lovitz, Phil Hartman, and Randy Quaid with their writing and delivery.

Behind the scenes on *Saturday Night Live*, many writers were competing to get their sketches on the show. "There was a Darwinian element," Meyer admits. "There might be ten sketches per show, and we would have thirty-five or forty sketches on the table. There was a bit of a battle, and I just tried to be a good collaborator." When big stars like Madonna were slated to appear on the show, his colleagues flocked to submit sketches. Meyer submitted material for those shows, but he also put in extra effort on sketches for less electric guests, who tended to attract fewer sketches. Meyer took it upon himself to develop compelling sketches for less glamorous guests like Jimmy Breslin because that was where the show needed him most. "I just wanted to be a good soldier," Meyer says. "When people weren't as excited, that's when I felt I had to step up my game." He rose to the occasion, cowriting a hilarious sketch for Breslin that had James Bond villains on a talk show. Breslin played Goldfinger, offering tips on designing fortresses and griping about having his schemes thwarted by Bond. The sketch predated the hit *Austin Powers* spoof of Bond movies by more than a decade.

Meyer's pattern of giving continued on *The Simpsons*. Among writers, the most popular task was typically to write the first draft of an episode, as it allowed them to put their creative stamp on it. Meyer would generate plenty of ideas for episodes, but he rarely wrote the first draft. Instead, feeling that his skills were needed more in rewriting, he took responsibility for the dirty work of spending months helping to rewrite and revise each episode. This is a defining feature of how givers collaborate: they take on the tasks that are in the group's best interest, not necessarily their own personal interests. This makes their groups better off: studies show that on average, from sales teams to paper mill crews to restaurants, the more giving group members do, the higher the quantity and quality of their groups' products and services. But it's not just their groups that get rewarded: like Adam Rifkin, successful givers expand the pie in ways that benefit themselves as well as their groups. Extensive research reveals that people who give their time and knowledge regularly to help their colleagues end up earning more raises and promotions in a wide range of settings, from banks to manufacturing companies. "On *The Simpsons,* I think George surrendered himself to the show," Tim Long says. "Intuitively, he understood that the best thing for him was for the show to be as good as possible."

There's a name for Meyer's actions: in the world of mountain-eering, it's called *expedition behavior*. The term was coined by the National Outdoor Leadership School (NOLS), which has provided wilderness education to thousands of people, including crews of NASA astronauts. Expedition behavior involves putting the group's goals and mission first, and showing the same amount of concern for others as you do for yourself. Jeff Ashby, a NASA space shuttle commander who has flown more than four hundred orbits around Earth, says that "expedition behavior—being selfless, generous, and putting the team ahead of yourself—is what helps us succeed in space more than anything else." John Kanengieter, who directs leadership at NOLS, adds that expedition behavior is "not a zero-sum game: when you give it away, you gain more in response."

Part of Meyer's success came from expanding the pie: the more he contributed to the success of his shows, the more success there was for the whole team to share. But Meyer's expedition behavior also changed the way his colleagues saw him. When givers put a group's interests ahead of their own, they signal that their primary goal is to benefit the group. As a result, givers earn the respect of their collaborators. If Meyer had competed to draft his strongest sketches for Madonna, his fellow writers might have viewed him as a threat to their own status and careers. By doing his best work for less coveted guests, Meyer was doing his colleagues a favor. Takers no longer felt that they needed to compete with him, matchers felt that they owed him, and givers saw him as one of them. "When you were breaking your story or rewriting your script in the room, George was always a welcome addition to the group," says Don Payne, a *Simpsons* writer since 1998. "He would always come up with something that would make your scripts better. That's what draws people to him; they respect and admire him."

In addition to building goodwill, volunteering for unpopular tasks and offering feedback gave Meyer the chance to demonstrate his comedic gifts without leading colleagues to feel insecure. In one study, University of Minnesota researchers Eugene Kim and Theresa Glomb found that highly talented people tend to make others jealous, placing themselves at risk of being disliked, resented, ostracized, and undermined. But if these talented people are also givers, they no longer have a target on their backs. Instead, givers are appreciated for their contributions to the group. By taking on tasks that his colleagues didn't want, Meyer was able to dazzle them with his wit and humor without eliciting envy.

Meyer summarizes his code of honor as "(1) Show up. (2) Work hard. (3) Be kind. (4) Take the high road." As he contributed in ways that revealed his skills without spawning jealousy, colleagues began to admire and trust his comedic genius. "People started to see him as somebody who wasn't just motivated personally," Tim Long explains. "You don't think of him as a competitor. He's someone you can think of on a higher plane, and can trust creatively." Carolyn Omine adds, "Compared to other writers' rooms I've been in, I would say *The Simpsons* tends to look longer for jokes. I think it's because we have writers, like George, who will say, 'No, that's not quite right,' even if it's late, even if we're all tired. I think that's an important quality. We need those people, like George, who aren't afraid to say, 'No, this isn't good enough. We can do better.'"

In a classic article, the psychologist Edwin Hollander argued that when people act generously in groups, they earn *idiosyncrasy credits*—positive impressions that accumulate in the minds of group members. Since many people think like matchers, when they work in groups, it's very common for them to keep track of each member's credits and debits. Once a group member earns idiosyncrasy credits through giving, matchers grant that member a license to deviate from a group's norms or expectations. As Berkeley sociologist Robb Willer summarizes, "Groups reward individual sacrifice." On *The Simpsons*, Meyer amassed plenty of idiosyncrasy credits, earning latitude to contribute original ideas and shift the creative direction of the show. "One of the best things about developing that credibility was if I wanted to try something that was fairly strange, people would be willing to at least give it a shot at the table read," Meyer reflects. "They ended up not rewriting my stuff as much as they had early on, because they knew I had a decent track record. I think people saw that my heart was in the right place—my intentions were good. That goes a long way."

In line with Meyer's experience, research shows that givers get extra credit when they offer ideas that challenge the status quo. In studies that I conducted with colleagues Sharon Parker and Catherine Collins, when takers presented suggestions for improvement, colleagues were skeptical of their intentions, writing them off as self-serving. But when ideas that might be threatening were proposed by givers, their colleagues listened and rewarded them for speaking up, knowing they were motivated by a genuine desire to contribute. "When I think about George in a writers' room, nice is not what I would say. He's spicier than that." Carolyn Omine laughs. "But when George is tough, you know it is only because he cares so much about getting it right."

In 1995, during the sixth *Simpsons* season, Meyer told his colleagues he would be leaving the show at the end of the season. Rather than seeing his departure as an opportunity for personal advancement, the writers didn't want to let him go. They quickly joined forces to recruit him back, persuading him to return as a consultant. Soon they had him all the way back as a full-time writer. "At a very early point, they realized that George was too important to let out of the room," Jon Vitti told the *Harvard Crimson*. "Nobody's opinion is more valued than George's." Looking back on his experiences working with Meyer, Tim Long adds that "there's something magical about getting the reputation as someone who cares about others more than yourself. It redounds to your benefit in countless ways."

Claiming the Lion's Share of the Credit

Although Meyer's giving strengthened his reputation in the inner circles of show business, he toiled in anonymity in the outside world. In Hollywood, there's an easy solution to this problem. Writers gain prominence by claiming credits on as many television episodes as possible, which proves that the ideas and scenes were their brain-child.

George Meyer shaped and sculpted more than three hundred *Simpsons* episodes, but in quiet defiance of Hollywood norms, he's only credited as a writer on twelve of them. On hundreds of episodes, other writers got the credit for Meyer's ideas and jokes. "George never took writing credits on *The Simpsons*, even though he was an idea machine," Tim Long told me. "People tend to come up with ideas and jealously guard them, but George would create ideas, give them to someone else and never take credit. There's a crucial stretch of *The Simpsons* over ten years where he's not credited with a single joke, even though he was responsible for a huge number of them."*

By giving away credit, Meyer compromised his visibility. "For a long time, George's towering contribution to what some see as the most important TV show of the period was not as well known as it should have been," Long recalls. "He was generating a tremendous amount of material, and not really getting credit." Should Meyer have claimed more credit for his efforts? Hogging credit certainly seemed to work for Frank Lloyd Wright: at Taliesin, Wright insisted

---

* Although my focus is on George Meyer, it's important to acknowledge that the comedy on *The Simpsons* has always been a collective achievement. In particular, Meyer is quick to praise Jon Swartzwelder, who has written five dozen episodes, more than double any other writer in show history. Other contributors with many writing credits include Joel Cohen, John Frink, Dan Greaney, Al Jean, Tim Long, Ian Maxtone-Graham, Carolyn Omine, Don Payne, Matt Selman, and Jon Vitti. Of course, Meyer notes, this list doesn't include the creators and many other writers, producers, and animators who have shaped the show's success. Meyer started sharing credit early on. "In *Army Man*, I felt if people were going to write, they should get credit for it, especially since they were doing it for free." He used a unique Army symbol to acknowledge each writer's contribution. "It was a bad decision," Meyer says, laughing, "because I had to cut all of them out with an X-Acto knife, and rubber-cement them to this board I was using. It was hard to find them in the pattern on my bedspread."

that his name be on every document as head architect, even when apprentices took the lead on a project. He threatened his apprentices that if they didn't credit him first and submit all documents for his approval, he would accuse them of forgery and take them to court.

Yet if we take a closer look at Meyer's experience, we might draw the conclusion that when Wright had success as an architect, it was in spite of taking credit—not because of it. Meyer's reluctance to take credit might have cost him some fame in the short run, but he wasn't worried about it. He earned credit as an executive producer, landing a half dozen Emmys for his work on *The Simpsons*, and felt there was plenty of credit to go around. "A lot of people feel they're diminished if there are too many names on a script, like everybody's trying to share a dog bowl," Meyer says. "But that's not really the way it works. The thing about credit is that it's not zero-sum. There's room for everybody, and you'll shine if other people are shining."

Time would prove Meyer right. Despite his short-term sacrifices, Meyer ended up receiving the credit he deserved. Meyer was virtually unknown outside Hollywood until 2000, when David Owen published his profile in the *New Yorker*, with the headline describing Meyer as "the funniest man behind the funniest show on TV." When Owen contacted key *Simpsons* writers for interviews, they jumped at the chance to sing Meyer's praises. As Tim Long puts it, "It makes me incredibly happy to extol George's virtues, even if I'm going to embarrass him."

Just as matchers grant a bonus to givers in collaborations, they impose a tax on takers. In a study of Slovenian companies led by Matej Cerne, employees who hid knowledge from their coworkers struggled to generate creative ideas because their coworkers responded in kind, refusing to share information with them. To illustrate, consider the career of the medical researcher Jonas Salk, who began working to develop a polio vaccine in 1948. The following year, scientists John Enders, Frederick Robbins, and Thomas Weller successfully grew the polio virus in test tubes, paving the way for mass-producing a vaccine based on a live virus. By 1952, Salk's research lab at the University of Pittsburgh had developed a vaccine that appeared to be effective. That year witnessed the worst polio epidemic in U.S. history. The virus infected more than 57,000 people, leading to more than 3,000 deaths and 20,000 cases of paralysis. Over the next three years, Salk's mentor, Thomas Francis, directed the evaluation of a field trial of the Salk vaccine, testing it on more than 1.8 million children with the help of 220,000 volunteers, 64,000 school workers, and 20,000 health care professionals. On April 12, 1955, in Ann Arbor, Michigan, Francis made an announcement that sent a ripple of hope throughout the country: the Salk vaccine was "safe, effective and potent." Within two years, the vaccine was disseminated through the herculean efforts of the March of Dimes, and the incidence of polio fell by nearly 90 percent. By 1961, there were just 161 cases in the United States. The vaccine had similar effects worldwide.

Jonas Salk became an international hero. But at the historic 1955 press conference, Salk gave a valedictory speech that jeopardized his relationships and his reputation in the scientific community. He didn't acknowledge the important contributions of Enders, Robbins, and Weller, who had won a Nobel Prize a year earlier for their groundbreaking work that enabled Salk's team to produce the vaccine. Even more disconcertingly, Salk gave no credit to the six researchers in his lab who were major contributors to his efforts to develop the vaccine—Byron Bennett, Percival Bazeley, L. James Lewis, Julius Youngner, Elsie Ward, and Francis Yurochko.

Salk's team left the press conference in tears. As historian David Oshinsky writes in *Polio: An American Story*, Salk never acknowledged "the people in his own lab. This group, seated proudly together in the packed auditorium, would feel painfully snubbed. . . . Salk's coworkers from Pittsburgh . . . had come expecting to be honored by their boss. A tribute seemed essential, and long overdue." This was especially true from a matcher's perspective. One colleague told a reporter, "At the beginning, I saw him as a father figure. And at the end, an evil father figure."

Over time, it became clear that Julius Youngner felt particularly slighted. "Everybody likes to get credit for what they've done," Youngner told Oshinsky. "It was a big shock." The snub fractured their relationship: Youngner left Salk's lab in 1957 and went on to make a number of important contributions to virology and immunology. In 1993, they finally crossed paths at the University of Pittsburgh, and Youngner shared his feelings. "We were in the audience, your closest colleagues and devoted associates, who worked hard and faithfully for the same goal that you desired," Youngner began. "Do you remember whom you mentioned and whom you left out? Do you realize how devastated we were at that moment and ever afterward when you persisted in making your coworkers invisible?" Youngner reflected that Salk "was clearly shaken by these memories and offered little response."

Jonas Salk's moment of taking sole credit haunted him for the rest of his career. He launched the Salk Institute for Biological Studies, where hundreds of researchers continue to push the envelope of humanitarian science today. But Salk's own productivity waned— later in his career, he tried unsuccessfully to develop an AIDS vaccine—and he was shunned by his colleagues. He never won a Nobel Prize, and he was never elected to the prestigious National Academy of Sciences.* "In the coming years, almost every prominent polio

---

* Many insiders believe that the credit-taking incident, coupled with the attention Salk gave to the media, was a major reason why the National Academy of Sciences never admitted Salk. But debate continues about why he wasn't awarded a Nobel Prize. Some scientists have argued that although the polio vaccine made an invaluable applied contribution to public health, it wasn't an original contribution to fundamental scientific knowledge.

researcher would gain entrance," Oshinsky writes. "The main exception, of course, was Jonas Salk. . . . As one observer put it, Salk had broken the 'unwritten commandments' of scientific research," which included "Thou shalt give credit to others." According to Youngner, "People really held it against him that he had grandstanded like that and really done the most un-collegial thing that you can imagine."

Salk thought his colleagues were jealous. "If someone does something and gets credit for it, then there is this tendency to have this competitive response," he acknowledged in rare comments about the incident. "I was not unscathed by Ann Arbor." But Salk passed away in 1995 without ever acknowledging the contributions of his colleagues. Ten years later, in 2005, the University of Pittsburgh held an event to commemorate the fiftieth anniversary of the vaccine announcement. With Youngner in attendance, Salk's son, AIDS researcher Peter Salk, finally set the record straight. "It was not the accomplishment of one man. It was the accomplishment of a dedicated and skilled team," Peter Salk said. "This was a collaborative effort."

It appears that Jonas Salk made the same mistake as Frank Lloyd Wright: he saw himself as independent rather than interdependent. Instead of earning the idiosyncrasy credits that George Meyer attained, Salk was penalized by his colleagues for taking sole credit.

Why didn't Salk ever credit the contributions of his colleagues to the development of the polio vaccine? It's possible that he was jealously guarding his own accomplishments, as a taker would naturally do, but I believe there's a more convincing answer: he didn't feel they deserved credit. Why would that be?

The Responsibility Bias

To understand this puzzle, we need to take a trip to Canada, where psychologists have been asking married couples to put their relationships on the line. Think about your marriage, or your most recent romantic relationship. Of the total effort that goes into the relationship, from making dinner and planning dates to taking out the garbage and resolving conflicts, what percentage of the work do you handle?

Let's say you claim responsibility for 55 percent of the total effort in the relationship. If you're perfectly calibrated, your partner will claim responsibility for 45 percent, and your estimates will add up to 100 percent. In actuality, psychologists Michael Ross and Fiore Sicoly found that three out of every four couples add up to significantly more than 100 percent. Partners overestimate their own contributions. This is known as the *responsibility bias*: exaggerating our own contributions relative to others' inputs. It's a mistake to which takers are especially vulnerable, and it's partially driven by the desire to see and present ourselves positively. In line with this idea, Jonas Salk certainly didn't avoid the spotlight. "One of his great gifts," Oshinsky writes, "was a knack for putting himself forward in a manner that made him seem genuinely indifferent to his fame. . . . Reporters and photographers would always find Salk grudging but available. He would warn them not to waste too much of his time; he would grouse about the important work they were keeping him from doing; and then, having lodged his formulaic protest, he would fully accommodate."

But there's another factor at play that's both more powerful and more flattering: information discrepancy. We have more access to information about our own contributions than the contributions of others. We see all of our own efforts, but we only witness a subset of our partners' efforts. When we think about who deserves the credit, we have more knowledge of our own contributions. Indeed, when asked to list each spouse's specific contributions to their marriage, on average, people were able to come up with eleven of their own contributions, but only eight of their partners' contributions.

When Salk claimed sole credit for the polio vaccine, he had vivid memories of the blood, sweat, and tears that he invested in developing the vaccine, but comparatively little information about his colleagues' contributions. He literally hadn't experienced what Youngner and the rest of the team did—and he wasn't present for the Nobel Prize–winning discovery that Enders, Robbins, and Weller made.

"Even when people are well intentioned," writes LinkedIn founder Reid Hoffman, "they tend to overvalue their own contributions and undervalue those of others." This responsibility bias is a major source of failed collaborations. Professional relationships disintegrate when entrepreneurs, inventors, investors, and executives feel that their partners are not giving them the credit they deserve, or doing their fair share.

In Hollywood, between 1993 and 1997 alone, more than four hundred screenplays—roughly a third of all submitted—went to credit arbitration. If you're a taker, your driving motivation is to make sure you get more than you give, which means you're carefully counting every contribution that you make. It's all too easy to believe that you've done the lion's share of the work, overlooking what your colleagues contribute.

George Meyer was able to overcome the responsibility bias. *The Simpsons* has contributed many words to the English lexicon, the most famous being Homer's *d'oh!* response to an event that causes mental or physical anguish. Meyer didn't invent that word, but he did coin *yoink*, the familiar phrase that *Simpsons* characters utter when they snatch an item from another character's hands. In 2007, the humor magazine *Cracked* ran a feature on the top words created by *The Simpsons*. Making the list were classics like *cromulent* (describing something that's fine, acceptable, or illegitimately legitimate) and *tomacco* (a crossbreed of tomato and tobacco made by Homer, first suggested in a 1959 *Scientific American* piece, and actually crossbred in 2003 by a *Simpsons* fan named Rob Bauer). But the top invented word on the list was *meh*, the expression of pure indifference that debuted in the sixth season of the show. In one episode, Marge Simpson is fascinated by a weaving loom at a Renaissance Fair, having studied weaving in high school. She weaves a message: "Hi Bart, I am weaving on a loom." Bart's response: "meh." Six years later, an episode aired in which Lisa Simpson actually spells out the word.

Meh has appeared in numerous dictionaries, from Macmillan ("used for showing that you do not care what happens or that you are not particularly interested in something") to Dictionary.com ("an expression of boredom or apathy") to *Collins English Dictionary* ("an interjection to suggest indifference or boredom—or as an adjective to say something is mediocre or a person is unimpressed"). Several years ago, George Meyer was caught by surprise when a *Simpsons* writer shared a memory with him about the episode in which *meh* first appeared. "He reminded me I had worked on that episode, and he thought I came up with the word *meh*. I didn't remember it." When I asked Tim Long who created *meh*, he was pretty confident it was George Meyer. "I'm almost sure he invented *meh*. It's everywhere—most people don't even realize it started with *The Simpsons*." Eventually, conversations with writers jogged Meyer's memory. "I was trying to think of a word that would be the easiest word to say with minimal effort—just a parting of the lips and air would come out."

Why didn't Meyer have a better memory of his contributions? As a giver, his focus was on achieving a collective result that entertained others, not on claiming personal responsibility for that result. He would suggest as many lines, jokes, and words as possible, letting others run with them and incorporate them into their scripts. His attention centered on improving the overall quality of the script, rather than on tracking who was responsible for it. "A lot of the stuff is just like a basketball assist. When somebody would say, 'George, that was yours,' I genuinely did not know," Meyer says. "I tended to not be able to remember the stuff that I had done, so I wasn't always saying when *I* did this and that. I was saying when *we* did this and that. I think it's good to get into the habit of doing that."

Research shows that it's not terribly difficult for matchers and takers to develop this habit. Recall that the responsibility bias occurs because we have more information about our own contributions than others'. The key to balancing our responsibility judgments is to focus our attention on what others have contributed. All you need to do is make a list of what your partner contributes *before* you estimate your own contribution. Studies indicate that when employees think about how much help they receive from their bosses before thinking about how much they contribute to their bosses, their estimates of their bosses' contributions double, from under 17 percent to over 33 percent. Bring together a work group of three to six people and ask each member to estimate the percentage of the total work that he or she does. Add up their estimates, and the average total is over 140 percent. Ask them to reflect on each member's contributions before their own, and the average total drops to 123 percent.

Givers like Meyer do this naturally: they take care to recognize what other people contribute. In one study, psychologist Michael McCall asked people to fill out a survey measuring whether they were givers or takers, and to make decisions in pairs about the importance of different items for surviving in the desert. He randomly told half of the pairs that they failed and the other half that they succeeded. The takers blamed their partners for failures and claimed credit for successes. The givers shouldered the blame for failures and gave their partners more credit for successes.

This is George Meyer's modus operandi: he's incredibly tough on himself when things go badly, but quick to congratulate others when things go well. "Bad comedy hurts George physically," Tim Long says. Meyer wants each joke to make people laugh—and many to make them think. Although he holds other people to the same high standards that he sets for himself, he's more forgiving of their mistakes. Early in his career, Meyer was fired from a show called *Not Necessarily the News* after six weeks. Twenty years later, he ran into the boss who fired him. She apologized—firing him was clearly a mistake—and braced herself for Meyer to be angry. As he shared the story with me, Meyer laughed: "It was just lovely to see her again. I said 'Come on, look where we are; all is forgiven.' There are a few people in Hollywood who thrive on driving their enemies' faces into the dirt. That's such a hollow motivation. And you don't want to have all these people out there trying to undermine you."

In the *Simpsons* rewrite room, being more forgiving of others than of himself helped Meyer get the best ideas out of others. "I tried to create a climate in the room where everybody feels that they can contribute, that it's okay to fall on your face many, many times," he says. This is known as *psychological safety*—the belief that you can take a risk without being penalized or punished. Research by Harvard Business School professor Amy Edmondson shows that in the type of psychologically safe environment that Meyer helped create, people learn and innovate more.* And it's givers who often

---

* Is there a dark side to psychological safety? Many managers believe that by tolerating mistakes, they're sending a message that it's okay to make mistakes. Such mistakes might not be disastrous on a television sitcom, but consider a setting where lives are on the line: hospital units. Edmondson asked members of eight hospital units to rate how much psychological safety they felt in the unit, and how many medication errors they made. Sure enough, the higher the psychological safety, the greater the number of errors reported. In units where health care professionals felt their mistakes would be forgiven, they seemed more likely to deliver the wrong medication to patients, putting them at risk for ineffective treatment or allergic reactions. It makes intuitive sense that tolerance for errors would cause people to become complacent and make more errors, but Edmondson wasn't convinced. She reasoned that psychological safety was increasing comfort with reporting errors, not causing errors. Sure enough, the higher a unit's psychological safety, the more errors reported. But when

create such an environment: in one study, engineers who shared ideas without expecting anything in return were more likely to play a major role in innovation, as they made it safe to exchange information. Don Payne recalls that when he and fellow writer John Frink joined *The Simpsons*, they were intimidated by the talented veterans on the show, but Meyer made it safe to present their ideas. "George was incredibly supportive, and took us under his wing. He made it very easy to join in and participate, encouraged us to pitch and didn't denigrate us. He listened, and asked for our opinions."

When revising scripts, many comedy writers cut material ruthlessly, leaving the people who wrote that material psychologically wounded. Meyer, on the other hand, says he "tried to specialize in the emotional support of other people." When writers were freaking out about their scripts being rewritten, he was often the one to console them and calm them down. "I was always dealing with people in extremis; I would often talk people down from panic," Meyer observes. "I got good at soothing them, and showing them a different way to look at the situation." At the end of the day, even if he was trashing their work, they knew he cared about them as people. Carolyn Omine comments that "George does not mince words; he'll come right out and tell you if he thinks the joke you pitched is dumb, but you never feel he's saying you're dumb." Tim Long told me that when you give Meyer a script to read, "It's as if you just handed him a baby, and it's his responsibility to tell you if your baby's sick. He really cares about great writing—and about you."

Edmondson examined more objective, independent data on medication errors, the psychologically safe units didn't actually make more errors. In fact, the higher the psychological safety in a unit, the *fewer* errors they made. Why? In the units that lacked psychological safety, health care professionals hid their errors, fearing retribution. As a result, they weren't able to learn from their mistakes. In the units with high psychological safety, on the other hand, reporting errors made it possible to prevent them moving forward.

The Perspective Gap

If overcoming the responsibility bias gives us a clearer understanding of others' contributions, what is it that allows us to offer support to colleagues in collaborations, where emotions can run high and people often take criticism personally? Sharing credit is only one piece of successful group work. Meyer's related abilities to console fellow writers when their work was being cut, and to create a psychologically safe environment, are a hallmark of another important step that givers take in collaboration: seeing beyond the perspective gap.

In an experiment led by Northwestern University psychologist Loran Nordgren, people predicted how painful it would be to sit in a freezing room for five hours. They made their predictions under two different conditions: warm and cold. When the warm group estimated how much pain they would experience in the freezing room, they had an arm in a bucket of warm water. The cold group also made their judgments with an arm in a bucket, but it was filled with ice water. Which group would expect to feel the most pain in the freezing room?

As you probably guessed, it was the cold group. People anticipated that the freezing room would be 14 percent more painful when they had their arm in a bucket of ice water than a bucket of warm water. After literally feeling the cold for a minute, they knew several hours would be awful. But there was a third group of people who experienced cold under different circumstances. They stuck an arm in a bucket of ice water, but then took the arm out and filled out a separate questionnaire. After ten minutes had passed, they estimated how painful the freezing room would be.

Their predictions should have resembled the cold group's, having felt the freezing temperature just ten minutes earlier, but they didn't. They were identical to the warm group. Even though they had felt the cold ten minutes earlier, once they weren't cold anymore, they could no longer imagine it. This is a *perspective gap*: when we're not experiencing a psychologically or physically intense state, we dramatically underestimate how much it will affect us. For instance, evidence shows that physicians consistently think their patients are feeling less pain than they actually are. Without being in a state of pain themselves, physicians can't fully realize what it's like to be in that state.

In a San Francisco hospital, a respected oncologist was concerned about a patient. "He's not as mentally clear as he was yesterday." The patient was old, and he had advanced metastatic cancer. The oncologist decided to order a spinal tap to see what was wrong, in the hopes of prolonging the patient's life. "Maybe he has an infection—meningitis, a brain abscess—something treatable."

The neurologist on call, Robert Burton, had his doubts. The patient's prognosis was grim, and the spinal tap would be extremely painful. But the oncologist was not ready to throw in the towel. When Burton entered the room with the spinal tap tray, the patient's family protested. "Please, no more," they said together. The patient—too frail to speak from a terminal illness—nodded, declining the spinal tap. Burton paged the oncologist and explained the family's wishes to avoid the spinal tap, but the oncologist was not ready to give up. Finally, the patient's wife grabbed Burton's arm, begging him for support in refusing the oncologist's plan to do the spinal tap. "It's not what we want," the wife pleaded. The oncologist was still determined to save the patient. He explained why the spinal tap was essential, and eventually, the family and patient gave in.

Burton performed the spinal tap, which was challenging to carry out and quite painful for the patient. The patient developed a pounding headache, fell into a coma and died three days later due to the cancer. Although the oncologist was a prominent expert in his field, Burton remembers him "mainly for what he taught me about uncritical acceptance of believing that you 'are doing good.' The only way you can really know is if you ask the patient and you have a dia-logue."

In collaborations, takers rarely cross this perspective gap. They're so focused on their own viewpoints that they never end up seeing how others are reacting to their ideas and feedback. On the other hand, researcher Jim Berry and I discovered that in creative work, givers are motivated to benefit others, so they find ways to put themselves in other people's shoes. When George Meyer was editing the work of *Simpsons* animators and writers, he was facing a perspective gap. He was cutting their favorite scenes and jokes, not his own. Recognizing that he couldn't literally feel what they were feeling, he found a close substitute: he reflected on what it felt like to receive feedback and have his work revised when he was in their positions.

When he joined *The Simpsons* in 1989, Meyer had written a Thanksgiving episode that included a dream sequence. He thought the sequence was hilarious, but Sam Simon, the show runner at the time, didn't agree. When Simon cut the dream from the script, Meyer was furious. "I flipped out. I was so enraged that Sam had to send me to do another task, just to get me out of the room." When criticizing and changing the work of animators and writers, Meyer would look back on this experience. "I could relate to that sense of being eviscerated when other people were rewriting their stuff," he told me. This made him more empathetic and considerate, helping other people to simmer down from intense states and accept his revisions.

Like Meyer, successful givers shift their frames of reference to the recipient's perspective. For most people, this isn't the natural starting point. Consider the common dilemma of giving a gift for a wedding or a new baby's arrival. When the recipient has created a registry, do you pick something from the registry or send a unique gift?

One evening, my wife was searching for a wedding gift for some friends. She decided it was more thoughtful and considerate to find something that wasn't on their registry, and chose to send candlesticks, assuming that our friends would appreciate the unique gift. Personally, I was perplexed. Several years earlier, when we received wedding gifts, my wife was often disappointed when people sent unique gifts, rather than choosing items from our registry. She knew she wanted particular items, and it was quite rare for anyone to send a gift that she preferred over the ones she had actually selected. Knowing that she preferred the registry gift when she was the recipient, why did she opt for a unique gift when she was in the giving role?

To get to the bottom of this puzzle, researchers Francesca Gino of Harvard and Frank Flynn of Stanford examined how senders and receivers react to registry gifts and unique gifts. They found that senders consistently underestimated how much recipients appreciated registry gifts. In one experiment, they recruited ninety people to either give or receive a gift from Amazon.com. The receivers had twenty-four hours to create a wish list of ten products in the price range of twenty to thirty dollars. The senders accessed the wish lists and were randomly assigned to either choose a registry gift (from the list) or a unique gift (an idea of their own).

The senders expected that the recipients would appreciate the unique gift as somewhat more thoughtful and personal. In fact, the opposite was true. The recipients reported significantly greater appreciation of the registry gifts than the unique gifts. The same patterns emerged with friends giving and receiving wedding gifts and birthday gifts. The senders preferred to give unique gifts, but the recipients actually preferred the gifts they solicited on their registries and wish lists.

Why? Research shows that when we take others' perspectives, we tend to stay within our own frames of reference, asking "How would *I* feel in this situation?" When we're giving a gift, we imagine the joy that we would experience in receiving the gifts that we're selecting. But this isn't the same joy that the recipient will experience, because the recipient has a different set of preferences. In the giver's role, my wife loved the candlesticks she picked out. But if our friends were enamored with those candlesticks, they would have put them on their gift registry.*

To effectively help colleagues, people need to step outside their own frames of reference. As George Meyer did, they need to ask, "How will *the recipient* feel in this situation?" This capacity to see the world from another person's perspective develops very early in life. In one experiment, Berkeley psychologists Betty Repacholi and Alison Gopnik studied fourteen-month-old and eighteen-month-old toddlers. The toddlers had two bowls of food in front of them: one with goldfish crackers and one with broccoli. The toddlers tasted food from both bowls, showing a strong preference for goldfish crackers over broccoli. Then, they watched a researcher express disgust while tasting the crackers and delight while tasting the broccoli. When the researcher held out her hand and asked for some food, the toddlers had a chance to offer either the crackers or the broccoli to the researcher. Would they travel outside their own perspectives and give her the broccoli, even though they themselves hated it?

The fourteen-month-olds didn't, but the eighteen-month-olds did. At fourteen months, 87 percent shared the goldfish crackers instead of the broccoli. By eighteen months, only 31 percent made this mistake while 69 percent had learned to share what others liked, even if it differed from what they liked. This ability to imagine other people's perspectives, rather than getting stuck in our own perspectives, is a signature skill of successful givers in collaborations.†

* Of course, my wife observed, our friends will love the candlesticks—they just didn't know that such an exquisite gift existed. If they did, the candlesticks surely would have been on their registry. And she was right.
† Growing up as the oldest child in his family, Meyer had plenty of opportunities to practice perspective taking. Studies show that having younger siblings develops our giver instincts by providing experience with teaching, child care,

Interestingly, when George Meyer first started his career as a comedy writer, he didn't use his perspective-taking skills in the service of helping his colleagues. He saw his fellow writers as rivals:

> When you start out, you see other people as obstacles to your success. But that means your world will be full of obstacles, which is bad. In the early years, when some of my colleagues and friends—even close friends—would have a rip-roaring success of some kind, it was hard for me. I would feel jealousy, that their success somehow was a reproach to me. When you start your career, naturally you're mainly interested in advancing yourself and promoting yourself.

But as Meyer worked on television shows, he began to run into the same people over and over. It was a small world, and a connected one. "I realized it's a very small pond. There are only a few hundred people at any one time writing television comedy for a living," Meyer says. "It's a good idea not to alienate these guys, and most of the jobs

---

feeding, and cleaning. Experts have long recognized that as older siblings, particularly if we're the firstborn, we're charged with taking care of our younger siblings, which requires acute attention to their unique needs and wants—and how they differ from our own. But Frank Lloyd Wright and Jonas Salk were firstborns: Wright had two younger sisters and Salk had two younger brothers. There's something else in Meyer's family background that may have nudged him in the giver direction. In a series of studies led by the Dutch psychologist Paul van Lange, givers had more siblings than the takers and matchers. The givers averaged two siblings; the takers and matchers averaged one and a half siblings. More siblings meant more sharing, which seemed to predispose people toward giving. It may not be a coincidence that George Meyer is the oldest of eight siblings. Interestingly, van Lange's data showed a sister effect, not just a sibling effect. The givers didn't have more brothers than the takers and matchers, but they were 50 percent more likely to have sisters. It is noteworthy that of Meyer's seven younger siblings, five are sisters. For more on how female family members—even infants—might tilt us in the giver direction, see my article "Why Men Need Women" in the *New York Times*.

you get are more or less through word of mouth, or a recommendation. It's really important to have a good reputation. I quickly learned to see other comedy writers as allies." Meyer began to root for other people to succeed. "It's not a zero-sum game. So if you hear that somebody got a pilot picked up, or one of their shows went to series, in a way that's really good, because comedy is doing better."

This wasn't the path that Frank Lloyd Wright followed. He was undoubtedly a genius, but he wasn't a genius maker. When Wright succeeded, it didn't multiply the success of other architects; it usually came at their expense. As Wright's son John reflected, "You do a good job building your buildings in keeping with your ideal. But you have been weak in your support of others in their desire for this same attainment." When it came to apprentices, his son charged, Wright never "stood behind one and helped him up." In one case, Wright promised his apprentices a drafting room so they could work, but it wasn't until seven years after starting the Taliesin fellowship that he made good on his promise. At one point, a client admitted that he preferred to hire Wright's apprentices over Wright himself, as the apprentices matched his talent but exceeded his conscientiousness when it came to completing work on schedule and within budget. Wright was enraged, and he forbade his architects from accepting independent commissions, requiring them to put his name at the top of all their work. A number of his most talented and experienced apprentices quit, protesting that Wright exploited them for personal gain and stole credit for their work. "It is amazing," de St. Aubin observes, "that few of the hundreds" of Wright's "apprentices went on to achieve significant, independent careers as practicing architects."

George Meyer's success had the opposite effect on his collaborators: it rippled, cascaded, and spread to the people around him. Meyer's colleagues call him a genius, but it's striking that he has also been a genius maker. By helping his fellow writers on *The Simpsons*,

George Meyer made them more effective at their jobs, multiplying their collective effectiveness. "He made me a better writer, inspiring me to think outside the box," Don Payne comments. Meyer's willingness to volunteer for unpopular tasks, help other people improve their jokes, and work long hours to achieve high collective standards rubbed off on his colleagues. "He makes everyone try harder," Jon Vitti told a *Harvard Crimson* reporter, who exclaimed that "Meyer's presence spurs other *Simpsons* writers to be funnier," extolling Meyer's gift for "inspiring greatness in those around him."

Meyer left *The Simpsons* in 2004 and is currently working on his first novel—tentatively titled *Kick Me 1,000,000 Times or I'll Die*—but his influence in the writers' room persists. Today, "George's voice is strongly in the DNA of the show," says Payne, "and he showed me that you don't have to be a jerk to get ahead." Carolyn Omine adds that "We all picked up a lot of George's comedic sense. Even though he's not here at *The Simpsons* anymore, we sometimes think in his way." Years later, Meyer is still working to lift his colleagues up. Despite winning five Emmy Awards, Tim Long hadn't achieved his lifelong dream: he wanted to be published in *The New Yorker*. In 2010, Long sent Meyer a draft of a submission. Meyer responded swiftly with incisive feedback. "He just went through it line by line, and he was incredibly generous. His notes helped me fix things that were bugging me at the bottom of my soul, but I couldn't articulate them." Then, Meyer took his giving one step further: he reached out to an editor at *The New Yorker* to help Long get his foot in the door. By 2011, Long's dream was fulfilled—twice.

By the time Meyer released the second issue of *Army Man*, he had thirty contributors. They all wrote jokes for free, and their careers soared along with Meyer's. At least seven of those contributors went on to write for *The Simpsons*. One contributor, Spike Feresten, wrote a single *Simpsons* episode in 1995, and became an Emmy-nominated writer and producer on *Seinfeld*, where he wrote the famous "Soup

Nazi" episode. And the *Army Man* contributors who didn't become *Simpsons* writers achieved success elsewhere. For example, Bob Odenkirk is a well-known writer and actor, Roz Chast is a staff cartoonist for *The New Yorker*, and Andy Borowitz became a bestselling author and creator of "The Borowitz Report," a satire column and website with millions of fans. Before that, Borowitz coproduced the hit movie *Pleasantville* and created *The Fresh Prince of Bel-Air*, which in turn launched Will Smith's career. By inviting them to write for *Army Man*, Meyer helped them soar. "I just asked the people who made me laugh to contribute," Meyer told Mike Sacks. "I didn't realize they would become illustrious."

4

Finding the Diamond in the Rough

The Fact and Fiction of Recognizing Potential

When we treat man as he is, we make him worse than he is; when we treat him as if he already were what he potentially could be, we make him what he should be.
—attributed to Johann Wolfgang von Goethe, German writer,
physicist, biologist, and artist

When Barack Obama entered the White House, a reporter asked him if he had a favorite app. Without hesitating, Obama named the iReggie, which "has my books, my newspapers, my music all in one place." The iReggie wasn't a piece of software, though. It was a man named Reggie Love, and no one would have guessed that he would become an indispensable resource to President Obama.

Love was a star athlete at Duke, where he accomplished the rare feat of playing key roles on both the football and basketball teams. But after two years of failed NFL tryouts following graduation, he decided to shift gears. Having studied political science and public policy at Duke, Love pursued an internship on Capitol Hill. With a background as a jock and little work experience, he ended up with a position in the mailroom of Obama's Senate office. Yet within a year, at the young age of twenty-six, Love was promoted up from the mailroom to become Obama's body man, or personal assistant.

Love worked eighteen-hour days and flew more than 880,000

miles with Obama. "His ability to juggle so many responsibilities with so little sleep has been an inspiration to watch," Obama said. "He is the master of what he does." When Obama was elected president, an aide remarked that Love "took care of the president." Love went out of his way to respond to every letter that came into his office. "I always wanted to acknowledge people, and let them know their voice was heard," Love told me. According to a reporter, Love is "known for his exceptional and universal kindness."

Decades earlier, in Love's home state of North Carolina, a woman named Beth Traynham decided to go back to school to study accounting. Beth was in her early thirties, and numbers were not her strong suit. She didn't learn to tell time on an analog clock until she was in third grade, and in high school, she leaned heavily on a boyfriend to get her through her math classes. Even in adulthood, she struggled with percentages.

When it came time to take the certified public accountant (CPA) exam, Beth was convinced that she would fail. Beyond the fact that she had trouble with math, she was facing serious time constraints. She was juggling a full-time job with taking care of three children at home—two of whom were toddlers, both of whom came down with chicken pox within two weeks of the exam. The lowest point came when she spent an entire weekend trying to understand pension accounting, and after three days, felt like she understood less than when she started. When Beth sat down to take the CPA exam, right off the bat, she had a panic attack when she looked at the multiple-choice questions. "I would rather go through natural childbirth (again) than ever have to sit for that exam again," Beth said. She left dejected, certain that she had failed.

On a Monday morning in August 1992, Beth's phone rang. The voice on the other end of the line said that she had earned the gold medal on the CPA exam in North Carolina. She thought it was a friend playing a joke on her, so she called the state board later that day to verify the news. It wasn't a joke: Beth had the single highest score in the entire state. Later, she was dumbfounded when she received another award: the national Elijah Watt Sells Award for Distinctive Performance, granted to the top ten CPA exam scores in the whole country, beating out 136,525 other candidates. Today, Beth is a widely respected partner at the accounting firm Hughes, Pittman & Gupton, LLC. She has been named an Impact 25 financial leader and one of the top twenty-five women in business in the Research Triangle.

Beth Traynham and Reggie Love have led dramatically different lives. Aside from their professional success and their North Carolina roots, there is one common thread that unites them. His name is C. J. Skender, and he is a living legend.

Skender teaches accounting, but to call him an accounting professor doesn't do him justice. He's a unique character, known for his trademark bow ties and his ability to recite the words to thousands of songs and movies on command. He may well be the only fifty-eight-year-old man with fair skin and white hair who displays a poster of the rapper 50 Cent in his office. And while he's a genuine numbers whiz, his impact in the classroom is impossible to quantify. Skender is one of a few professors for whom Duke University and the University of North Carolina look past their rivalry to cooperate: he is in such high demand that he has permission to teach simultaneously at both schools. He has earned more than two dozen major teaching awards, including fourteen at UNC, six at Duke, and five at North Carolina State. Across his career, he has now taught close to six hundred classes and evaluated more than thirty-five thousand students. Because of the time that he invests in his students, he has developed what may be his single most impressive skill: a remarkable eye for talent.

In 2004, Reggie Love enrolled in C. J. Skender's accounting class at Duke. It was a summer course that Love needed to graduate, and while many professors would have written him off as a jock, Skender recognized Love's potential beyond athletics. "For some reason, Duke football players have never flocked to my class," Skender explains, "but I knew Reggie had what it took to succeed." Skender went out of his way to engage Love in class, and his intuition was right that it would pay dividends. "I knew nothing about accounting before I took C. J.'s class," Love says, "and the fundamental base of knowledge from that course helped guide me down the road to the White House." In Obama's mailroom, Love used the knowledge of inventory that he learned in Skender's class to develop a more efficient process for organizing and digitizing a huge backlog of mail. "It was the number-one thing I implemented," Love says, and it impressed Obama's chief of staff, putting Love on the radar. In 2011, Love left the White House to study at Wharton. He sent a note to Skender: "I'm on the train to Philly to start the executive MBA program and one of the first classes is financial accounting—and I just wanted to say thanks for sticking with me when I was in your class."

A dozen years earlier, after Beth Traynham took the CPA exam, she approached Skender to warn him about her disappointing performance. She told him she was sure she flunked the entire exam, but Skender knew better. He promised: "If you didn't pass, I'll pay your mortgage." Skender was right again—and he wasn't just right about Beth. That spring, the silver and bronze medalists on the CPA exam in North Carolina were also his students. Skender's students earned the top three scores of all 3,396 CPA candidates who took the exam. It was the first time in North Carolina that any school had swept the medals, and although accounting was a male-dominated field, all three of Skender's medalists were women. In total, Skender has had more than forty different students win CPA medals by placing in the top three in the state. He has also demonstrated a knack for identifying future teachers: more than three dozen students have followed in his footsteps into university teaching. How does he know talent when he sees it?

It may sound like pure intuition, but C. J. Skender's skill in recognizing potential has rigorous science behind it. Spotting and cultivating talent are essential skills in just about every industry; it's difficult to overstate the value of surrounding ourselves with stars. As with networking and collaboration, when it comes to discovering the potential in others, reciprocity styles shape our approaches and effectiveness. In this chapter, I want to show you how givers succeed by recognizing potential in others. Along with tracing Skender's techniques, we'll take a look at how talent scouts identify world-class athletes, why people end up overinvesting in low-potential candidates, and what top musicians say about their first teachers. But the best place to start is the military, where psychologists have spent three decades investigating what it takes to identify the most talented cadets.

Star Search

In the early 1980s, a psychologist named Dov Eden published the first in a series of extraordinary results. He could tell which soldiers in the Israel Defense Forces (IDF) would become top performers before they ever started training.

Eden is a physically slight but psychologically intense man who grew up in the United States. After finishing his doctorate, he immigrated to Israel and began conducting research with the IDF. In one study, he examined comprehensive assessments of nearly a thousand soldiers who were about to arrive for training with their platoons. He had their aptitude test scores, evaluations during basic training, and appraisals from previous commanders. Using this information alone, which was gathered before the beginning of training for their current roles, Eden was able to identify a group of high-potential trainees who would emerge as stars.

Over the next eleven weeks, the trainees took tests measuring their expertise in combat tactics, maps, and standard operating procedures. They also demonstrated their skill in operating a weapon, which was evaluated by experts. Sure enough, the candidates Eden spotted as high-potentials at the outset did significantly better than their peers over the next three months: they scored 9 percent higher on the expertise tests and 10 percent higher on the weapons evaluation. What information did Eden use to identify the high-potentials? If you were a platoon leader in the IDF, what characteristics would you value above all others in your soldiers?

It's helpful to know that Eden drew his inspiration from a classic study led by the Harvard psychologist Robert Rosenthal, who teamed up with Lenore Jacobson, the principal of an elementary school in San Francisco. In eighteen different classrooms, students from kindergarten through fifth grade took a Harvard cognitive ability test. The test objectively measured students' verbal and reasoning skills, which are known to be critical to learning and problem solving. Rosenthal and Jacobson shared the test results with the teachers: approximately 20 percent of the students had shown the potential for intellectual blooming, or spurting. Although they might not look different today, their test results suggested that these bloomers would show "unusual intellectual gains" over the course of the school year.

The Harvard test was discerning: when the students took the cognitive ability test a year later, the bloomers improved more than the rest of the students. The bloomers gained an average of twelve IQ points, compared with average gains of only eight points for their classmates. The bloomers outgained their peers by roughly fifteen IQ points in first grade and ten IQ points in second grade. Two years later, the bloomers were still outgaining their classmates. The intelligence test was successful in identifying high-potential students: the bloomers got smarter—and at a faster rate—than their classmates.

Based on these results, intelligence seems like a strong contender as the key differentiating factor for the high-potential students. But it wasn't—at least not in the beginning. Why not?

The students labeled as bloomers didn't actually score higher on the Harvard intelligence test. Rosenthal chose them at random.

The study was designed to find out what happened to students when teachers *believed* they had high potential. Rosenthal randomly selected 20 percent of the students in each classroom to be labeled as bloomers, and the other 80 percent were a control group. The bloomers weren't any smarter than their peers—the difference "was in the mind of the teacher."

Yet the bloomers became smarter than their peers, in both verbal and reasoning ability. Some students who were randomly labeled as bloomers achieved more than 50 percent intelligence gains in a single year. The ability advantage to the bloomers held up when the students had their intelligence tested at the end of the year by separate examiners who weren't aware that the experiment had occurred, let alone which students were identified as bloomers. And the students labeled as bloomers continued to show gains after two years, even when they were being taught by entirely different teachers who didn't know which students had been labeled as bloomers. Why?

Teachers' beliefs created self-fulfilling prophecies. When teachers believed their students were bloomers, they set high expectations for their success. As a result, the teachers engaged in more supportive behaviors that boosted the students' confidence and enhanced their learning and development. Teachers communicated more warmly to the bloomers, gave them more challenging assignments, called on them more often, and provided them with more feedback. Many experiments have replicated these effects, showing that teacher expectations are especially important for improving the grades and intelligence test scores of low-achieving students and members of stigmatized minority groups. In a comprehensive review of the evidence, psychologists Lee Jussim and Kent Harber concluded, "Self-fulfilling prophecies in the classroom are real."

But we all know that children are impressionable in the early phases of intellectual development. When Dov Eden began his research at the IDF, he wondered whether these types of self-fulfilling prophecies could play out with more fully formed adults. He told some platoon leaders that he had reviewed aptitude test scores, evaluations during basic training, and appraisals from previous commanders, and that the "average command potential of your trainees is appreciably higher than the usual level . . . Therefore, you can expect unusual achievements from the trainees in your group."

As in the elementary school study, Eden had selected these trainees as high-potentials at random. He was testing the effect of leaders believing that their trainees were high-potentials. Amazingly, the trainees randomly labeled as high-potentials did significantly better on expertise tests and weapons evaluations than the trainees who were not arbitrarily designated as high-potentials. Just like the teachers, when the platoon leaders believed in the trainees' potential, they acted in ways that made this potential a reality. The platoon leaders who held high expectations of their trainees provided more help, career advice, and feedback to their trainees. When their trainees made mistakes, instead of assuming that they lacked ability, the platoon leaders saw opportunities for teaching and learning. The supportive behaviors of the platoon leaders boosted the confidence and ability of the trainees, enabling and encouraging them to achieve higher performance.

Evidence shows that leaders' beliefs can catalyze self-fulfilling prophecies in many settings beyond the military. Management researcher Brian McNatt conducted an exhaustive analysis of seventeen different studies with nearly three thousand employees in a wide range of work organizations, from banking to retail sales to manufacturing. Overall, when managers were randomly assigned to see employees as bloomers, employees bloomed. McNatt concludes that these interventions "can have a fairly large effect on performance." He encourages managers to "recognize the possible power and influence in (a) having a genuine interest and belief in the potential of their employees . . . and (b) engaging in actions that support others and communicate that belief . . . increasing others' motivation and effort and helping them achieve that potential."

Some managers and teachers have already internalized this message. They see people as bloomers naturally, without ever being told. This is rarely the case for takers, who tend to place little trust in other people. Because they assume that most people are takers, they hold relatively low expectations for the potential of their peers and subordinates. Research shows that takers harbor doubts about others' intentions, so they monitor vigilantly for information that others might harm them, treating others with suspicion and distrust. These low expectations trigger a vicious cycle, constraining the development and motivation of others. Even when takers are impressed by another person's capabilities or motivation, they're more likely to see this person as a threat, which means they're less willing to support and develop him or her. As a result, takers frequently fail to engage in the types of supportive behaviors that are conducive to the confidence and development of their peers and subordinates.

Matchers are better equipped to inspire self-fulfilling prophecies. Because they value reciprocity, when a peer or subordinate demonstrates high potential, matchers respond in kind, going out of their way to support, encourage, and develop their promising colleagues and direct reports. But the matcher's mistake lies in waiting for signs of high potential. Since matchers tend to play it safe, they often wait to offer support until they've seen evidence of promise. Consequently, they miss out on opportunities to develop people who don't show a spark of talent or high potential at first.

Givers don't wait for signs of potential. Because they tend to be trusting and optimistic about other people's intentions, in their roles as leaders, managers, and mentors, givers are inclined to see the potential in everyone. By default, givers start by viewing people as bloomers. This is exactly what has enabled C. J. Skender to develop so many star students. He isn't unusual in recognizing talented people; he simply starts by seeing everyone as talented and tries to bring out the best in them. In Skender's mind, every student who walks into his classroom is a diamond in the rough—able and willing to be mined, cut, and polished. He sees potential where others don't, which has set in motion a series of self-fulfilling prophecies.

Polishing the Diamond in the Rough

In 1985, a student of Skender's named Marie Arcuri sat for the CPA exam. She wasn't a good standardized test taker, and she didn't pass the first time. A few days later, she received a letter in the mail from Skender. He wrote to every single student who had taken the exam, congratulating those who passed and encouraging those who didn't. For the past quarter century, Marie has saved the letter:

> Your husband, family, and friends love you because of the beautiful person you have made yourself—not because of a performance on an examination. Remember that . . . Focus on November. Concentrate on practice . . . I want what's best for you. You WILL get through this thing, Marie. I write on my tests, "The primary purpose has already been served by your preparation for this exam" . . . Success doesn't measure a human being, effort does.

Studies show that accountants are more likely to achieve their potential when they receive the type of encouragement that Skender provided. Several years ago, seventy-two new auditors joined a Big Four accounting firm. Half of the auditors were randomly assigned to receive information that they had high potential to succeed. The study was led by researcher Brian McNatt, who had a doctorate, two accounting degrees, a CPA certification, and five years of experience as an accountant and auditor. McNatt read the résumés of the auditors who were randomly assigned to believe in their potential. Then, he met with each of the auditors and informed them that they were hired after a highly competitive selection process, management had high expectations for their success, and they had the skills to overcome challenges and be successful. Three weeks later, McNatt sent them a letter reinforcing this message. For a full month, the auditors who received McNatt's message earned higher performance ratings than the auditors in the control group, who never met with McNatt or received a letter from him. This was true even after controlling for the auditors' intelligence test scores and college grades.

This is the effect that Skender's letter had on Marie Arcuri. He encouraged her to believe in her potential and set high expectations for her to succeed. "He saw the best in his students, and still sees the best in his students," Marie says. She took the exam again and passed two sections, leaving two more to go. Along the way, Skender continued encouraging her. "He wasn't going to let me slack off one bit. He would call me and check in on my progress." She passed the final section and earned her CPA in 1987, two years after she started taking the four sections of the exam. "The difference he made in my life [was in] making sure my priorities were in order, keeping me on track, and preventing me from throwing in the towel," Marie explains. "I knew how much he'd invested in me, and I was not going to let him down." Today, Marie owns two Lexus automobile dealerships. "The accounting background and the skills in reading financial statements have been valuable. But more than C. J. taught me material for my job, he built my character, my passion, and my determination. His commitment to making sure that I got through led me to realize that I'd rather be defined by perseverance than by whether or not I passed an exam."

Skender's approach contrasts with the basic model most companies follow when it comes to leadership development: identify high-potential people, and then provide them with the mentoring, support, and resources needed to grow to achieve their potential. To identify these high-potential future leaders, each year companies spend billions of dollars assessing and evaluating talent. Despite the popularity of this model, givers recognize that it is fatally flawed in one respect. The identification of talent may be the wrong place to start.

For many years, psychologists believed that in any domain, success depended on talent first and motivation second. To groom world-class athletes and musicians, experts looked for people with the right raw abilities, and then sought to motivate them. If you want to find people who can dunk like Michael Jordan or play piano like Beethoven, it's only natural to start by screening candidates for leaping ability and an ear for music. But in recent years, psychologists have come to believe that this approach may be backward.

In the 1960s, a pioneering psychologist named Raymond Cattell developed an investment theory of intelligence. He proposed that interest is what drives people to invest their time and energy in developing particular skills and bases of knowledge. Today, we have compelling evidence that interest precedes the development of talent. It turns out that motivation is the reason that people develop talent in the first place.

In the 1980s, the psychologist Benjamin Bloom led a landmark study of world-class musicians, scientists, and athletes. Bloom's team interviewed twenty-one concert pianists who were finalists in major international competitions. When the researchers began to dig into the eminent pianists' early experiences with music, they discovered an unexpected absence of raw talent. The study showed that early on most of the star pianists seemed "special only when comparing one child with others in the family or neighborhood." They didn't stand out on a local, regional, or national level—and they didn't win many early competitions.

When Bloom's team interviewed the world-class pianists and their parents, they stumbled upon another surprise. The pianists didn't start out learning from piano teachers who were experts. They typically took their first piano lessons with a teacher who lived nearby in their neighborhoods. In *The Talent Code*, Daniel Coyle writes that "From a scientific perspective, it was as if the researchers had traced the lineage of the world's most beautiful swans back to a scruffy flock of barnyard chickens." Over time, even without an expert teacher at the outset, the pianists managed to become the best musicians in the world. The pianists gained their advantage by practicing many more hours than their peers. As Malcolm Gladwell showed us in *Outliers*, research led by psychologist Anders Ericsson reveals that attaining expertise in a domain typically requires ten thousand hours of deliberate practice. But what motivates people to practice at such length in the first place? This is where givers often enter the picture.

When the pianists and their parents talked about their first piano teachers, they consistently focused on one theme: the teachers were caring, kind, and patient. The pianists looked forward to piano lessons because their first teachers made music interesting and fun. "The children had very positive experiences with their first lessons. They made contact with another adult, outside their home, who was warm, supportive, and loving," Bloom's team explains. The world-class pianists had their initial interest sparked by teachers who were givers. The teachers looked for ways to make piano lessons enjoyable, which served as an early catalyst for the intense practice necessary to develop expertise. "Exploring possibilities and engaging in a wide variety of musical activities took precedence" over factors such as "right or wrong or good or bad."

The same patterns emerged for world-class tennis players. When Bloom's team interviewed eighteen American tennis players who had been ranked in the top ten in the world, they found that although their first coaches "were not exceptional coaches, they tended to be very good with young children . . . What this first coach provided was motivation for the child to become interested in tennis and to spend time practicing."

In roles as leaders and mentors, givers resist the temptation to search for talent first. By recognizing that anyone can be a bloomer, givers focus their attention on motivation. The top-ranked tennis players tended to have a first coach who took "a special interest in the tennis player," Bloom's team notes, "usually because he perceived the player as being motivated and willing to work hard, rather than because of any special physical abilities."

In the accounting classroom, looking for motivation and work ethic, not only intellectual ability, is part of what has made C. J. Skender so successful in recognizing talent. When Skender bet Beth Traynham that she would pass the CPA exam, it wasn't because she was unusually gifted in accounting. It was because he noticed "how hard she worked all semester." When Skender recognized that Reggie Love had promise, whereas others wrote him off as just another jock, it was because Love "worked diligently, and was always prepared for class," Skender says. "He was interested in learning and bettering himself." When Skender encouraged Marie Arcuri, it was because she was "the most involved and committed individual I have ever met. Her persistence set her apart."

The psychologist Angela Duckworth calls this *grit*: having passion and perseverance toward long-term goals. Her research shows that above and beyond intelligence and aptitude, gritty people—by virtue of their interest, focus, and drive—achieve higher performance. "Persistence is incredibly important," says psychologist Tom Kolditz, a brigadier general who headed up behavioral sciences and leadership at the U.S. Military Academy for a dozen years. The standard selection rate for Army officers to key command positions is 12 percent; Kolditz's former faculty have been selected at rates as high as 75 percent, and he chalks much of it up to selecting candidates based on grit. As George Anders writes in *The Rare Find*, "you can't take motivation for granted."

Of course, natural talent also matters, but once you have a pool of candidates above the threshold of necessary potential, grit is a major factor that predicts how close they get to achieving their potential. This is why givers focus on gritty people: it's where givers have the greatest return on their investment, the most meaningful and lasting impact. And along with investing their time in motivating gritty people, givers like Skender strive to cultivate grit in the first place. "Setting high expectations is so important," Skender says. "You have to push people, make them stretch and do more than they think possible. When they take my tests, I want them thinking it was the toughest exam they've ever seen in their lives. It makes them better learners." To encourage effort, he gives them a half dozen past exams for practice. "They need to make a significant investment, and it pays off. Forcing them to work harder than they ever have in their lives benefits them in the long run."

One of the keys to cultivating grit is making the task at hand more interesting and motivating. In Bloom's study, across the board, the talented musicians and athletes were initially taught by givers, teachers who

> liked children and rewarded them with praise, signs of approval, or even candy when they did anything right. They were extremely encouraging. They were enthusiastic about the talent field and what they had to teach these children. In many cases . . . they treated the child as a friend of the family might. Perhaps the major quality of these teachers was that they made the initial learning very pleasant and rewarding.

This description could have been written about Skender. At first glance, he seems to fit the stereotype of an accounting whiz.* But at various stages in his life, Skender aspired to be a disc jockey, musician, actor, talk show host, and stand-up comedian. Set foot in his classroom, and you'll see that he hasn't quite given up on these dreams. True to his compulsive nature and eclectic taste, he punctuates his courses with entertaining routines to keep his students engaged, playing four songs at the start of each class and tossing candy bars to the first students who shout out the correct answers to music trivia. This is how a poster of a rapper ended up on his wall. "If you want to engage your audience, if you really want to grab their attention, you have to know the world they live in, the music they listen to, the movies they watch," he explains. "To most of these kids, accounting is like a root canal. But when they hear me quote Usher or Cee Lo Green, they say to themselves, 'Whoa, did that fat old

---

* Skender compulsively makes lists of everything, from his favorite songs to the ten best days of his life, and arranges the dollar bills in his wallet according to the order of their serial numbers. He owns more than eight hundred pairs of suspenders, each of which has a unique name and number. He alphabetizes his socks and his underwear and lays out his clothes weeks in advance. For more than two decades, he has worn a bow tie every Monday, Thursday, and Saturday—even when mowing his lawn. He is religious about being the first to arrive in his parking garage at work, usually before five A.M., yet he is known for staying past midnight at review sessions to help students prepare for exams. He translates his advice about reciprocity into the language of accounting: "I'd rather have a large accounts receivable than a large accounts payable." To put his teaching load in perspective, a typical college professor teaches between three and eight classes a year. Over a career, that amounts to somewhere between one hundred and three hundred classes. Skender has nearly doubled this, and he recently told his dean that he intends to teach thirty-five more years. In calendar year 2012 alone, more than two thousand students took Skender's courses. To accommodate the demand, the university once moved his class to a special oversized room away from the main campus. Even when he teaches early in the morning, his classroom is packed, and many more students wish they could enroll. For one eight A.M. class, he had 190 students on the waiting list.

white-haired guy just say what I thought he said?' And then you've got 'em."

By cultivating interest in accounting, Skender believes that his students will be more likely to invest the time and energy necessary to master the discipline. "C. J. is the epitome of someone who is empathetic," Reggie Love says. "He knows more about music than anyone, and he's always able to weave it into the lecture to help people connect with the material. When you think about having to take a hard course, which typically isn't very interesting, having to keep up with it is challenging. C. J. made it interesting, and I ended up working harder as a result." Love earned an A in Skender's class. David Moltz, a former student of Skender's who works at Google, elaborates that Skender "helps every single student (and person) he comes across in any way possible. He sacrifices hundreds of hours of his personal life to make an impact on the lives of students and teach as many of them as possible. He goes out of his way to make everyone that he engages with feel special."

Throwing Good Money After Bad Talent

Because they see potential all around them, givers end up investing a lot of their time in encouraging and developing people to achieve this potential. These investments don't always pay off; some candidates lack the raw talent, and others don't sustain their passion or maintain the requisite level of grit. Skender once wrote more than one hundred recommendation letters for a student who was applying to graduate programs outside of accounting. She was rejected by all of the programs in her first year, and she decided to apply again, so he dutifully rewrote the recommendation letters. When the schools turned her down once more, Skender revised his recommendation letters for a third year in a row. Finally, after three strikes, Skender encouraged her to pursue a different route.

If Skender were more of a taker or a matcher, would he have given up sooner, saving his own time and the student's? Do givers overinvest in people who possess loads of passion but fall short on aptitude, and how do they manage their priorities to focus on people who show promise while investing less in those who don't? To find out, there's nowhere better to look than professional basketball, where the annual NBA draft tests talent experts on an international stage.

The late Stu Inman is remembered as the man behind two of the worst draft mistakes in the history of the National Basketball Association. In 1972, the Portland Trail Blazers had the first pick in the draft. Inman was serving as the director of player personnel, and he picked center LaRue Martin, who turned out to be a disappointment, averaging just over five points and four rebounds per game in four seasons with the Blazers. In drafting Martin, Inman passed up two of the greatest players in NBA history. The second pick that year was Bob McAdoo, who scored more points in his first season than Martin did in his entire career. McAdoo was named Rookie of the Year, and two years later, he was the NBA's Most Valuable Player. In his fourteen-year NBA career, McAdoo won the league scoring title twice, played on two championship teams, and made five All-Star teams. In that draft, Inman also missed out on Julius Erving—better known as Dr. J.—who was selected twelfth. Erving ended up leading his teams to three championships, winning four MVP awards, making sixteen All-Star teams, and becoming one of the top five leading scorers in the history of professional basketball. Both McAdoo and Erving are members of the Basketball Hall of Fame.

A dozen years later, after being promoted to general manager of the Blazers, Stu Inman had the chance to redeem himself. In the 1984 NBA draft, Inman had the second pick. He chose another center, Sam Bowie, who was over seven feet tall, but athletic and coordinated: he could shoot, pass, and steal, not to mention block shots and grab rebounds. But Bowie never lived up to his potential. When he retired from basketball, ESPN named him the worst draft pick in the history of North American professional sports. In 2003, *Sports Illustrated*, whose cover Bowie had graced years earlier, called him the second-biggest draft flop in the history of the NBA. The biggest? LaRue Martin.

In selecting Bowie second, Inman passed up on a shooting guard from North Carolina named Michael Jordan. With the third pick, the Chicago Bulls selected Jordan, and the rest is history. After being named Rookie of the Year, Jordan racked up six championships, ten scoring titles, and eleven MVP awards while making fourteen All-Star teams and averaging more points than any player ever. He was recognized as the greatest North American athlete of the twentieth century by ESPN.

Inman recognized Jordan's potential, but the Blazers already had two strong guards. They needed a center, so he drafted Sam Bowie. With that choice, he didn't just miss out on Michael Jordan; he also passed up future Hall of Famers Charles Barkley (drafted fifth) and John Stockton (drafted sixteenth). It was bad enough that Inman chose Martin over McAdoo and Erving, and Bowie over Jordan, Barkley, and Stockton. But drafting professional basketball players is at best an imperfect science, and even great managers and coaches make mistakes.

What was worse was that the Blazers held on to both players far longer than they should have. They kept LaRue Martin for four seasons, and by the time they decided to trade him, he had virtually no value. The Blazers couldn't even get an actual player in exchange for Martin—they gave him away in exchange for "future considerations" from the Seattle SuperSonics, who ended up letting him go before the season even started. That was the end of Martin's basketball career, and it was an embarrassing outcome for Inman. "It was a sore subject," said Jack Ramsay, who was the Blazers' coach in Martin's last year and now serves as an ESPN analyst. "Because LaRue couldn't play. He was trying to make the team when I got there, but we had no place for him. He had no offensive game. And he wasn't a rebounder or shot blocker even though he was six-eleven. So he had no skills." The Blazers followed a similar path with Sam Bowie. In 1989, after five lackluster seasons, the Blazers finally traded Bowie to the New Jersey Nets. Why did the Blazers hold on to Sam Bowie and LaRue Martin for so long?

Stu Inman was widely known as a giver. After playing college basketball and coaching high school basketball for a few years, Inman made the leap to college coach, eventually becoming the head coach at his alma mater, San Jose State. In this role, Inman seemed to prioritize players' interests ahead of his own success. One of Inman's star recruits was Tommie Smith, an exceptional athlete who came to San Jose State to run track and play football and basketball. On the freshman basketball team, Smith was the top scorer and rebounder, so in his sophomore year, he began practicing with the varsity basketball team under Inman. One day, Smith came by Inman's office and announced that he was going to quit basketball to focus on track. "I thought he was going to blow up at me," Smith writes, "but he didn't. Coach Inman said, 'Okay, Tom, I understand,' he shook my hand and told me to be sure to come by to see him whenever I wanted to, and that I was always welcome back if I changed my mind. That was the greatest thing in the world for me."

It wasn't so great for Inman. Smith's speed could have added a great deal to the San Jose State basketball team; a few years later, in 1968, Smith won the Olympic gold medal in the 200-meter dash, setting a world record. But Inman had wanted what was best for Smith. Along with letting top talent walk away, Inman made room for gritty players even if they lacked talent. When a skinny white player named Terry Murphy tried out for the varsity team, Inman respected his work ethic and invited him on board. Murphy recalls being one of the worst players Inman had ever coached: "I scored four points the whole year."

Despite this lackluster performance, Inman told Murphy, "I'm never gonna cut you, you're enthusiastic and you play hard and you're a good guy." Inman was "continually giving advice to any basketball junkie who sought it," writes Wayne Thompson, a reporter who covered the Blazers throughout Inman's tenure. He couldn't help it: "Teaching at any level on any subject is the most rewarding thing you can do," Inman told Thompson. "I just love to see the expression on the face of a student who gets it for the first time. Just watching the learning process come to full bloom gives me such a rush."

Once Inman developed a positive impression of players, was he too committed to teaching and developing them, so much that he invested in motivated players even if they lacked the requisite talent? In the classroom, C. J. Skender can afford to dedicate his time to students who demonstrate interest and drive, as he can teach and mentor a large number of students each semester. Conversely, in professional basketball and most work organizations, we face more limits: making a bet on one person's potential means passing on others.

Inman had made a commitment to developing LaRue Martin and Sam Bowie. If Inman had been more of a taker, doesn't it seem obvious that he would have cut his losses much more quickly and moved on to other players? The moment he realized that Martin and Bowie weren't contributing to his team's success, a taker wouldn't feel any sense of responsibility to them. And if Inman had been more of a matcher, wouldn't he have been more willing to let them go? Surely a matcher would grow frustrated that his investments in Martin and Bowie were not being reciprocated or rewarded.

It might seem that givers have a harder time letting go. But in reality, the exact opposite is true. It turns out that givers are the *least* vulnerable to the mistake of overinvesting in people—and that being a giver is what prevented Stu Inman from making far worse mistakes.

Facing the Mirror: Looking Good or Doing Good?

Barry Staw is a world-renowned organizational behavior professor at the University of California at Berkeley, and he has spent his career trying to understand why people make bad decisions in organizations. In an ingenious study, Staw and Ha Hoang collected data on all 240-plus players who were picked in the first two rounds of the NBA draft between 1980 and 1986, in hopes of seeing what effect draft position had on a player's career. They measured each player's performance with a series of different metrics: scoring (points per minute, field goal percentage, and free throw percentage), toughness (rebounds and blocks per minute), and quickness (assists and steals per minute). Staw and Hoang controlled for each player's performance on all of these metrics, as well as for the player's injuries and illnesses, whether the player was a guard, forward, or center, and the quality of the player's team based on win/loss records. Then they examined how much time on the court the players received and how long their teams kept them before trading them, to see if teams made the mistake of overinvesting in players just because they drafted them early.

The results produced a devastating conclusion: teams couldn't let go of their big bets. They stuck with the players whom they drafted early, giving them more playing time and refusing to trade them even if they played poorly. After taking performance out of the equation, players who were drafted earlier still spent more minutes on the court and were less likely to be traded. For every slot higher in the draft, players were given an average of twenty-two more minutes in their second season, and their teams were still investing more in them by their fifth season, when each draft slot higher accounted for eleven more minutes on the court. And for every slot higher in the draft, players were 3 percent less likely to be traded.

This study is a classic case of what Staw calls *escalation of commitment* to a losing course of action. Over the past four decades, extensive research led by Staw shows that once people make an initial investment of time, energy, or resources, when it goes sour, they're at risk for increasing their investment. Gamblers in the hole believe that if they just play one more hand of poker, they'll be able to recover their losses or even win big. Struggling entrepreneurs think that if they just give their start-ups a little more sweat, they can turn it around. When an investment doesn't pay off, even if the expected value is negative, we invest more.

Economists explain this behavior using a concept known as the "sunk cost fallacy": when estimating the value of a future investment, we have trouble ignoring what we've already invested in the past. Sunk costs are part of the story, but new research shows that other factors matter more. To figure out why and when escalation of commitment happens, researchers at Michigan State University analyzed 166 different studies. Sunk costs do have a small effect—decision makers are biased in favor of their previous investments—but three other factors are more powerful. One is anticipated regret: will I be sorry that I didn't give this another chance? The second is project completion: if I keep investing, I can finish the project. But the single most powerful factor is *ego threat*: if I don't keep investing, I'll look and feel like a fool. In response to ego threat, people invest more, hoping to turn the project into a success so they can prove to others—and themselves—that they were right all along.

In one study led by Staw, when California bank customers defaulted on loans, the managers who originally funded the loans struggled to let go and write off the losses. "Bankers who have been closely associated with decisions to fund problem loans are the ones to show the greatest difficulty in acknowledging the subsequent risks of these loans and the likelihood of default," Staw and colleagues write. The study showed that when managers who originally funded the problem loans left the bank, the new managers were significantly more likely to write the loans off. The new managers had no personal responsibility for the problem loans, so their egos weren't under threat; they didn't feel compelled to justify the original decisions as wise.

Research suggests that due to their susceptibility to ego threat, takers are more vulnerable to escalation of commitment than givers. Imagine that you're running an aircraft company, and you have to decide whether or not to invest $1 million in a plane that's invisible to radar technology. You find out that the project is not doing well financially, and a competitor has already finished a better model. But you've made significant investments: the project is 50 percent complete, and you've already spent $5 million and eighteen months working on it. How likely are you to invest the extra $1 million?

In this study by Henry Moon at London Business School, before making their investment decisions, 360 people completed a questionnaire that included giver statements such as "I keep my promises" and taker statements such as "I try to get others to do my duties." The takers were significantly more likely to invest the extra $1 million than the givers. They felt responsible for an investment that was going bad, so they committed more to protect their pride and save face. As University of South Carolina management professors Bruce Meglino and Audrey Korsgaard explain, "although the organization itself might be better off if the decision were abandoned, such action would cause the decision maker to incur significant personal costs (e.g., loss of career mobility, loss of reputation). Because escalating his or her commitment allows the decision maker to keep the prospect of failure hidden, such behavior is personally rational" from the perspective of a taker.

The givers, on the other hand, were primarily concerned about protecting other people and the organization, so they were more willing to admit their initial mistakes and de-escalate their commitment. Other studies show that people actually make more accurate and creative decisions when they're choosing on behalf of others than themselves. When people make decisions in a self-focused state, they're more likely to be biased by ego threat and often agonize over trying to find a choice that's ideal in all possible dimensions. When people focus on others, as givers do naturally, they're less likely to worry about egos and miniscule details; they look at the big picture and prioritize what matters most to others.

Armed with this understanding, it's worth revisiting the story of Stu Inman. As a giver, although he felt invested in the players he drafted first, he felt a stronger sense of responsibility to the team. "Stu was a kind person, considerate of other people's feelings," Wayne Thompson told me. "But he never let that influence selections. If he didn't think a guy could play, he put his arm around him and wished him well." Inman wasn't the one responsible for keeping Sam Bowie on board; Inman left the Blazers in 1986, just two years after drafting Bowie. A taker might have continued to defend the bad decision, but Inman admitted his error in choosing Bowie over Jordan. "All our scouts thought Bowie was the answer to our problems, and I did, too," Inman said, but "it was a mistake."*

---

* To be fair, Bowie's career was hampered by injuries. In college, he missed two full seasons due to shin injuries. Before the draft, to make sure Bowie was completely healthy, Inman subjected him to a seven-hour physical examination. Bowie had a solid first season, but after that, injuries caused him to miss 81 percent of the games in the next four seasons, including nearly two entire seasons. And Inman and his scouts weren't the only ones to bet on Bowie over Jordan. In June 1984, after the draft, a *Chicago Tribune* headline read "Apologetic Bulls 'Stuck' with Jordan." The general manager of the Bulls, Rod Thorn, seemed disappointed. "We wish he were 7 feet, but he isn't," Thorn lamented. "There just wasn't a center available. What can you do? Jordan isn't going to turn this franchise around . . . He's a very good offensive player, but not an overpowering offensive player." Even Jordan seemed to endorse the Bowie selection: "Bowie fits in better than I would," he said during his rookie year, as Portland had "an overabundance of big guards and small forwards." Perhaps the best defense of Inman's choice was offered by Ray Patterson, who ran the Houston Rockets in 1984,

Inman didn't escalate his commitment to LaRue Martin either. Although the Blazers kept Martin for four seasons, Inman and his colleagues took early action in response to Martin's poor performance. In his rookie season, when there were clear signs that Martin was floundering, a taker might have given him extra playing time in an effort to justify choosing him ahead of Bob McAdoo and Julius Erving. But this wasn't what happened. The Blazers granted the starting center position to the hardworking Lloyd Neal, who was just 6'7", putting Martin at backup. In his rookie season, Martin averaged less than thirteen minutes per game on the court, compared with thirty-two for McAdoo and forty-two for Erving. In his second season, Martin continued to underperform, and instead of escalating commitment by giving him more time on the court, the Blazers gave him less—under eleven minutes per game, whereas McAdoo played forty-three and Erving played over forty. Inman and his colleagues managed to overcome the temptation to keep betting on Martin.

A major reason why givers are less vulnerable than takers to escalation of commitment has to do with responses to feedback, as demonstrated in research by Audrey Korsgaard, Bruce Meglino, and Scott Lester on how givers and takers react to information about their performance. In one study, people filled out a survey indicating whether they were givers or takers and made ten decisions about how to solve problems. Then, all participants received a performance score and a suggestion to delegate their authority more when making decisions. The score was randomly assigned so that half of the participants learned that their performance was above average, whereas the other half were told that they were below average. Then, all

---

having selected Hakeem Olajuwon first in that draft before Bowie and Jordan: "Anybody who says they'd have taken Jordan over Bowie is whistling in the dark. Jordan just wasn't that good."

participants made ten more decisions. Would they use the suggestion to delegate more?

When they believed they were above average, the takers followed the suggestion, delegating 30 percent more often. But when they believed they were below average, the takers only delegated 15 percent more often. Once they felt criticized, they were less willing to accept the recommendation for improvement. They protected their pride by refusing to believe that they made poor decisions, discounting the negative feedback. The givers, on the other hand, accepted the criticism and followed the suggestion. Even when they received negative feedback indicating that they were below average, the givers delegated 30 percent more often.

In escalation situations, takers often struggle to face the reality that an initial choice has gone bad. Takers tend to "discount social information and performance feedback that does not support their favorable view of themselves," write Meglino and Korsgaard, whereas givers "may be more apt to accept and act on social information without carefully evaluating the personal consequences." Givers focus more on the interpersonal and organizational consequences of their decisions, accepting a blow to their pride and reputations in the short term in order to make better choices in the long term.

This receptivity to negative feedback helped Stu Inman recognize when he had made a bad investment. Inman was admired around the league for his openness to criticism. Many coaches "took issue with my more incendiary critiques," writes reporter Steve Duin, but "they never bothered Inman," who was "patient and generous," and "one of the most gracious men ever associated with the NBA." When LaRue Martin underperformed, the Blazers coach at the time, Jack McCloskey, voiced his concerns to Inman. "He worked hard and was a very nice young man, but he wasn't skilled. It was that simple. I tried to develop his skills around the basket, and he wasn't an outside player. He didn't have the skills to be the number-one pick." A taker might have rejected the negative feedback, but Inman listened to it.

After Martin's second season, in 1974, the Blazers landed the first pick in the draft again. Having de-escalated their commitment to Martin, they needed another center to replace him, so Inman drafted one, a young man from UCLA named Bill Walton. In his rookie season, Walton was the starting center, averaging thirty-three minutes a game, roughly twice as many as Martin in the backup position. This arrangement continued for another year, after which Inman unloaded Martin.

The next season was 1976–1977, and Walton led the Blazers to the NBA championship over the Philadelphia 76ers, who were led by Julius Erving. Walton was the Finals MVP, and the next year, he was the league MVP. After he retired, he made the Basketball Hall of Fame and was named one of the fifty greatest players in NBA history. Inman was the architect of the 1977 championship team, which had been last in the division the previous year, and remains the only team in the Blazers' four-decade history to win the title. According to Jack Ramsay, who coached the winning team, Inman was "never in the spotlight, and never taking proper credit for the team he assembled."

Glimpsing Glimmers in Chunks of Coal

As a giver, Inman built this championship team with an approach that mirrored C. J. Skender's: seeing potential in players where others didn't. "Inman wanted a complete portfolio on everybody he was interested in," writes Wayne Thompson. "No doubt that is what made him so successful in finding diamonds in the rough." Half of the top six scorers on the championship team—and five of the top nine—were drafted late by Inman, in the second or third round. "He was way ahead of the curve in seeing potential," noted Steve Duin. "Stu, in the subculture of basketball gurus, was near the apex. He was considered a genius," said Mavericks president Norm Sonju. In a chronicle of the 1984 draft, Filip Bondy writes that Inman was viewed by many as "the best personnel man in the league. He was so good, so respected, that other clubs would track his scouting missions and listen very carefully to rumors about which players might interest him."

In the 1970s, most basketball teams were focusing heavily on observable physical talents such as speed, strength, coordination, agility, and vertical leap. Inman thought it was also important to pay attention to the inner attributes of players, so he decided to begin evaluating their psychological makeup. Before a draft, along with reviewing a player's statistics and watching him play, Inman wanted to understand him as a person. He would watch players closely during the pregame warm-up to see how hard they worked, and he would interview their coaches, family members, friends, and teachers about issues of motivation, mind-set, and integrity. According to the *Oregonian*, "Inman made his reputation by finding undervalued players. . . . His eye for talent was as sharp as his feel for people. He wanted players whose character and intelligence were as high as their vertical jumps."

In 1970, Inman joined the Blazers, then a brand-new NBA team, as chief talent scout. That summer, he held an open tryout for people to put their basketball skills to the test. It was partially a public relations stunt to generate local excitement about basketball, but Inman was also looking for players who had gone overlooked by other teams. None of the guys from the open tryout made the team, but Inman's fascination with unlikely candidates would bear fruit several years later. In 1975, with the twenty-fifth pick in the second round of the draft, Inman selected a little-known Jewish forward named Bob Gross. Coaches and fans thought it was a mistake. Gross had played college basketball at Seattle, averaging ten points a game, and then transferred to Long Beach State, where he averaged just six and a half points in his junior year. "The story of Bob Gross's collegiate and professional basketball life was that nobody noticed him," wrote Frank Coffey in a book about the Blazers, "until they really started looking hard."

Inman happened to see a game between Long Beach and Michigan State, and his interest was piqued when Gross hustled to block a shot on what should have been an easy Spartan layup on a fast break. Inman took a closer look and saw more evidence of Gross's work ethic: he more than doubled his scoring average from his junior to senior year, when he put in more than sixteen points a game. Inman "discovered a jewel, a consistent, hardworking, extraordinarily effective basketball player," Coffey wrote. Gross was praised by one of his college coaches for "unselfish dedication to the team." When the Blazers made the Finals in his third NBA season, Gross delivered, pouring in an average of seventeen points per game. In the pivotal games five and six, he guarded Julius Erving and led the Blazers by scoring twenty-five and twenty-four points. According to Bill Walton, "Bob Gross was the 'grease guy' for that team. He made it flow . . . Bob would run relentlessly, guard and defend . . . Without Bob . . . Portland could not have won the championship."

Inman recognized that givers were undervalued by many teams, since they didn't hog the spotlight or use the flashiest of moves. His philosophy was that "It's not what a player is, but what he can become . . . that will allow him to grow." When Inman saw a guy practice with grit and play like a giver, he classified him as a diamond in the rough. In fact, there's a close connection between grit and giving. In my own research, I've found that because of their dedication to others, givers are willing to work harder and longer than takers and matchers. Even when practice is no longer enjoyable, givers continue exerting effort out of a sense of responsibility to their team.

This pattern can be seen in many other industries. Consider Russell Simmons, the cofounder of the hip-hop label Def Jam

Records, which launched the careers of LL Cool J and the Beastie Boys. Simmons is often called the godfather of hip-hop, and he was giving away music for free as early as 1978, long before most labels started doing that. When I asked him about his success, he attributed it to finding and promoting givers. "Good givers are great getters; they make everybody better," Simmons explains. One of his favorite givers is Kevin Liles, who started working for free as an intern and rose all the way up to become president of Def Jam. As an intern, Liles was the first to arrive at work and the last to leave. As a promotion director, Liles was responsible for one region, but he went out of his way to promote other regions too. "Everybody started to look at Kevin as a leader, because they all looked to him for direction. He gave until people couldn't live without him." In selecting and promoting talent, Simmons writes, "The most important quality you can show me is a commitment to giving."

Stu Inman knew that gritty givers would be willing to put the good of the team above their own personal interests, working hard to fulfill the roles for which they were needed. In the fabled 1984 draft, after selecting Sam Bowie, Inman took a forward named Jerome Kersey in the second round with the forty-sixth pick overall. Kersey came from Longwood College, a little-known Division II school in Virginia, yet blossomed into an excellent NBA player. A Longwood sports administrator said that Kersey "had the best work ethic of anyone that's ever been here," which is what led Inman to recognize his promise when few NBA insiders did. The next year, in 1985, Inman found another hidden gem of a point guard with the twenty-fourth pick in the draft: Terry Porter, a gritty giver who earned acclaim for his hustle and selflessness. He made two All-Star teams with the Blazers and played seventeen strong NBA seasons, and in 1993, he won the J. Walter Kennedy Citizenship Award, awarded annually to one player, coach, or trainer who demonstrates "outstanding service and dedication to the community." Along with providing tickets for disadvantaged children to attend games and promoting graduation parties free of drugs and alcohol, Porter has given extensively to boys' and girls' clubs, working in partnership with his former teammate Jerome Kersey.

Perhaps Inman's best investment occurred in the 1983 draft, when the Blazers had the fourteenth pick. Inman selected shooting guard Clyde Drexler, who was passed up by other teams because he wasn't regarded as a very strong shooter. Although he was the fifth shooting guard chosen, Drexler is now widely regarded as the steal of the 1983 draft. He outscored all other players in the draft, averaging more than 20 points a game in his career, and was the only player in that draft to make the all-NBA team, at least one All-Star game (he made ten of them), the Olympics, and the Basketball Hall of Fame. By the time he retired, Drexler joined legends Oscar Robertson and John Havlicek as the third player in NBA history to rack up more than 20,000 points, 6,000 rebounds, and 3,000 assists. Like Walton, Drexler was designated one of the fifty greatest players of all time. How did Inman know Drexler would be such a star when so many other teams let him slide by?

As a giver, Inman was open to outside advice. While at San Jose State, Inman met Bruce Ogilvie, a pioneer in sports psychology who "came onto the sports scene when psychologists were referred to as 'shrinks' and any player going to visit one was seen as a problem." Most general managers and coaches avoided psychologists like Ogilvie, approaching the so-called science skeptically. Some viewed psychological assessment as irrelevant; others worried that it would threaten their own expertise and standing.

Whereas takers often strive to be the smartest people in the room, givers are more receptive to expertise from others, even if it challenges their own beliefs. Inman embraced Ogilvie and his methods with open arms, requiring players to undergo several hours of evaluation before the draft. Inman worked with Ogilvie to assess players on their selflessness, desire to succeed, willingness to persevere, receptivity to being coached, and dedication to the sport. Through these assessments, Inman could develop a deep understanding of a player's tendencies toward grit and giving. "Other NBA teams were taking psychological looks at draftable players, but none to the degree that we used it and trusted it," Inman said. "You had to like the talent before you would consider it in your evaluation. But it provided a clear barometer as to whether the guy would fulfill his potential."

When Ogilvie assessed Drexler, Inman was impressed with his psychological profile. Inman interviewed the coaches who had seen Drexler play at Houston, and there was a consistent theme: Drexler played like a giver. "Clyde was the glue on that team. I was taken by the almost unanimous reaction from other coaches in that league," Inman explained. "They said he did what he had to do to win a game. His ego never interfered with his will to win." According to Bucky Buckwalter, who was then a scout, "There was some reluctance from teams . . . He was not a great shooter." But Inman and his team decided that Drexler could "learn to shoot from the perimeter, or somehow make up for it with his other talents." Inman was right: Drexler "turned out to be a more skilled player . . . than I would have expected," Buckwalter said.

Even Inman's bad bets on the basketball court have gone on to success elsewhere; the man knew a giver when he saw one. LaRue Martin has worked at UPS for twenty-five years, most recently as the community services director in Illinois. In 2008, he received a letter out of the blue from former Blazers owner Larry Weinberg: "you certainly are a wonderful role model in the work you are doing for UPS." Martin has played basketball with President Obama, and in 2011, he was elected to the board of directors of the Retired Players Association. "I would love to be able to give back," Martin said.

And remember Terry Murphy, Inman's worst player at San Jose State? Inman gave Murphy a chance but didn't see a future for him in basketball, so he encouraged him to go out for volleyball. Inman was spot-on about his work ethic: Murphy ended up making the U.S. national volleyball team. But Murphy didn't leave basketball behind altogether: in 1986, to raise money for the Special Olympics, he started a three-on-three street basketball tournament in Dallas. By 1992, Hoop It Up had more than 150,000 players and a million fans. Five years later, there were 302 events in twenty-seven different countries, raising millions of dollars for charity.

Perhaps the best testament to Inman's success is that although he missed out on Michael Jordan as a player, he outdid Jordan as a talent evaluator. As a basketball executive, Jordan has developed a reputation that conveys more taker cues than giver. This was foreshadowed on the court, where Jordan was known as self-absorbed and egotistical. As Jordan himself once remarked, "To be successful you have to be selfish."* Coaches had to walk on eggshells to give him constructive feedback, and in his Hall of Fame speech, Jordan was widely criticized for thanking few people and vilifying those who doubted him. Back in his playing days, he was a vocal advocate for a greater share of team revenues going to players. Now, as an owner, he has pushed for greater revenue to owners, presumably to put more money in his own pockets.†

---

* Significantly, it was a shift from taking toward giving that appeared to elevate Jordan's success as a player. When Jordan played for the Chicago Bulls, his coach Phil Jackson emphasized that if Jordan focused on "making his team members more successful, he would expand his impact and ultimate success, and thereby become the best individual basketball player and also the leader of the best basketball team," writes Stephen Roulac. Jordan became "more giver than taker," Roulac explains, and "became even more dominant and prominent. As he did less alone, when game circumstances dictated the appropriateness of more selfish play, he was even more effective."

† Interestingly, Jordan's basketball coach at the University of North Carolina, the

When it comes to betting on talent for too long, Jordan's moves as an executive offer a fascinating contrast with Inman's. When Jordan became president of basketball operations for the Washington Wizards, he used the first pick in the 2001 draft to select center Kwame Brown. Brown was straight out of high school, loaded with talent, but seemed to lack grit, and never came anywhere near his potential. Later, he would be called the second-biggest NBA draft bust of the decade and one of the one hundred worst picks in sports history. After Brown, the second and third picks in the drafts were also centers, and they fared far better. The second pick was Tyson Chandler, who went on to make the 2012 U.S. Olympic team. The third pick was Pau Gasol, another young center less than a year and a half older than Brown. Gasol won the Rookie of the Year award, and in the coming decade, he would make four All-Star teams, win two NBA championships, and earn the J. Walter Kennedy Citizenship Award. Both Gasol and Chandler swamped Brown's performance in scoring, rebounding, and blocking shots.

---

legendary Dean Smith, had more of a giver style. Against his own interests, and strong resistance from his assistants, Smith advised Jordan to enter the NBA draft early, before his senior year. Smith had a rule: "We do what's best for the player out of season and what's best for the team in season." As NBA salaries skyrocketed, Smith encouraged every player who had a good shot at being picked in the top five or ten to leave college early and secure his financial future, as long as he promised to come back and finish his education later. In his thirty-six years as head coach, Smith sent nine athletes to the draft early, and seven made good on their promises. Although Smith was encouraging his best players to leave the team, putting his players' interests first seemed to help him recruit top talent and build trust and loyalty. Smith retired with 879 wins, then more than any coach in NCAA history; his teams made eleven Final Fours and won two national championships. As Chris Granger, executive vice president at the NBA, explains, "Talented people are attracted to those who care about them. When you help someone get promoted out of your team, it's a short-term loss, but it's a clear long-term gain. It's easier to attract people, because word gets around that your philosophy is to help people."

Brown's disappointing results appeared to threaten Jordan's ego. When Jordan came out of retirement to play for the Wizards alongside Brown, he routinely berated and belittled Brown, whose poor performance was hurting the team—and making Jordan's draft choice look foolish. In his first season, Brown put up paltry numbers, averaging less than five points and four rebounds per game. Yet in his second season, Brown's minutes on the court doubled.

Jordan was fired from the Wizards after that season, but he wasn't ready to give up on Brown. Nearly a decade later, in 2010, Brown signed a contract with the Charlotte Bobcats, a team owned by none other than Michael Jordan. "Michael was very much a part of this," Brown's agent said. "He wanted this to happen."

By that point, Brown had played ten seasons for four different teams, averaging under seven points and six rebounds in more than five hundred games. In his previous season, he was spending just thirteen minutes on the court. When Brown joined Jordan's Bobcats, his playing time was doubled to twenty-six minutes a game. The Bobcats gave Brown more minutes than he had played in the prior two seasons combined, yet he continued to struggle, averaging under eight points and seven rebounds. Jordan "wanted to give Kwame another opportunity," Brown's agent said. "There's been so much written about the fact that this was Michael's first pick and so much criticism directed at both of them when it didn't work out." A giver might admit the mistake and move on, but Jordan was still trying to turn the bad investment around. "I love Michael, but he just has not done a good job," says friend and former Olympic teammate Charles Barkley. "I don't think Michael has hired enough people around him who will disagree." Under Jordan's direction, in 2012, the Bobcats finished with the worst winning percentage in NBA history.

Conversely, Inman's teams achieved surprising levels of success. In addition to building the 1977 team that went from last place to the title in just a year with a large number of unknowns, Inman's draft picks made the Blazers a formidable team for years to come. After he left the Blazers in 1986, the team flourished under the leadership of Drexler, Porter, and Kersey. The three hidden gems, discovered by Inman in three consecutive years, led the Blazers to the Finals twice. Once again, Inman rarely received the credit. To the casual fan, it may appear that Inman was a failure, but basketball insiders regard him as one of the finest talent evaluators the sport has ever seen. Inman's experience, coupled with research evidence, reveals that givers don't excel only at recognizing and developing talent; they're also surprisingly good at moving on when their bets don't work out.

Stu Inman spent the last four years of his life volunteering as an assistant coach for the Lake Oswego High School basketball team in Oregon. "He had them to a T," said Lake Oswego's head coach. "Not only did he have them as basketball players, he had their characters, too. He took time not to prejudge people but to see them as they really are." At Lake Oswego, Stu Inman helped to groom a young player named Kevin Love, who has gone on to pursue the legacy that Sam Bowie and LaRue Martin never fulfilled: thrive as a big man who can shoot. As a 6'10" center, Love has made the U.S. Olympic team and two All-Star teams in his first four seasons, been named the NBA's most improved player, and won the three-point shooting championship.

"If you choose to champion great talent, you will be picking one of the most altruistic things a person can do," writes George Anders. "In any given year, quick-hit operators may make more money and win more recognition, at least briefly. Over time, though, that dynamic reverses."

5

The Power of
Powerless Communication

How to Be Modest and Influence People

Speak softly, but carry a big stick.
—Theodore Roosevelt, U.S. president

Dave Walton took a deep breath. He was an employment law expert who specialized in trade secrets and employee competition cases. As a partner at the firm Cozen O'Connor, Dave was one of the youngest lawyers to be elected shareholder, and he had been named a Pennsylvania Super Lawyer—Rising Star for several years. But he was about to stand up and give his first closing argument in front of a jury.

It was 2008, and Dave was representing a company that owned Acme-Hardesty, a Pennsylvania castor oil distributor that received its supplies from Jayant Oils and Derivatives in Mumbai, India. In December 2006, the CEO of Acme's parent company was informed that Jayant was setting up a U.S. office and sales organization, and would no longer supply Acme with castor oil. During the following month, Acme executives learned that Jayant was planning to sell castor oil products directly to customers in the U.S. market, competing with Acme for business.

In the summer of 2006, two Acme employees had jumped ship to Jayant and helped them set up the competing company. Acme's parent company filed suit against Jayant and the two employees, accusing them of stealing trade secrets and confidential information.

Dave prepared diligently and spoke passionately. He presented evidence that in March 2006, while still working for Acme, the employees agreed to financial terms to help Jayant start the competing distributor. In June, each of the two received initial payments of $50,000 from Jayant for consulting services.

The employees gave notice that they were leaving and went straight to India without informing Acme of their new positions. Dave argued that in India, they incorporated knowledge from Acme into Jayant's business plan. One employee provided Jayant with a list of U.S. customer prospects that he was paid to develop for Acme, Dave claimed, and the Jayant president admitted that Acme's documents were used to generate projections for investors. Dave further argued that while the employees were setting up the plan for Jayant in India, they used false e-mail aliases that gave them continued access to Acme's orders.

The defendants were represented by three different prominent law firms, and Dave's opponent in the trial was highly articulate. He had twenty-five years of experience, a law degree from Columbia and an undergraduate degree from Cornell, and a slew of awards under his belt, including being named one of the top one hundred lawyers in Pennsylvania and the litigator of the week for the entire country. One source described him as an "accomplished, knowledgeable, and sophisticated lawyer who is amazing on his feet in court."

The defense attorney was eloquent and polished, telling the jury that Jayant engaged in legitimate competition, as it was entitled to do. Acme did lose some customers, the lawyer admitted, but it wasn't because the employees did anything wrong. Acme was the middle man distributing Jayant's castor oil products to customers. By cutting out the middleman, Jayant was able to sell the products more cheaply, which is precisely the point of fair competition. The employees were being treated poorly at Acme. The defense attorney nailed his key arguments, and he questioned the credibility of Dave's main witnesses. Dave was impressed with the skill that the defense attorney demonstrated. "He was really good. He made better arguments than we anticipated."

Dave knew the trial could go either way. On the one hand, he had painted a compelling portrait that Jayant and the two employees were guilty. On the other hand, this was a high-pressure, high-profile case. It was Dave's first time taking the lead in a jury trial; he was by far the youngest lawyer there. During one of his examinations, an old foe reared its head: Dave started stammering. This happened a few more times, and it signaled that he lacked confidence.

Dave was particularly concerned about the effect on one particular juror. During the trial, this juror made it clear that he was in favor of the defendants: he felt that Jayant and the employees had done nothing wrong. The juror responded enthusiastically to the defense attorney, nodding appreciatively throughout his arguments and laughing loudly at his jokes. In contrast, when Dave spoke, the juror avoided eye contact, smirked, and made dismissive gestures. Throughout the trial, the juror came to court wearing blue jeans. But on the day of the closing arguments, the juror arrived wearing a suit and tie. When Dave watched the juror waltz in, his heart sank. The juror wanted to be the foreman, and he was obviously vying to turn the jury against Dave's case.

Dave finished his closing, and the jury went into deliberation. When they came out, the antagonistic juror walked out first. He had been elected foreman, and he read the verdict.

The jury ruled in favor of Dave's client, to the tune of $7 million. Dave's victory set a record for the largest trade-secret verdict in Pennsylvania. There's no doubt that Dave presented a brilliant case, speaking with conviction as a true expert in his field. But there was another factor that gave him the slightest edge.

There's something that separates Dave Walton from other distinguished lawyers—and it's something that he shares with former GE CEO Jack Welch, Vice President Joe Biden, singer Carly Simon, *20/20* anchor John Stossel, actor James Earl Jones, and Bill Walton of the Portland Trail Blazers, who is now a basketball announcer.

They all stutter.

Stuttering is a speech disorder that affects about 1 percent of the population. Growing up, Dave Walton was teased and ridiculed for stuttering. When he graduated from college, he applied for a sales job, but was turned down. "The interviewer told him he would never make it in sales because of his stutter," his wife Mary says. When Dave decided to apply to law school, many of his friends and family members raised their eyebrows, hoping he wouldn't have to do any public speaking. In law school, it seemed that their fears were prescient. Dave recalls that during his first mock court argument, the judge started crying. "She felt bad for me."

Most people see stuttering as a disability, and we marvel at people like Jack Welch and James Earl Jones, whose confident demeanors typically bear little trace of their speech difficulties. But the truth is far more interesting and complex. Many people who stutter end up becoming quite successful, and it's not always because they have conquered their stuttering. In the trade secrets trial, when Dave stammered and tripped over a couple of arguments, something strange happened.

The jurors *liked* him.

At the end of the trial, several jurors approached him. "They told me that they really respected me because they knew that I had a stutter," Dave says. "They stressed that my stutter was minor but that they noticed it and that they talked about it. The jurors said they admired my courage in being a trial lawyer."

Dave didn't win the trial because of his stutter. But it may have created a stronger connection with the jury, helping to tip the balance in his favor. When the jurors commended him, Dave was "surprised and a little embarrassed . . . My first thought was, 'I don't remember stuttering that much.' As the jurors walked away from me, I realized that I had something that was natural and genuine. It was an epiphany—my stutter could be an advantage."

In this chapter, I want to explore how Dave Walton's experience reveals critical but counterintuitive clues about influencing others— and how Dave exemplifies what givers do differently when they seek influence. In *To Sell Is Human*, Daniel Pink argues that our success depends heavily on influence skills. To convince others to buy our products, use our services, accept our ideas, and invest in us, we need to communicate in ways that persuade and motivate. But the best method for influence may not be the one that first comes to mind.

Research suggests that there are two fundamental paths to influence: dominance and prestige. When we establish dominance, we gain influence because others see us as strong, powerful, and authoritative. When we earn prestige, we become influential because others respect and admire us.

These two paths to influence are closely tied to our reciprocity styles. Takers are attracted to, and excel in, gaining dominance. In an effort to claim as much value as possible, they strive to be superior to others. To establish dominance, takers specialize in *powerful communication*: they speak forcefully, raise their voices to assert their authority, express certainty to project confidence, promote their accomplishments, and sell with conviction and pride. They display strength by spreading their arms in dominant poses, raising their eyebrows in challenge, commanding as much physical space as possible, and conveying anger and issuing threats when necessary. In the quest for influence, takers set the tone and control the conversation by sending powerful verbal and nonverbal signals. As a result, takers tend to be much more effective than givers in gaining dominance. But is that the most sustainable path to influence?

When our audiences are skeptical, the more we try to dominate them, the more they resist. Even with a receptive audience, dominance is a zero-sum game: the more power and authority I have, the less you have. When takers come across someone more dominant, they're at risk of losing their influence. Conversely, prestige isn't zero-sum; there's no limit to the amount of respect and admiration that we can dole out. This means that prestige usually has more lasting value, and it's worth examining how people earn it.

The opposite of a taker's powerful communication style is called *powerless communication*. Powerless communicators tend to speak less assertively, expressing plenty of doubt and relying heavily on advice from others. They talk in ways that signal vulnerability, revealing their weaknesses and making use of disclaimers, hedges, and hesitations. In Western societies, Susan Cain writes in *Quiet*, people expect us to communicate powerfully. We're told that great leaders use "power talk" and "power words" to forcefully convey their messages. By using powerless communication, surely people wind up at a disadvantage when it comes to influence.

Um, well, not quite.

I think.

In this chapter, my aim is to challenge traditional assumptions about the importance of assertiveness and projecting confidence in gaining influence. It turns out this style doesn't always serve us well, and givers instinctively adopt a powerless communication style that proves surprisingly effective in building prestige. I want to trace how givers develop prestige in four domains of influence: presenting, selling, persuading, and negotiating. Because they value the perspectives and interests of others, givers are more inclined toward asking questions than offering answers, talking tentatively than boldly, admitting their weaknesses than displaying their strengths, and seeking advice than imposing their views on others. Is it possible that these forms of powerless communication can become powerful?

Presenting: The Value of Vulnerability

At age twenty-six, two years after finishing my doctorate in organizational psychology, I was asked to teach senior military leaders how to motivate their troops. The military was trying to transition from a command-and-control model to a more collaborative approach, and I happened to be doing research related to the topic. My first assignment was a four-hour class for twenty-three colonels in the U.S. Air Force. They were former fighter pilots, having logged an average of more than 3,500 flight hours and 300 combat hours. Their aircraft of choice: F-16s carrying rockets and precision-guided munitions. And just as *Top Gun* had taught me, they had badass nicknames.

Striker was in charge of more than 53,000 officers and a $300 million operating budget. Sand Dune was an aerospace engineer who flew combat missions in operations Desert Storm, Iraqi Freedom, and Enduring Freedom. Boomer was running programs that cost more than $15 billion, including unmanned aircraft that could be flown from New Mexico to Afghanistan by remote control.

The colonels were in their forties and fifties—twice my age. They had spent their careers in an organization that rewarded seniority, and I had none. Although I had some relevant knowledge and a doctorate, I was way out of my league, and it showed. At the end of the day, the colonels completed course feedback forms. Two comments were particularly revealing:

- Stealth: "More quality information in audience than on podium."
- Gunner: "The instructor was very knowledgeable, but not yet experienced enough . . . slightly missed the needs of the

audience. The material was very academic . . . I gained very little from the session. I trust the instructor did gain useful insight."

Others were gentler, but the message still came through loud and clear. Bomber said, "The professors get younger every year," and Stingray added, "I prefer that my professors be older than I am or I start to believe that I am approaching middle age and we all know that is not true . . . don't we?"

I had started my presentation to the colonels with powerful communication: I talked confidently about my credentials. This wasn't how I usually opened in the classroom. In my role as a professor, I've always felt a strong sense of responsibility to give to my students, and I tend to be more concerned about connecting with students than establishing my authority. When I teach undergraduates, I open my very first class with a story about my biggest failures. With the Air Force colonels, though, I was worried about credibility, and I only had four hours—instead of my usual four months—to establish it. Deviating from my typical vulnerable style, I adopted a dominant tone in describing my qualifications. But the more I tried to dominate, the more the colonels resisted. I failed to win their respect, and I felt disappointed and embarrassed.

I had another session with Air Force colonels coming up on my schedule, so I decided to try a different opening. Instead of talking confidently about my credentials, I opened with a more powerless, self-deprecating remark:

"I know what some of you are thinking right now:

'What can I possibly learn from a professor who's twelve years old?'"

There was a split second of awkward silence, and I held my breath.

Then the room erupted with bursts of laughter. A colonel named

Hawk piped up: "Come on, that's way off base. I'm pretty sure you're thirteen." From there, I proceeded to deliver a near carbon copy of my first presentation—after all, the information I had to deliver on motivation hadn't changed. But afterward, when I looked at the feedback, it differed night and day from my previous session:

- "Spoke with personal experience. He was the right age! High energy; clearly successful already."
- "Adam was obviously knowledgeable regarding the topic and this translated into his passion and interest. This allowed him to be very effective. One word—EXCELLENT!"
- "Although junior in experience, he dealt with the studies in an interesting way. Good job. Very energetic and dynamic."
- "I can't believe Adam is only twelve! He did a great job."

Powerless communication had made all the difference. Instead of working to establish my credentials, I made myself vulnerable, and called out the elephant in the room. Later, I adopted the same approach when teaching Army generals and Navy flag officers, and it worked just as well. I was using my natural communication style, and it helped me connect with a skeptical audience.

Takers tend to worry that revealing weaknesses will compromise their dominance and authority. Givers are much more comfortable expressing vulnerability: they're interested in helping others, not gaining power over them, so they're not afraid of exposing chinks in their armor. By making themselves vulnerable, givers can actually build prestige.

But there's a twist: expressing vulnerability is only effective if the audience receives other signals establishing the speaker's competence. In a classic experiment led by the psychologist Elliot Aronson, students listened to one of four tapes of a candidate auditioning for a Quiz Bowl team. Half of the time, the candidate was an expert, getting 92 percent of questions right. The other half of the time, the candidate had only average knowledge, getting 30 percent right.

As expected, audiences favored the expert. But an interesting wrinkle emerged when the tape included a clumsy behavior by the candidate. Dishes crashed, and the candidate said, "Oh, my goodness—I've spilled coffee all over my new suit."

When the average candidate was clumsy, audiences liked him even less.

But when the expert was clumsy, audiences liked him even more.

Psychologists call this the *pratfall effect*. Spilling a cup of coffee hurt the image of the average candidate: it was just another reason for the audience to dislike him. But the same blunder helped the expert appear human and approachable—instead of superior and distant.* This explains why Dave Walton's stuttering made a positive impression on the jury. The fact that Dave was willing to make himself vulnerable, putting his stutter out for the world to see, earned their respect and admiration. The jurors liked and trusted him, and they listened carefully to him. This set the stage for Dave to convince them with the substance of his arguments.

Establishing vulnerability is especially important for a lawyer like Dave Walton. Dave has a giver tendency: he spends a great deal of time mentoring junior associates, and he fights passionately for justice on behalf of his clients. But these aren't the first attributes that a jury sees: his appearance doesn't exactly ooze warmth. "I'm a big guy with a military look," Dave explains,

---

* It's worth noting that the pratfall effect depends on the audience's self-esteem. Powerless communication humanizes the communicator, so it should be most appealing to audiences who see themselves as human: those with average self-esteem. Indeed, Aronson and colleagues found that when competent people make blunders, audiences with average self-esteem respond more favorably than audiences with high and low self-esteem.

and I have an intense streak. In the trade secrets trial, I wouldn't say stuttering is why I won, but it helped my credibility: it made me a real person. It gave them an insight into my character that they liked. It humanized me: this is a guy we can pull for. It made me seem less polished, and more credible as an advocate. People think you have to be this polished, perfect person. Actually, you don't want a lawyer who is too slick. Good trial lawyers aim to be an expert and a regular guy at the same time.

When Dave Walton stands in front of a jury in spite of his stutter, they can see that he cares deeply about his clients—he believes in them enough that he's willing to expose his own vulnerability to support them. This sends a powerful message to his audience that helps win them over by increasing his prestige and softening the dominance in his natural appearance.

Selling: Separating the Swindlers from the Samaritans

Expressing vulnerability in ways that are unrelated to competence may build prestige, but it's only a starting point for givers to exercise influence. To effectively influence people, we need to convert the respect that we earn into a reason for our audiences to change their attitudes and behaviors. Nowhere is this clearer than in sales, where the entire job depends on getting people to buy—and buy more. We often stereotype salespeople as manipulative and Machiavellian, thinking of great sellers as intimidating, confrontational, self-serving, or even sometimes deceitful. Daniel Pink finds that the first words that come to mind when we think of salespeople are *pushy*, *ugh*, and *yuck*. In one study, people ranked the forty-four most commonly chosen MBA occupations in terms of how socially responsible they were. Salesperson ranked forty-third, barely above stockbroker at the very bottom of the social responsibility list. This sets up the expectation that top salespeople must be takers, yet in the opening chapter, we saw a preview of evidence that many highly productive salespeople are givers. How do givers sell effectively?

Bill Grumbles is a powerful executive, but if you met him, you probably wouldn't realize it. He speaks so softly that you might find yourself leaning forward just to hear him. After working his way up to a vice presidency at HBO, he became the president of worldwide distribution for TBS. Throughout his career, Grumbles has gone out of his way to help and mentor others. Today, he spends his time coaching business students on leadership and volunteering to give them career advice. Early on, powerless communication actually helped him rise to the top of HBO's sales charts.

Back in 1977, HBO was an unknown brand; most Americans didn't even have cable. Grumbles was in his late twenties, and he was sent to open an HBO sales office in Kansas City. He had no sales experience, so he started doing what he did best as a giver: asking questions. His questions were sincere, and customers responded. "I would be on a sales call, and I'd look at the walls, around the office, and see their interests. I'd ask about their grandchildren, or their favorite sports team. I would ask a question, and customers would talk for twenty minutes." Other salespeople were bringing in one contract a month. Grumbles was four times as productive: he brought in one contract a week.

By asking questions and listening to the answers, Grumbles showed his customers that he cared about their interests. This built prestige: customers respected and admired the concern that he showed. After one of his early sales calls, a customer took him aside to tell him he was a "great conversationalist." Grumbles laughs: "I'd hardly said a thing!"

Asking questions opened the door for customers to experience what the psychologist James Pennebaker calls the joy of talking. Years ago, Pennebaker divided strangers into small groups. Imagine that you've just joined one of his groups, and you have fifteen minutes to talk with strangers about a topic of your choice. You might chat about your hometown, where you went to college, or your career.

After the fifteen minutes are up, you rate how much you like the group. It turns out that the more you talked, the more you like the group. This isn't surprising, since people love to talk about themselves. But let me ask you another question: How much did you learn about the group?

Logically, learning about the people around you should depend on listening. The less you talk, the more you should discover about the group. But Pennebaker found the opposite: the *more* you talk, the *more you think you've learned about the group*. By talking like a taker and dominating the conversation, you believe you've actually come to know the people around you, even though they barely spoke. In *Opening Up*, Pennebaker muses, "Most of us find that communicating our thoughts is a supremely enjoyable learning experience."

It's the givers, by virtue of their interest in getting to know us, who ask us the questions that enable us to experience the joy of learning from ourselves. And by giving us the floor, givers are actually learning about us and from us, which helps them figure out how to sell us things we already value.

To shed further light on how givers sell successfully, I want to take you on a journey to Raleigh, North Carolina, where I'm posing as a mystery shopper. I'm working with an innovative optometry company called Eye Care Associates, with the goal of figuring out what distinguishes star sellers from the rest of the pack. Every employee in the company has filled out a survey about whether they're givers, takers, or matchers, and now it's time for me to see them in action.

I enter an eye care office and express an interest in replacing a pair of broken sunglass frames that I purchased at LensCrafters. I walk over to a display case, and I'm approached by my very first salesman. He shows me a snazzy pair of glasses, and swiftly launches into a compelling pitch with powerful communication. The lenses are tailor-made for driving. The contours of the frames accentuate the shape of my face. The color matches my skin tone. I've never been mistaken for cool, but I briefly flirt with the fantasy that these shades could transform me into James Bond—or at least James Woods. When I express concerns about the price, the salesman confidently assures me that they're worth it. They fit me so perfectly, he says, that the designers must have had a winning face like mine in mind when they created these shades. I develop a sneaking suspicion that he's flattering me to make the sale. *Taker?*

At another office, the salesperson offers to do me a favor. He'll replace my frames for free, if I switch over to his office for eye exams. *Matcher . . . and I have the survey data to back it up.*

Who's the more successful seller: the taker or the matcher?

Neither. Both are right in the middle of the pack.

At a third office in Knightdale, North Carolina, I meet Kildare Escoto. Kildare is an imposing figure, with thick eyebrows and a thin goatee. He's a serious weightlifter, and if you asked him right now, he could drop and do a hundred push-ups without breaking a sweat. His parents are from the Dominican Republic, and he grew up in rough-and-tumble New York City. He has the same title as the two salespeople I met at other offices, but his style couldn't be more different.

We're the exact same age, but Kildare calls me "sir," and I sense that he means it. He speaks softly and asks me some basic questions before he even pulls out a single tray of sunglasses from the case. Have I ever been here before? Do I have a prescription to fill? What's my lifestyle like—do I play sports? He listens carefully to my answers and gives me some space to contemplate.

I have 20/20 vision, but Kildare is so good that I suddenly feel the urge to buy a pair of shades. I blow my cover. I tell him I'm studying the techniques of outstanding salespeople—is he willing to discuss his approach? Kildare objects. "I don't look at it as selling," he explains. "I see myself as an optician. We're in the medical field first, retail second, sales maybe third. My job is to take the patient, ask the patient questions, and see what the patient needs. My mind-set is not to sell. My job is to help. My main purpose is to educate and inform patients on what's important. My true concern in the long run is that the patient can see."

The data reveal two striking facts about Kildare Escoto. First, in my survey, he had the single highest giver score of any employee in the company. Second, he was also the top-selling optician in the entire company, bringing in more than double the average sales revenue.

It's not a coincidence. The second-highest seller also more than doubled the average, and she's a giver too. Her name is Nancy Phelps, and she has the same philosophy as Kildare. "I get involved with patients, ask where they work, what their hobbies are, what they like to do on vacations. It's about the patients and their needs." It's revealing that when patients walk in the door, they ask for Nancy. "I'm a real believer in giving patients their new fresh eyes that they're going to see their best in," she says.

To see whether Kildare and Nancy are exceptions to the rule, Dane Barnes and I asked hundreds of opticians to complete a survey measuring whether they were takers, matchers, or givers. We also gave them an intelligence test, assessing their ability to solve complex problems. Then we tracked their sales revenue over the course of an entire year.

Even after controlling for intelligence, the givers outsold the matchers and takers. The average giver brought in over 30 percent more annual revenue than matchers and 68 percent more than takers. Even though matchers and takers together represented over 70 percent of the sellers, half of the top sellers were givers. If all opticians were givers, the average company's annual revenue would spike from approximately $11.5 million to more than $15.1 million.

Givers are the top sellers, and a key reason is powerless communication.

Asking questions is a form of powerless communication that givers adopt naturally. Questions work especially well when the audience is already skeptical of your influence, such as when you lack credibility or status, or when you're in a highly competitive negotiation situation. Neil Rackham spent nine years studying expert and average negotiators. He identified expert negotiators as those who were rated as highly effective by both sides, and had a strong track record of success with few failures. He recorded more than one hundred negotiations and combed through them to see how the experts differed from average negotiators. The expert negotiators spent much more time trying to understand the other side's perspective: questions made up over 21 percent of the experts' comments but less than 10 percent of the average negotiators' comments.

If Kildare were a taker, he'd be more interested in leading with his own answers than asking questions. But instead of telling patients what they want, he asks them what they want. One day, Mrs. Jones comes out of an eye exam, and Kildare approaches her to find out if she's interested in a new pair of glasses. In one eye, she's nearsighted. In the other eye, she's farsighted. Her doctor has prescribed a multifocal lens, but she's clearly skeptical. She's there to get her eyes examined, and has no intention of making an expensive purchase. She tells Kildare she doesn't want to try the new lens.

Instead of delivering an assertive pitch, Kildare starts asking her questions. "What kind of work do you do?" He learns that she works at a computer, and he notices that when she's trying to read, she turns her head to privilege her nearsighted eye. When she's looking at something in the distance, as when driving, she turns her head the other way to rely on her farsighted eye. Kildare asks why the doctor has prescribed a new lens, and she mentions that she's struggling with distance, computer work, and reading. He sees that she's getting frustrated and reassures her: "If you feel you don't need corrective lenses, I'm not going to waste your time. Let me just ask you one more question: when will you wear these glasses?" She says they would really only be useful at work, and they're awfully expensive if she can only wear them part of the day.

As he listens to her answer, Kildare realizes that his customer has a misconception about how multifocal lenses can be used. He gently explains that she can use multifocal lenses not only at work, but also in the car and at home. She's intrigued, and she tries them on. A few minutes later, she decides to get fitted for her very first pair of multifocal glasses, spending $725. A taker might have lost the sale. By asking questions, Kildare was able to understand her concerns and address them.

But maybe we're stacking the deck in favor of givers. After all, opticians are selling in the health care industry, where it's easy to believe in the product and care about patients in need. Can givers succeed in sales jobs where customers are more skeptical, like insurance? In one study, managers rated the giving behaviors of more than a thousand insurance salespeople. Even in insurance, the higher the salesperson's giver score, the greater that salesperson's revenue, policies sold, applications, sales quotas met, and commissions earned.

By asking questions and getting to know their customers, givers build trust and gain knowledge about their customers' needs. Over time, this makes them better and better at selling. In one study, pharmaceutical salespeople were assigned to a new product with no existing client base. Each quarter, even though the salespeople were paid commission, the givers pulled further ahead of the others.*

---

* The same pattern showed up in another study, where more than six hundred salespeople responsible for women's products completed a questionnaire that revealed whether they were givers: did they try to offer the product that was best suited to customers' needs? When researchers tracked their sales revenue, the givers initially had no advantage. As they came to understand their customers,

Moreover, giving was the only characteristic to predict performance: it didn't matter whether the salespeople were conscientious or care-free, extroverted or introverted, emotionally stable or anxious, and open-minded or traditional. The defining quality of a top pharmaceu-tical salesperson was being a giver. And powerless communication, marked by questions, is the defining quality of how givers sell.

Out of curiosity, are you planning to vote in the next presidential election?

By asking you that one question, I've just increased the odds that you will actually vote by 41 percent.

That's another benefit of powerless communication. Many people assume that the key to persuasive skill is to deliver a confident, asser-tive pitch. But in daily life, we're bombarded by advertisers, telemar-keters, salespeople, fund-raisers, and politicians trying to convince us that we want to buy their products, use their services, and support their causes. When we hear a powerful persuasive message, we get suspicious. In some cases, we're concerned about being tricked, duped, or manipulated by a taker. In other situations, we just want to make our own free choices, rather than having our decisions con-trolled by someone else. So if I tell you to go out and vote, you might resist. But when I ask if you're planning to vote, you don't feel like I'm trying to influence you. It's an innocent query, and instead of resisting my influence, you reflect on it. "Well, I do care about being a good citizen, and I want to support my candidate." This doesn't feel like I'm persuading you. As Aronson explains, you've been convinced by someone you already like and trust:

Yourself.

Dave Walton knows why questions are effective persuasive

---

the givers pulled further and further ahead. By the third and fourth quarters, the givers were bringing in significantly more revenue. The givers gathered more information about customers' needs and were more flexible in how they responded to customers.

devices. He sees great lawyers as salespeople, and it's important that they don't sell their arguments too assertively, like takers. "The art of advocacy is to lead you to my conclusion *on your terms*. I want you to form your own conclusions: you'll hold on to them more strongly. I try to walk jurors up to that line, drop them off, and let them make up their own minds." Thoughtful questions pave the way for jurors to persuade themselves. According to Aronson, "in direct persuasion, the audience is constantly aware of the fact that they have been persuaded by another. Where self-persuasion occurs, people are convinced that the motivation for change has come from within."

By asking people questions about their plans and intentions, we increase the likelihood that they actually act on these plans and intentions. Research shows that if I ask you whether you're planning to buy a new computer in the next six months, you'll be 18 percent more likely to go out and get one. But it only works if you already feel good about the intention that the question targets. Studies show that asking questions about your plans to floss your teeth and avoid fatty foods significantly enhances the odds that you will actually floss and eat healthy. These are desirable actions, so questions open the door for you to persuade yourself to engage in them.* But if I ask about your plans to do something undesirable, questions don't work. For example, are you planning to eat some chocolate-covered grasshoppers this month?

After thinking about it, you're probably even less likely to do it. In the examples that we've covered so far, the givers were selling desirable products to interested customers. When Bill Grumbles was selling HBO, he had customers who were open to a better cable

---

* Part of the reason that intention questions work is that they elicit commitment: once people say yes, they feel compelled to follow through. But interestingly, research suggests that intention questions can work even when people initially say no. The questions trigger reflection, and if the behavior is attractive, some people change their mind and decide to do it.

product. When Kildare Escoto and Nancy Phelps sell glasses, they have patients who need new frames or lenses. How do givers change the minds of audiences who aren't so receptive?

Persuading: The Technique of Tentative Talk

In 2004, Volkswagen's retail theme was "Drive it. You'll get it." Consumers connected with the double meaning. The line conveyed that to fully appreciate a Volkswagen's performance features, you had to sit behind the wheel. It also carried another message: if you take the car for a test drive, you'll love it so much that you'll end up buying it. It was just one of a string of memorable campaigns from Arnold Worldwide, Volkswagen's advertising agency. But Don Lane, the man who generated the clever "Drive it. You'll get it" theme, never appeared in the credits.

Lane was a senior account executive, not a member of the creative department. His job was to package and sell the creative team's ideas. One day, while stuck on a strategic brief for the creative team, an idea popped into his head. Instead of writing the strategy, he wrote a sample script that ended with the line, "Drive it. You'll get it."

It wasn't standard practice for an account person to come to the creative team with a solution, instead of a problem to solve. In fact, it was forbidden for an account guy to contribute to the creative process. So Lane had a dilemma: how could he get the creative team to listen? If he were a taker, he might have stormed into the creative director's office to pitch the line, lobby powerfully for it, and demand full credit. If he were a matcher, he might have offered a favor to the creative team and hoped for reciprocity, or called in a favor owed. But Lane leaned in the giver direction. He wasn't concerned about the credit; he just wanted to help the creative team and see a good line get implemented. "In our business, creative people are gifted and deserve to get most of, if not all of, the credit. Some account management people resent that," Lane says. "I knew that my job was to help creative people and provide space for them to come up with ideas. I didn't really care if anyone knew it was my idea. It didn't matter where the idea came from. If it worked, we would all share in the success."

Lane walked into the creative director's office. Instead of using powerful communication—"I have a great line, you should use it"—he went with a softer approach. He presented a sample radio script to show how it would work. Then he said to the creative director, "I know this is against the rules, but I want to give you a sense of what I'm talking about. What do you think of this line? 'Drive it, you'll get it.'"

The creative director got it. He looked up at Lane, smiled, and said, "That's our campaign." The campaign sold many cars and won several advertising awards.

Alison Fragale, a professor at the University of North Carolina, is an expert on the form of powerless communication that Don Lane used effectively. Fragale finds that speech styles send signals about who's a giver and who's a taker. Takers tend to use powerful speech: they're assertive and direct. Givers tend to use more powerless speech, talking with tentative markers like these:

- Hesitations: "well," "um," "uh," "you know"
- Hedges: "kinda," "sorta," "maybe," "probably," "I think"
- Disclaimers: "this may be a bad idea, but"
- Tag questions: "that's interesting, isn't it?" or "that's a good idea, right?"
- Intensifiers: "really," "very," "quite"

These markers send a clear message to the audience: the speaker lacks confidence and authority. Lacking confidence is a bad thing, right?

If we break down how Don Lane pitched his idea, we can see two markers of powerless speech: a disclaimer and a tag question. His disclaimer was "I know this is against the rules, but," and his tag question was "What do you think?" Fragale shows that when people have to work closely together, such as in teams and service relationships, powerless speech is actually more influential than powerful speech.

To illustrate one of her studies, imagine that your plane has just crash-landed in the desert. You're with your coworker, Jamie. You have to prioritize twelve items, including a flashlight and a map, in order of importance for survival. You share your rankings with Jamie, who disagrees. You're not a fan of the flashlight. But Jamie thinks it's critical, and decides to deliver a forceful message:

> The flashlight needs to be rated higher. It is the only reliable night signaling device; also, the reflector and lens could be used to start a fire, which is another way to signal for help. Put it higher.

Jamie sounds like a taker—and probably is, since takers are inclined to give orders like this. Are you willing to listen to Jamie?

If you're like most people, the answer is no. You're supposed to be collaborating, and you don't want to be told what to do, so you resist Jamie's influence. In trying to establish dominance, Jamie has lost prestige. But what if Jamie makes the same suggestion, talking more tentatively, and adding some questions and hedges?

> Do you think the flashlight should maybe be rated higher? It may be a pretty reliable night signaling device. Also, maybe the reflector and lens could be used to start a fire, which could possibly be another way to signal for help.

In Fragale's study, people were much more receptive to this version. Powerless speech signals that Jamie is a giver. By talking tentatively, Jamie shows a willingness to defer to you, or at least take your opinion into consideration. Fragale finds that even when Jamie delivers the exact same message in the exact same tone both times, adding markers of tentative talk such as hedges, tag questions, and intensifiers earns greater respect and influence. This is why the creative director was so open to Don Lane's idea: Lane signaled that he wasn't trying to threaten the director's authority. It was clear to the creative director that Lane was just trying to share a good idea, and the director knew a good idea when he saw it.*

Over time, talking tentatively paid off for Lane. He brought ideas up gently and didn't ask for credit. "Creative people responded to this approach, and it gave me credibility when I had a creative idea worth sharing," Lane explains. Whereas many of his peers had conflicts with creative people, Lane developed a reputation for being a rare account guy with whom creative people enjoyed working. Instead of seeing him as an outsider stepping on their toes, they saw him as a helpful contributor. They frequently requested him on projects, often saying, "He's helping us. He's not a typical account guy. Let's keep him involved and give him more opportunities." Knowing that he was generous and open, creative teams were willing to share ideas with him and welcome his input, rather than guarding their turf more closely.

Lane's ability to contribute to creative teams attracted the attention of senior management. At an unusually early stage in his career, Lane was invited to play a key role in the world-renowned "Drivers wanted" campaign for Volkswagen. "Givers fear that they'll become invisible," Lane says. "But I've seen givers thrive because people like

---

* Disclaimer: Certain types of disclaimers are riskier than other forms of power-less communication. For example, it's common for people to start a sentence with "I don't mean to sound selfish, but . . ." Psychologists have shown that this type of disclaimer backfires: it heightens the expectation that the speaker is going to say something selfish, which leads the listener to search for—and find—information that confirms the speaker's selfishness.

working with and trust them. Realizing this was a major turbo boost early in my career." Lane was promoted more quickly than many of his peers, and he is now an executive vice president and executive director at Arnold. In the words of one creative vice president, "Don is a complete team player . . . If I have another opportunity to work with Don—I would jump at the chance."

An analysis of tentative talk points to another reason why Dave Walton's stutter might have helped him connect with the jury in the trade secrets trial. Hesitations, hedges, and intensifiers are built-in features of stuttering. When a jury hears Dave Walton stutter, he no longer sounds dominant and imposing. They don't feel that he's trying to convince them, so they lower their resistance. They become just a bit more open to being persuaded by him.

When givers use powerless speech, they show us that they have our best interests at heart. But there's one role in which people tend to avoid talking tentatively: leadership. Not long ago, a marketing manager named Barton Hill found out why. He was leading a business unit at a financial services firm, and he was invited to interview for a major promotion to a higher-level position, where he would lead multiple business units. The interviewer opened with a softball question: tell us about your successes. Hill started talking about his team's accomplishments, which were quite impressive.

Although Hill was the front-runner for the position, he didn't get it. The interviewer told him he didn't sound like a leader. "I kept using words like *we* and *us*," Hill says. "I didn't use enough first-person singular pronouns, like *I* and *me*. I found out later that it didn't seem like I was a leader. He thought I didn't drive the team's success, and wanted someone who could." The interviewer expected Hill to speak more assertively, and powerless communication cost him the job.

By speaking with greater speed, volume, assertiveness, and certainty, takers convince us that they know what they're talking about.

In one study conducted by psychologists in California, takers were judged by group members as more competent, but in reality, they weren't more competent. Takers, the study's authors report, "attain influence because they behave in ways that make them appear competent—even when they actually lack competence."

By failing to use powerful speech in his interview, Barton Hill failed to create the impression of dominance. Yet the same powerless communication that cost him the promotion ended up earning prestige, making his teams successful. Whereas powerful communication might be effective in a one-shot job interview, in a team or a service relationship, it loses the respect and admiration of others. Psychologists in Amsterdam have shown that although group members perceive takers as highly effective leaders, takers actually undermine group performance. Speaking dominantly convinces group members that takers are powerful, but it stifles information sharing, preventing members from communicating good ideas. "Teams love it when their leader presents a work product as a collaborative effort. That's what inspires them to contribute," Hill reflects. "The paradox comes from people thinking an inclusive leader isn't strong enough to lead a team, when in fact that leader is stronger, because he engenders the support of the team. People bond to givers, like electromagnetism." Eventually, Hill left for another company, and three of his former employees approached him about joining his team. This type of loyalty has paid off in the long run: Hill's teams have been wildly successful. He is now a managing director and global head of marketing at Citi Transaction Services, a division of more than twenty thousand people.

Of course, there's a time and a place for leaders to use powerful speech. In a study of pizza franchises, colleagues Francesca Gino, Dave Hofmann, and I found that when most employees in a store are dutiful followers, managers are well served to speak powerfully. But when most employees are proactive, generating new ideas for cooking and delivering pizzas more efficiently, powerful speech backfires. When employees were proactive, managers who talked forcefully led their stores to 14 percent lower profits than managers who talked less assertively and more tentatively. By conveying dominance, the powerful speakers discouraged their proactive employees from contributing. When people use powerful communication, others perceive them as "preferring and pursuing individual accomplishments," Fragale writes, "at the expense of group accomplishments." Through talking tentatively, the powerless speakers earned prestige: they showed openness to proactive ideas that would benefit the group.

To see if this effect would hold up in a more controlled setting, my colleagues and I brought teams of people together to fold T-shirts. We instructed half of the team leaders to talk forcefully, and asked the other half to talk more tentatively. Once again, when team members were passive followers, the powerful speakers did just fine. But when team members were highly proactive, taking initiative to come up with a faster way to fold T-shirts, the powerless speakers were much more effective. Proactive teams had 22 percent higher average output under leaders who spoke powerlessly than powerfully. Team members saw the powerful speakers as threatened by ideas, viewing the powerless speakers as more receptive to suggestions. Talking tentatively didn't establish dominance, but it earned plenty of prestige. Team members worked more productively when the tentative talkers showed that they were open to advice.

To a taker, this receptivity to advice may sound like a weakness. By listening to other people's suggestions, givers might end up being unduly influenced by their colleagues. But what if seeking advice is actually a strategy for influencing other people? When givers sit down at the bargaining table, they benefit from advice in unexpected ways.

Negotiating: Seeking Advice in the Shadow of a Doubt

In 2007, a *Fortune* 500 company closed a plant in the Midwest United States. One of the people to lose her position was an effervescent research scientist named Annie. The company offered Annie a transfer to the East Coast, but it would require her to give up on her education. While working full time, Annie was enrolled in a night-time MBA program. She couldn't afford to quit her job, and if she did, the company would no longer pay for her degree. Yet if she accepted the transfer, she wouldn't be able to continue studying. She was in a bind, with little time and few options.

Two weeks later, something extraordinary happened: she was offered a seat on the company's private jet, which was normally available only to top executives, with unlimited access until she finished her MBA. She accepted the transfer and spent the next nine months riding the corporate jet back and forth, twice a week, until she finished her degree. The company also paid for her rental car every week and commercial plane tickets when the corporate jet wasn't running. How did she get the company to make such a big investment in her?

Annie landed all of these perks without ever negotiating. Instead, she used a form of powerless communication that's quite familiar to givers.

Entering negotiations, takers typically work to establish a dominant position. Had Annie been a taker, she might have compiled a list of all of her merits and attracted counteroffers from rival companies to strengthen her position. Matchers are more inclined to see negotiating as an opportunity for quid pro quo. If Annie were a matcher, she would have gone to a senior leader who owed her a favor and asked for reciprocity. But Annie is a giver: she mentors dozens of colleagues, volunteers for the United Way, and visits elementary school classes to interest students in science. When her colleagues make a mistake, she's regularly the one to take responsibility, shielding them from the blame at the expense of her own performance. She once withdrew a job application when she learned that a friend was applying for the same position.

As a giver, Annie wasn't comfortable bargaining like a taker or a matcher, so she chose an entirely different strategy. She reached out to a human resources manager and asked for advice. "If you were in my shoes, what would you do?"

The manager became Annie's advocate. She reached out to the heads of Annie's department and site, and started to lobby on Annie's behalf. The department head, in turn, called Annie and asked what he could do to keep her. Annie mentioned that she wanted to finish her MBA, but couldn't afford to fly back and forth. In response, the department head offered her a seat on the jet.

New research shows that advice seeking is a surprisingly effective strategy for exercising influence when we lack authority. In one experiment, researcher Katie Liljenquist had people negotiate the possible sale of commercial property. When the sellers focused on their goal of getting the highest possible price, only 8 percent reached a successful agreement. When the sellers asked the buyers for advice on how to meet their goals, 42 percent reached a successful agreement. Asking for advice encouraged greater cooperation and information sharing, turning a potentially contentious negotiation into a win-win deal. Studies demonstrate that across the manufacturing, financial services, insurance, and pharmaceuticals industries, seeking advice is among the most effective ways to influence peers, superiors, and subordinates. Advice seeking tends to be significantly more persuasive than the taker's preferred tactics of pressuring subordinates and ingratiating superiors. Advice seeking is also consistently more influential than the matcher's default approach of trading favors.

This is true even in the upper echelons of major corporations. Recently, strategy professors Ithai Stern and James Westphal studied executives at 350 large U.S. industrial and service firms, hoping to find out how executives land seats on boards of directors. Board seats are coveted by executives, as they often pay six-figure salaries, send clear status signals, and enrich networks by granting access to the corporate elite.

Takers assume that the best path to a board seat is ingratiation. They flatter a director with compliments, or track down his friends to praise him indirectly. Yet Stern and Westphal found that flattery only worked when it was coupled with advice seeking. Instead of just complimenting a director, executives who got board seats were more likely to seek advice along with the compliment. When praising a director's skill, the advice-seeking executives asked how she mastered it. When extolling a director's success in a task, these executives asked for recommendations about how to replicate his success. When executives asked a director for advice in this manner, that director was significantly more likely to recommend them for a board appointment—and they landed more board seats as a result.

Advice seeking is a form of powerless communication that combines expressing vulnerability, asking questions, and talking tentatively. When we ask others for advice, we're posing a question that conveys uncertainty and makes us vulnerable. Instead of confidently projecting that we have all the answers, we're admitting that others might have superior knowledge. As a result, takers and matchers tend to shy away from advice seeking. From a taker's perspective, asking for advice means acknowledging that you don't have all the answers. Takers may fear that seeking advice might make them look weak, dependent, or incompetent. They're wrong: research shows that people who regularly seek advice and help from knowledgeable colleagues are actually rated more favorably by supervisors than those who never seek advice and help.

Appearing vulnerable doesn't bother givers, who worry far less about protecting their egos and projecting certainty. When givers ask for advice, it's because they're genuinely interested in learning from others. Matchers hold back on advice seeking for a different reason: they might owe something in return.

According to Liljenquist, advice seeking has four benefits: learning, perspective taking, commitment, and flattery. When Annie asked for advice, she discovered something she didn't know before: the company's jet had extra seats, and it traveled back and forth between her two key locations. Had she lobbied more assertively instead of seeking advice, she might never have gained this information. In fact, Annie had several previous conversations in which no one mentioned the jet.

This brings us to the second benefit of advice seeking: encouraging others to take our perspectives. In Annie's previous conversations, where she didn't ask for advice, the department head focused on the company's interest in transferring her while saving as much money as possible. The advice request changed the conversation. When we ask for advice, in order to give us a recommendation, advisers have to look at the problem or dilemma from our point of view. It was only when Annie sought guidance that the department head ended up considering the problem from her perspective, at which point the corporate jet dawned on him as a solution.

Once the department head proposed this solution, the third benefit of advice seeking kicked in: commitment. The department head played a key role in generating the jet solution. Since it was his idea and he had already invested some time and energy in trying to help Annie, he was highly motivated to help her further. He ended up paying for the rental car that she used in the Midwest and agreeing to fund commercial flights if the corporate jet was not running.

There's no doubt that Annie earned these privileges through a combination of hard work, talent, and generosity. But a clever study sheds further light on why the department head was so motivated to offer Annie more than just the corporate jet. Half a century ago, the psychologists Jon Jecker and David Landy paid people for succeeding on a geometry task. In the control group, the participants kept the money, and visited the department secretary to fill out a final questionnaire. But when another group of participants started to leave, the researcher asked them for help. "I was wondering if you would do me a favor. The funds for this experiment have run out and I am using my own money to finish the experiment. As a favor to me, would you mind returning the money you won?"

Nearly all of the participants gave the money back. When questioned about how much they liked the researcher, the people who had done him the favor liked him substantially *more* than the people who didn't. Why?

When we give our time, energy, knowledge, or resources to help others, we strive to maintain a belief that they're worthy and deserving of our help. Seeking advice is a subtle way to invite someone to make a commitment to us. Once the department head took the time to offer advice to Annie, he became more invested in her. Helping Annie generate a solution reinforced his commitment to her: she must be worthy of his time. If she wasn't important to him, why would he have bothered to help her? As Benjamin Franklin wrote in his autobiography, "He that has once done you a kindness will be more ready to do you another than he whom you yourself have obliged."

When we ask people for advice, we grant them prestige, showing that we respect and admire their insights and expertise. Since most people are matchers, they tend to respond favorably and feel motivated to support us in return. When Annie approached the human resources manager for advice, the manager stepped up and went to bat for her. According to biographer Walter Isaacson, Benjamin Franklin saw advice seeking as a form of flattery. Franklin "had a fundamental rule for winning friends," Isaacson writes: appeal to "their pride and vanity by constantly seeking their opinion and advice, and they will admire you for your judgment and wisdom."

Regardless of their reciprocity styles, people love to be asked for advice. Giving advice makes takers feel important, and it makes givers feel helpful. Matchers often enjoy giving advice for a different reason: it's a low-cost way of racking up credits that they can cash in later. As a result, when we ask people for advice, they tend to respond positively to us.

But here's the catch: advice seeking only works if it's genuine. In her research on advice seeking, Liljenquist finds that success "depends on the target perceiving it as a sincere and authentic gesture." When she directly encouraged people to seek advice as an influence strategy, it fell flat. Their counterparts recognized them as fakers: they could tell that the advice seekers were ingratiating based on ulterior motives. "People who are suspected of strategically managing impressions are more likely to be seen as selfish, cold, manipulative, and untrustworthy," Liljenquist writes. Advice seeking was only effective when people did it spontaneously. Since givers are more willing to seek advice than takers and matchers, it's likely that many of the spontaneous advice seekers in her studies were givers. They were actually interested in other people's perspectives and recommendations, and they were rated as better listeners.

I believe this applies more generally to powerless communication: it works for givers because they establish a sincere intent to act in the best interests of others. When presenting, givers make it clear that they're expressing vulnerability not only to earn prestige but also to make a genuine connection with the audience. When selling, givers ask questions in a way that conveys the desire to help customers, not take advantage of them. When persuading and negotiating, givers speak tentatively and seek advice because they truly value the ideas and viewpoints of others.

Powerless communication is the natural language of many givers, and one of the great engines behind their success. Expressing vulnerability, asking questions, talking tentatively, and seeking advice can open doors to gaining influence, but the way we direct that influence will reverberate throughout our work lives, including some we've already discussed, like building networks and collaborating with colleagues. As you'll see later, not every giver uses powerless communication, but those who do often find that it's useful in situations where we need to build rapport and trust. It can't easily be faked, but if you fake it long enough, it might become more real than you expected. And as Dave Walton discovered, powerless communication can be far more powerful and effective than meets the ear.

6

The Art of Motivation Maintenance

Why Some Givers Burn Out but Others Are On Fire

---

*The intelligent altruists, though less altruistic than the unintelligent altruists,
will be fitter than both unintelligent altruists and selfish individuals.*

—Herbert Simon, Nobel Prize winner in economics

Up to this point, we've been focusing on how givers climb to the top of the success ladder through the unique ways that they build networks, collaborate, communicate, influence, and help others achieve their potential. But as you saw in the opening chapter, givers are also more likely to end up at the bottom of the success ladder. Success involves more than just capitalizing on the strengths of giving; it also requires avoiding the pitfalls. If people give too much time, they end up making sacrifices for their collaborators and network ties, at the expense of their own energy. If people give away too much credit and engage in too much powerless communication, it's all too easy for them to become pushovers and doormats, failing to advance their own interests. The consequence: givers end up exhausted and unproductive.

Since the strategies that catapult givers to the top are distinct from those that sink givers to the bottom, it's critical to understand what differentiates successful givers from failed givers. The next three chapters examine why some givers burn out while others are on fire;

how givers avoid being exploited by takers; and what individuals, groups, and organizations can do to protect givers and spread their success.

Recently, the Canadian psychologists Jeremy Frimer and Larry Walker led an ambitious effort to figure out what motivates highly successful givers. The participants were winners of the Caring Canadian Award, the country's highest honor for giving, recognizing people who have devoted many years of their lives to help their communities or advance a humanitarian cause. Many winners of this award have sustained extraordinary giving efforts for decades in order to make a difference.

To reveal what drove them, all of the participants filled out a questionnaire asking them to list ten goals in response to "I typically try to . . ." Then, Walker conducted in-depth interviews with twenty-five Caring Canadian winners and a comparison group of twenty-five people who matched the winners in gender, age, ethnicity, and education, but had not sustained the same level or duration of giving. Walker spent a hundred hours interviewing all fifty people about their lives, covering key periods and critical events in childhood, adolescence, and adulthood. From there, independent raters read the goal lists, listened to the interview tapes, and rated the degree to which the participants expressed two key motivations: self-interest and other-interest. Self-interest involved pursuing power and achievement, whereas other-interest focused on being generous and helpful. On which set of motivations did the Caring Canadian winners score higher than the comparison group?

The intuitive answer is other-interest, and it's correct. In their life stories, the Caring Canadians mentioned giving and helping more than three times as often as the comparison group. When they listed their goals, the Caring Canadians listed nearly twice as many goals related to other-interest as the comparison group. The Caring Canadians highlighted goals like "serve as a positive role model to young people" and "advocate for women from a low-income bracket." The comparison participants were more likely to mention goals like "get my golf handicap to a single digit," "be attractive to others," and "hunt the biggest deer and catch big fish."

But here's the surprise: the Caring Canadians also scored higher on self-interest. In their life stories, these highly successful givers mentioned a quest for power and achievement almost twice as often as the comparison group. In their goals, the Caring Canadians had roughly 20 percent more objectives related to gaining influence, earning recognition, and attaining individual excellence. The successful givers weren't just more other-oriented than their peers; they were also more self-interested. Successful givers, it turns out, are just as ambitious as takers and matchers.

These results have fascinating implications for our understanding of why some givers succeed but others fail. Up until this point, we've looked at reciprocity styles on a continuum from taking to giving: is your primary concern for your own interests or others' interests? Now I want to complicate that understanding by looking at the interplay of self-interest and other-interest. Takers score high in self-interest and low in other-interest: they aim to maximize their own success without much concern for other people. By contrast, givers always score high on other-interest, but they vary in self-interest. There are two types of givers, and they have dramatically different success rates.

Selfless givers are people with high other-interest and low self-interest. They give their time and energy without regard for their own needs, and they pay a price for it. Selfless giving is a form of pathological altruism, which is defined by researcher Barbara Oakley as "an unhealthy focus on others to the detriment of one's own needs," such that in the process of trying to help others, givers end up harming themselves. In one study, college students who scored high on selfless giving declined in grades over the course of the semester.

These selfless givers admitted "missing class and failing to study because they were attending to friends' problems."

Most people assume that self-interest and other-interest are opposite ends of one continuum. Yet in my studies of what drives people at work, I've consistently found that self-interest and other-interest are completely independent motivations: you can have both of them at the same time. As Bill Gates argued at the World Economic Forum, "there are two great forces of human nature: self-interest, and caring for others," and people are most successful when they are driven by a "hybrid engine" of the two. If takers are selfish and failed givers are selfless, successful givers are *otherish*: they care about benefiting others, but they also have ambitious goals for advancing their own interests.

Concern for Others' Interests

		LOW	HIGH
	LOW	Apathetic	*Selfless:* Self-sacrificing Givers
Concern for **Self-interest**			
	HIGH	*Selfish:* Takers	*Otherish:* Successful Givers

Selfless giving, in the absence of self-preservation instincts, easily becomes overwhelming. Being otherish means being willing to give more than you receive, but still keeping your own interests in sight, using them as a guide for choosing when, where, how, and to whom you give. Being otherish is very different from matching. Matchers expect something back from each person they help. Otherish givers help with no strings attached; they're just careful not to overextend themselves along the way. Instead of seeing self-interest and other-interest as competing, the Caring Canadians found ways to integrate them, so that they could do well by doing good. As you'll see, when concern for others is coupled with a healthy dose of concern for the self, givers are less prone to burning out and getting burned—and they're better positioned to flourish.

* * *

"In West Philadelphia, born and raised, on the playground is where I spent most of my days . . . I got in one little fight and my mom got scared . . ."

When Will Smith wrote these famous lyrics for the theme song of *The Fresh Prince of Bel-Air*, the hit sitcom that launched his career, he had just graduated from Overbrook High School in Philadelphia. Overbrook has a majestic façade, its five-story building resembling a castle perched atop a hill. During his time in the castle, Smith was treated like royalty, earning the nickname "Prince" from teachers for his ability to charm his way out of trouble. Years later, when he started a production company, he named it Overbrook Entertainment. Smith is not the only accomplished person to attend Overbrook, whose alumni include astronaut Guion Bluford Jr., the first African American in space, and Jon Drummond, an Olympic gold medalist in track. Overbrook is one of just six high schools in the entire United States that has seen more than ten students go on to play in the National Basketball Association, one of whom was the legendary Wilt Chamberlain.

But for most students, Overbrook is no fairy tale.

Located at the corner of Fifty-ninth and Lancaster in the heart of West Philadelphia, Overbrook is just a few blocks from one of the top ten drug corners in the country. Take a stroll past the school, and it's not uncommon to see the drivers of passing cars rolling up their windows and locking their doors. In 2006, Overbrook was one of twenty-eight schools in the United States that was identified as "persistently dangerous" based on crime statistics. As of 2011, there were roughly 1,200 students enrolled at Overbrook, and nearly 500 were suspended at some point during the school year, racking up nearly fifty assaults and twenty weapons or drugs charges. The educational prospects for students are similarly dismal. On the SAT, Overbrook's average hovers more than three hundred points below the national average, with more than three quarters of students in the bottom 25 percent in the country. Nearly half of all students who start high school at Overbrook will never finish: the graduation rate is just 54 percent.

In the hopes of turning this tragic situation around, a corps of talented, passionate young educators has arrived at Overbrook from Teach For America (TFA), the renowned nonprofit organization that sends college graduates to spend two years fighting educational inequity as teachers in some of the most disadvantaged schools in the country. TFA is filled with givers: research shows that the vast majority of teachers join to make a difference in students' lives. Many come from privileged backgrounds, and they're determined to help students who are less fortunate. As one anonymous teacher put it:

> I knew throughout my life that I wanted to do something where I help . . . Social justice issues burn within me and the fact that so many students have been so viciously failed by the school systems in this country is infuriating and invigorating. I want every child to grow up able to make choices . . . education can be an equalizer . . . it's a justice issue, and by joining TFA I saw a way to help make it my issue too.

In the past twenty years, more than twenty thousand teachers have worked for TFA, making tremendous strides toward promoting educational equity. But sheltered lives in suburbs and sororities leave many teachers dramatically unprepared for the trials and tribulations of inner-city schools.

In the Overbrook hallways, the school's massive difficulties fell hard on the shoulders of a twenty-four-year-old TFA neophyte named Conrey Callahan. With white skin and blond hair, Conrey stood out in the halls like a sore thumb: 97 percent of Overbrook's students are African American. Conrey—a dog lover who lives with Louie, the mutt she rescued—grew up in a cozy Maryland suburb, attending a high school that was named one of the best in the country. Calling her a ball of energy would be an understatement: she runs half-marathons, captained her high school soccer and lacrosse teams, and competed for six years in jump rope competitions, making the junior Olympics. Although her intellectual prowess led her Vanderbilt professors to encourage her to pursue history, Conrey set her sights on more practical matters: "I set out to make a difference, improving education and opportunities for kids in low-income communities."

But Conrey's idealistic dreams of inspiring the next generation of students were quickly crushed by the harsh realities of arriving at school at 6:45 A.M., staying up until 1:00 A.M. to finish grading and lesson plans for her Spanish classes, and days marked by breaking up fights, battling crime, and trying to track down truant students who only showed up for two days of class in an entire year. One of Conrey's most promising students was living in a foster home, and had to drop out of school after giving birth to a child with developmental problems.

Conrey was constantly complaining to one of her closest friends, an investment banker who worked a hundred hours a week and couldn't grasp why teaching at Overbrook was so stressful. In an act of desperation, Conrey invited the friend to join her on a school field trip. The friend finally understood: "she couldn't believe the sheer exhaustion that she felt at the end of the day," Conrey recalls. Finally, Conrey hit rock bottom. "It was awful. I was burned out, overwhelmed, and ready to give up. I never wanted to set foot in a school again. I was disgusted with the school, the students, and myself."

Conrey was displaying the classic symptoms of burnout, and she wasn't alone. Berkeley psychologist Christina Maslach, the pioneer of research on job burnout, reports that across occupational sectors, teaching has the highest rates of emotional exhaustion. One TFA teacher admires the organization but says it is "focused on hard work and dedication almost to a fault . . . you leave training with the mindset that unless you pour every waking hour of your life into the job then you're doing a disservice to your kids." Of all TFA teachers, more than half leave after their two-year contract is up, and more than 80 percent are gone after three years. About a third of all TFA alumni walk away from education altogether.

Since givers tend to put others' interests ahead of their own, they often help others at the expense of their own well-being, placing themselves at risk for burnout. Four decades of extensive research shows that when people become burned out, their job performance suffers. Exhausted employees struggle to focus their attention and lack the energy to work their hardest, longest, and smartest, so the quality and quantity of their work takes a nosedive. They also suffer from poorer emotional and physical health. Strong evidence reveals that burned-out employees are at heightened risk for depression, physical fatigue, sleep disruptions, impaired immune systems, alcohol abuse, and even cardiovascular disease.

When Conrey hit rock bottom at Overbrook High School, she felt that she was giving too much. She was arriving at work early, staying up late, and working weekends, and she could hardly keep up. In this situation, it seems that the natural way to recover and recharge would be to reduce her giving. But that wasn't what she did. Instead, Conrey gave *more*.

While maintaining her overwhelming teaching workload, Conrey began volunteering her time as a TFA alumni mentor. As a content support specialist, every other week she helped ten different teachers create tests and design new lesson plans. Then, in her limited spare time, she founded a mentoring program. With two friends, she created a Philadelphia chapter of Minds Matter, a national nonprofit organization that helps high-achieving, low-income students prepare for college. Conrey spent her nights and weekends filing for nonprofit status, finding a pro-bono law firm and accountant, and applying for national approval. Finally, after a year, she was able to start recruiting students and mentors, and she created the plans for weekly sessions. From then on, Conrey added five hours a week mentoring high school students.

All told, Conrey was spending more than ten extra hours per week giving. This meant even less room in her schedule for relaxation or restorative downtime, and even more responsibility to others. And yet, when she started giving more, Conrey's burnout faded, and her energy returned. Suddenly, in fact, she seemed to be a renewed bundle of energy at Overbrook, finding the strength to serve as the coordinator for gifted students and create a Spanish 3 program from scratch. Unlike many of her peers, she didn't quit. Of the five teachers who joined Overbrook from TFA with her, Conrey was the only one still teaching there after four years. Of the dozen teachers who arrived in the same three-year window as her, Conrey was one of just two left. She became one of the rare TFA teachers who continued teaching for at least four years, and she was nominated for a national teaching award. How is it possible that giving more revitalized her, instead of draining her?

The Impact Vacuum: Givers Without a Cause

A decade ago, Howard Heevner, a dynamic director of a university call center, invited me to help him figure out how to maintain the motivation of his callers. The callers were charged with contacting university alumni and asking them to donate money. They were required to ask for donations three times before hanging up, and still faced a rejection rate exceeding 90 percent. Even the most seasoned and successful callers were burning out. As one experienced caller put it: "I found the calls I was making to be extremely difficult. Many of the prospects cut me off in my first couple of sentences and told me they were not interested in giving."

I assumed that the takers were dropping like flies: they wouldn't be as committed as the givers. So during training, I measured whether each caller was a giver, matcher, or taker. In their first month on the job, the takers were bringing in an average of more than thirty donations a week. Contrary to my expectation, the givers were much less productive: they were struggling to maintain their motivation, making fewer calls and bringing in under ten donations a week. I was mystified: why were the callers who wanted to make a difference actually making the least difference?

I got my answer one day when I paid a visit to the call center, and noticed a sign one of the callers had posted above his desk:

> ### DOING A GOOD JOB HERE
>
> *Is Like Wetting Your Pants*
>
> *in a Dark Suit*
>
> ### YOU GET A WARM FEELING
>
> ### BUT NO ONE ELSE NOTICES

According to my data, the caller who proudly displayed this sign was a strong giver. Why would a giver feel unappreciated? In reflecting on this sign, I began to think that my initial assumption was correct after all: based on the motivational structure of the job, the givers should be outpacing the takers. The problem was that the givers were being deprived of the rewards they find most energizing.

The takers were motivated by the fact that they were working at the highest-paying job on campus. But the givers lacked the rewards that mattered most to them. Whereas takers tend to care most about benefiting personally from their jobs, givers care deeply about doing jobs that benefit other people. When the callers brought in donations, most of the money went directly to student scholarships, but the callers were left in the dark: they had no idea who was receiving the money, and how it affected their lives.

At the next training session, I invited new callers to read letters from students whose scholarships had been funded by the callers' work. One scholarship student named Will wrote:

> When it came down to making the decision, I discovered that the out-of-state tuition was quite expensive. But this university is in my blood. My grandparents met here. My dad and his four brothers all went here. I even owe my younger brother to this school—he was conceived the night we won the NCAA basketball tournament. All my life I have dreamed of coming here. I was ecstatic to receive the scholarship, and I came to school ready to take full advantage of the opportunities it afforded me. The scholarship has improved my life in many ways . . .

After reading the letters, it took the givers just a week to catch up to the takers. The takers did show some improvement, but the givers responded most powerfully, nearly tripling in weekly calls and donations. Now, they had a stronger emotional grasp of their impact: if they brought in more money, they could help more scholarship students like Will. By spending just five minutes reading about how the job helped other people, the givers were motivated to achieve the same level of productivity as the takers. "The greatest untapped source of motivation," writes Susan Dominus, "is a sense of service to others."

But the givers still weren't seeing the full impact of their jobs. Instead of reading letters, what if they actually met a scholarship recipient face-to-face? When callers interacted with one scholarship recipient in person, they were even more energized. The average caller doubled in calls per hour and minutes on the phone per week. By working harder, the callers reached more alumni, resulting in 144 percent more alumni donating each week. Even more strikingly, revenue quintupled: callers averaged $412 before meeting the scholarship recipient and more than $2,000 afterward. One caller soared from averages of five calls and $100 per shift to nineteen calls and $2,615 per shift. Several control groups of callers, who didn't meet a scholarship recipient, showed no changes in calls, phone time, donations, or revenue. Overall, just five minutes interacting with one scholarship recipient motivated twenty-three callers to raise an extra $38,451 for the university in a single week.* Although the givers, takers, and matchers were all motivated by meeting the scholarship recipient, the gains in effort and revenue were especially pronounced among the givers.

The turnaround highlights a remarkable principle of giver burnout: it has less to do with the amount of giving and more with the amount of feedback about the impact of that giving. Researchers have drawn the same conclusion in health care, where burnout is often described as compassion fatigue, "the stress, strain, and weariness of caring for others." Originally, experts believed that compassion fatigue was caused by expressing too much compassion. But new research has challenged this conclusion. As researchers Olga Klimecki and Tania Singer summarize, "More than all other factors, including . . . the time spent caregiving, it is the perceived suffering that leads to depressive symptoms in the caregiver." Givers don't

---

* Interestingly, when leaders and managers delivered the same message, it didn't work. The scholarship students were able to speak from firsthand experience about the importance of the callers' work, and what it meant to them personally. Although we often look to leaders and managers to inspire employees, when it comes to combating giver burnout, there may be an advantage of outsourcing inspiration to the clients, customers, students, and other end users who can attest to the impact of givers' products and services.

burn out when they devote too much time and energy to giving. They burn out when they're working with people in need but are unable to help effectively.

Teachers are vulnerable to giver burnout because of the unique temporal experience that defines education. Even though teachers interact with their students on a daily basis, it can take many years for their impact to sink in. By then, students have moved on, and teachers are left wondering: did my work actually matter? With no clear affirmation of the benefits of their giving, the effort becomes more exhausting and harder to sustain. These challenges are pervasive in a setting like Overbrook, where teachers must fight many distractions and disadvantages to stimulate the attention—let alone attendance—of students. When Conrey Callahan was emotionally exhausted, it wasn't because she was giving too much. It was because she didn't feel her giving was making a difference. "In teaching, do I have an impact? It's kind of dicey," Conrey told me. "I often feel like I'm not doing anything effective, that I'm wasting my time and I'm not making a difference."

When Conrey launched Minds Matter Philadelphia, she may have been bulking up her schedule, but the net effect was to fill the impact vacuum that she experienced in her teaching job at Overbrook. "With my mentoring program, there's no doubt; I know that I have a more direct impact," she says. By mentoring low-income students who were high achievers, she felt able to make more of a difference than in her Overbrook classroom, where each student presented specific challenges. When she mentored high-achieving students, the positive feedback came more rapidly and validated her effort. She watched one mentee, David, blossom from a shy, reserved loner into an outspoken young man with a close group of friends. As with the fund-raising callers meeting a scholarship student who benefited from their work, seeing the impact of her program had an energizing effect.

But that effect wasn't limited to the mentoring program. Thanks to the energy boost, Conrey developed renewed hope that she could have an impact in her job at Overbrook. Observing the progress of her high-achieving mentees instilled confidence that she could help the students struggling in her own classroom. "I know what I've started is really making a difference with these kids. What I've seen in three months is a big change for them, and they make me realize how great kids can be." As she spent more time mentoring students at Minds Matter, she walked into her Overbrook classroom with greater enthusiasm, fueled by a revitalized sense of purpose.

In research with two colleagues, I've discovered that the perception of impact serves as a buffer against stress, enabling employees to avoid burnout and maintain their motivation and performance. In one study, a student and I found that high school teachers who perceived their jobs as stressful and demanding reported significantly greater burnout. But upon closer inspection, job stress was only linked to higher burnout for teachers who felt they didn't make a difference. A sense of lasting impact protected against stress, preventing exhaustion.

In the classroom, it sometimes takes years for a teacher's lesson to hit home with students. By that time, many teachers have lost contact with their students. But at least for a while, teachers have the opportunity to see their short-term impact as they interact face-to-face with their students. Many other jobs provide no contact at all with the people who benefit from our work. In health care, for example, many medical professionals provide critical diagnoses without ever meeting the patients on the other end of their test results. In Israel, a group of radiologists evaluated nearly a hundred computed tomography (CT) exams from patients. After three months passed, the radiologists had forgotten the original CT exams, and they evaluated them again. Some of the radiologists got better, showing 53 percent improvement in detecting abnormalities unrelated to the primary reason for the exams. But other radiologists got worse: their accuracy dropped by 28 percent—on the exact same CT exams, in just three months. Why did some radiologists get better while others got worse?

Their patients had been photographed before their exams. Half of the radiologists completed their first CT exams without a patient's photo. When they did their second CT exams three months later, they saw the photo. These were the radiologists who improved by 53 percent. The other half of the radiologists saw the patient photo in their first CT exams, and then completed their second CT exams three months later with no photo. These were the radiologists who deteriorated by 28 percent.

Attaching a single patient's photo to a CT exam increased diagnostic accuracy by 46 percent. And roughly 80 percent of the key diagnostic findings came *only when the radiologists saw the patient's photo*. The radiologists missed these important findings when the photo was absent—even if they caught them three months earlier. When the radiologists saw the patient's photo, they felt more empathy. By encouraging empathy, the photos motivated the radiologists to conduct their diagnoses more carefully. Their reports were 29 percent longer when the CT exams included patient photos. When the radiologists saw a photo of a patient, they felt a stronger connection to the human impact of their work. A patient photo "makes each CT scan unique," said one radiologist.

In a recent study, researcher Nicola Bellé found similar patterns in a study of ninety Italian nurses who were invited to assemble surgical kits. After being randomly assigned to meet health-care practitioners who would use the kits, nurses were significantly more productive and more accurate. This effect was particularly pronounced among nurses who had reported strong giver tendencies in a survey. Interestingly, a week after meeting the health-care practitioners who benefited from the surgical kits, all of the nurses actually felt more inclined toward giving. Along with reducing burnout among givers, a firsthand connection to impact can tilt people of all reciprocity styles in the giver direction. When people know how their work makes a difference, they feel energized to contribute more.

Building on this idea that seeing impact can reduce the burnout of givers and motivate others to give, some organizations have designed initiatives to connect employees to the impact of their products and services. At Wells Fargo, a vice president named Ben Soccorsy created videos of customers talking about how the company's low-interest loans helped them reduce and eliminate their unwanted debt. "In many cases, customers felt like they had a massive weight lifted off their shoulders: they now had a plan for paying down their debt," Soccorsy says. When bankers watched the videos, "it was like a light switch turned on. Bankers realized the impact their work could have—that this loan can really make a difference in customers' lives. It was a really compelling motivator." At Medtronic, employees across the company—from engineers to salespeople—pay visits to hospitals to see their medical technologies benefiting patients. "When they're exhausted," former Medtronic CEO Bill George told me, "it's very important that they get out there and see procedures. They can see their impact on patients, which reminds them that they're here to restore people to full life and health." Medtronic also holds an annual party for the entire company, more than thirty thousand employees, at which six patients are invited to share their stories about how the company's products have changed their lives. When they see for the first time how much their work can matter, many employees break down into tears.

Having a greater impact is one of the reasons why, counterintuitive as it might seem, giving more can actually help givers avoid burnout. But it's not the whole story. There's a second reason why

Conrey's extra giving was energizing, and it has to do with where and to whom she gave. Nearly a century ago, the psychologist Anitra Karsten invited people to work on repetitive tasks for as long as they enjoyed them, but to stop when they were tired. For long periods of time, the participants toiled away at tasks like drawing pictures and reading poems aloud, until they couldn't handle it any longer. One man's task was to write *ababab* over and over. As the Harvard psychologist Ellen Langer retells it, "He went on until he was mentally and physically exhausted. His hand felt numb, as though it couldn't move to make even one more mark. At that moment the investigator asked him to sign his name and address for a different purpose. He did so quite easily."

The same strange thing happened to other participants. One woman said she was so drained that she couldn't lift her arm to make another mark. But she then lifted her arm to adjust her hair, apparently without any difficulty or discomfort. And when participants read poems aloud until their voices were hoarse, they had no trouble complaining about the task—and when they complained, they didn't sound hoarse anymore. According to Langer, they weren't faking it. Rather, "the change of context brought renewed energy."

When Conrey volunteered as a mentor to TFA teachers, it created a change of context that made giving feel fresh. "Working with adults, doing something that is kind of teaching, that doesn't burn me out. That invigorates me," Conrey says. Giving more can be exhausting if it's in the same domain. Instead of giving more in the same way, over and over, she expanded her contributions to a different group of people. The same thing happened when she started mentoring high school students at Minds Matter: she had a new setting and a new group of people to help. Instead of teaching them Spanish, she was getting them ready for college. By shifting her giving to a novel domain, she was able to recharge her energy.

Otherish Choices: Chunking, Sprinkling, and the 100-Hour Rule of Volunteering

We discussed otherish behavior at the beginning of this chapter, and in both Conrey's example and that of the fund-raising callers, the distinction between selfless givers and otherish givers begins to come into play. In these contexts, decisions about how, where, and how much to give clearly make a difference when it comes to burning out or firing up. It might seem that by giving more, Conrey was being selfless. But what she actually did was create an opportunity for giving that was also personally rewarding, drawing energy from the visible impact of her contributions. To be more selfless, in this case, would have meant giving even more at school, where endless help was needed, but where she felt limited in her ability to make a difference. Instead, Conrey thought more about her own well-being and found a way to improve it by giving in a new way.

That choice has real consequences for givers. In numerous studies, Carnegie Mellon psychologist Vicki Helgeson has found that when people give continually without concern for their own well-being, they're at risk for poor mental and physical health.* Yet when they give in a more otherish fashion, demonstrating substantial concern for themselves as well as others, they no longer experience health costs. In one study, people who maintained equilibrium between benefiting themselves and others even achieved significant increases in happiness and life satisfaction over a six-month period.†

---

* Research shows that on the job, people who engage in selfless giving end up feeling overloaded and stressed, as well as experiencing conflict between work and family. This is even true in marriages: in one study of married couples, people who failed to maintain an equilibrium between their own needs and their partner's needs became more depressed over the next six months. By prioritizing others' interests and ignoring their own, selfless givers exhaust themselves.

† The salutary effects of being otherish may even be visible in our writing. The

To gain a deeper understanding of otherish and selfless givers, it's worth looking more closely at the decisions they make about when and how much to give. It turns out that Conrey's giving helped her avoid burnout not only due to the variety but also because of how she planned it.

Imagine that you're going to perform five random acts of kindness this week. You'll be doing things like helping a friend with a project, writing a thank-you note to a former teacher, donating blood, and visiting an elderly relative. You can choose one of two different ways to organize your giving: chunking or sprinkling. If you're a chunker, you'll pack all five acts of giving into a single day each week. If you're a sprinkler, you'll distribute your giving evenly across five different days, so that you give a little bit each day. Which do you think would make you happier: chunking or sprinkling?

In this study, led by the psychologist Sonja Lyubomirsky, people performed five random acts of kindness every week for six weeks. They were randomly divided into two groups: half chunked their giving into a single day each week, and the other half sprinkled it across all five days each week. At the end of the six weeks, despite performing the same number of helping acts, only one group felt significantly happier.

The chunkers achieved gains in happiness; the sprinklers didn't. Happiness increased when people performed all five giving acts in a

---

psychologist James Pennebaker has been able to trace gains in health to the words that people use in their journal entries. "The writings of those whose health improved showed a high rate of the use of I-words on one occasion and then high rates of the use of other pronouns on the next occasion, and then switching back and forth in subsequent writings," Pennebaker explains in *The Secret Life of Pronouns*, such that "healthy people say something about their own thoughts and feelings in one instance and then explore what is happening with other people before writing about themselves again." The people whose journal entries are purely selfish or selfless, on the other hand, are much less likely to show health improvements.

single day, rather than doing one a day. Lyubomirsky and colleagues speculate that "spreading them over the course of a week might have diminished their salience and power or made them less distinguishable from participants' habitual kind behavior."

Like the participants who became happier, Conrey was a chunker. At Minds Matter, Conrey packed her volunteering into one day a week, giving all five weekly hours of mentoring high school students on Saturdays. By chunking her giving into weekly blocks, she was able to experience her impact more vividly, leading her efforts to feel like "more than a drop in the bucket."

Chunking giving is an otherish strategy. Instead of mentoring students after school, when she was already exhausted, Conrey reserved it for the weekend, when her energy was recharged and it was more convenient in her schedule. In contrast, selfless givers are more inclined to sprinkle their giving throughout their days, helping whenever people need them. This can become highly distracting and exhausting, robbing selfless givers of the attention and energy necessary to complete their own work.

One September, seventeen software engineers at a *Fortune* 500 company were charged with developing code for a major new product. It was a color laser printer that would sell for 10 percent of the cost of other products on the market. If it succeeded, the company would be a dominant player in the market and could release an entire family of products to follow the printer. The division was losing money rapidly, and if the printer wasn't ready on time, the division would fold. To finish the project, the engineers were working nights and weekends, but they were still behind schedule. The odds were against them: only once in the division's history had a product been launched on time. They were "stressed" and "exhausted," writes Harvard professor Leslie Perlow, with "insufficient time to meet all the demands on them."

The engineers had fallen into a pattern of selfless giving: they were constantly helping their colleagues solve problems. One engineer reported that "The biggest frustration of my job is always having to help others and not getting my own work done"; another lamented that "The problem with my work style is that responsiveness breeds more need for responsiveness, and I am so busy responding, I cannot get my own work done." On a typical day, an engineer named Andy worked from 8:00 A.M. until 8:15 P.M. It wasn't until after 5:00 P.M. that Andy found a block of time longer than twenty minutes to work on his core task. In the hopes of carving out time to get their own work done, engineers like Andy began arriving at work early in the morning and staying late at night. This was a short-lived solution: as more engineers burned the midnight oil, the interruptions occurred around the clock. The engineers were giving more time without making more progress, and it was exhausting.

Perlow had an idea for turning these selfless givers into otherish givers. She proposed that instead of sprinkling their giving, they could chunk it. She worked with the engineers to create dedicated windows for quiet time and interaction time. After experimenting with several different schedules, Perlow settled on holding quiet time three days a week, starting in the morning and lasting until noon. During quiet time, the engineers worked alone, and their colleagues knew to avoid interrupting them. The rest of the time, colleagues were free to seek help and advice.

When Perlow polled the engineers about quiet time, two thirds reported above-average productivity. When Perlow stepped back and left it to the engineers to manage their own quiet time for a full month, 47 percent maintained above-average productivity. By chunking their helping time, the engineers were able to conserve time and energy to complete their own work, making a transition from selfless to otherish giving. In the words of one engineer, quiet time enabled "me to do some of the activities during the day which I would have normally deferred to late evening." After three months, the engineers launched the laser printer on time, for only the second time in division history. The vice president of the division chalked the success up to the giving boundaries created by quiet time: "I do not think we could have made the deadline without this project."*

Since the engineers were facing an urgent need to finish their product on time, they had a strong justification for making their giving more otherish. But in many situations, the appropriate boundaries for giving time are much murkier. Sean Hagerty is a principal in investment management at Vanguard, a financial services company that specializes in mutual funds. Sean is a dedicated mentor with a long-standing passion for education, and he has made a habit of volunteering his time at least a week each year to teach employees at Vanguard's corporate university. When Vanguard's chief learning officer counted his hours, she noticed that Sean was spending a large amount of time in the classroom. She was worried that he would burn out, and Sean recognized that he might be at risk: "It's a pretty significant commitment given that I have a day job." But instead of scaling back his hours, Sean asked for more: "It's among the most valuable things that I do." The more hours he volunteered teaching, the more energized he felt, until he approached two weeks and cleared one hundred hours of annual volunteering on educational initiatives.

One hundred seems to be a magic number when it comes to giving. In a study of more than two thousand Australian adults in their mid-sixties, those who volunteered between one hundred and eight hundred hours per year were happier and more satisfied with their lives than those who volunteered fewer than one hundred or

---

* New research shows that when employees spend a great deal of time helping colleagues, it only detracts from their productivity if they lack time management skills. When employees have strong time management skills, the more they help others, the more productive they are—perhaps in part due to the energy benefits.

more than eight hundred hours annually. In another study, American adults who volunteered at least one hundred hours in 1998 were more likely to be alive in 2000. There were no benefits of volunteering more than one hundred hours. This is the *100-hour rule* of volunteering. It appears to be the range where giving is maximally energizing and minimally draining.

A hundred hours a year breaks down to just two hours a week. Research shows that if people start volunteering two hours a week, their happiness, satisfaction, and self-esteem go up a year later. Two hours a week in a fresh domain appears to be the sweet spot where people make a meaningful difference without being overwhelmed or sacrificing other priorities. It's also the range in which volunteering is most likely to strike a healthy balance, offering benefits to the volunteer as well as the recipients.* In a national study, several thousand Canadians reported the number of hours that they volunteered per year, and whether they gained new technical, social, or organizational knowledge and skills from volunteering. For the first few hours a week, volunteers gained knowledge and skills at a consistent rate. By five hours a week, volunteering had diminishing returns: people were learning less and less with each additional hour. After eleven hours a week, additional time volunteered no longer added new knowledge and skills.

When Conrey started volunteering as an alumni mentor for TFA, she was giving about seventy-five hours a year. When she launched Minds Matter, the nonprofit mentoring program for high school students, she sailed over the 100-hour mark. Perhaps it's not a coincidence

---

* The optimal number of hours per year may drop below one hundred as we age. In one study of American adults over sixty-five, those who volunteered between one and forty hours in 1986 were more likely to be alive in 1994 than those who volunteered zero or more than forty hours. This was true even after controlling for health conditions, physical activity, religion, income, and a host of other factors that might influence survival.

that her energy was restored right around that point. But it wasn't just the amount of time that mattered; there's another form of chunking in Conrey's giving that's also apparent in Sean Hagerty's giving, and it reveals a key contrast between selfless and otherish giving.

As Sean Hagerty spent more time teaching in the Vanguard classroom, he began to crave more opportunities for giving. "I want to leave the place better than I entered it in my small way," he says, and he began asking himself how he could have an impact on the world. As he reflected on different ways of giving, he noticed a pattern in how he was spending his free time. "I found myself reading more and more about education. I had a natural passion for it." Sean decided to lead and launch two new programs around education. One program is called The Classroom Economy, and it has a national focus: Sean and his colleagues teach the basics of money management to kindergartners around the United States. The other program, Team Vanguard, is local: Sean has partnered with a charter school in Philadelphia to administer a four-year mentoring program, where employees volunteer their time on evenings, weekends, and lunch breaks. Despite the substantial time commitment, Sean found that both programs "have a tremendously positive impact on my energy. It's the selling point I have with senior staff who worry about volunteer hours, which take time out of the day. It does sometimes, but my point of view is that it creates a much more highly engaged employee, including me. I love that work is giving me an outlet for philanthropic interests."

If Sean were a purely selfless giver, he might sprinkle his energy across many different causes out of a sense of duty and obligation, regardless of his own level of interest and enthusiasm for them. Instead, he adopts an otherish approach, choosing to chunk his giving to focus on education, a cause about which he's passionate. "I get incredible personal satisfaction out of giving back to the community in this way," Sean says.

Psychologists Netta Weinstein and Richard Ryan have demonstrated that giving has an energizing effect only if it's an enjoyable, meaningful choice rather than undertaken out of duty and obligation. In one study, people reported their giving every day for two weeks, indicating whether they had helped someone or done something for a good cause. On days when they gave, they rated why they gave. On some days, people gave due to enjoyment and meaning—they thought it was important, cared about the other person, and felt they might enjoy it. On other days, they gave out of duty and obligation—they felt they had to and would feel like a bad person if they didn't. Each day, they reported how energized they felt.

Weinstein and Ryan measured changes in energy from day to day. Giving itself didn't affect energy: people weren't substantially happier on days when they helped others than on days that they didn't. But the reasons for giving mattered immensely: on days that people helped others out of a sense of enjoyment and purpose, they experienced significant gains in energy.* Giving for these reasons conferred a greater sense of autonomy, mastery, and connection to others, and it boosted their energy. When I studied firefighters and fund-raising callers, I found the same pattern: they were able to work much harder and longer when they gave their energy and time due to a sense of enjoyment and purpose, rather than duty and obligation.

For Conrey, this is a major difference between teaching at Overbrook and volunteering with Minds Matter and TFA. In the Overbrook classroom, giving is an obligation. Her job requires her to

---

* Interestingly, the emotional boost from giving doesn't always kick in right away. When psychologist Sabine Sonnentag and I surveyed European firefighters and rescue workers, we found that on days when they had a substantial positive impact on others, they were energized at home after work, but not during work. Seeing their impact helped them experience greater meaning and mastery, but it was only after reflecting on the impact of their actions that they experienced the full charge from giving.

break up fights and maintain order, tasks that—although important—don't align with the passion that drew her into teaching. In her volunteer work, giving is an enjoyable choice: she loves helping high-achieving underprivileged students and mentoring less experienced TFA teachers. This is another way giving can be otherish: Conrey focused on benefiting students and teachers, but doing so in a way that connects to her core values and fuels her enthusiasm. The energy carried over to her classroom, helping her maintain her motivation.

But at Overbrook, Conrey couldn't avoid the obligation to give to her students in ways that she didn't find naturally exciting or energizing. What did she do to stay energized despite the sense of duty?

During one particularly stressful week, Conrey was struggling to get through to her students. "I was feeling miserable, and the kids were being awful." She approached a teacher named Sarah for help. Sarah recommended an activity that was a hit in her classroom: they got to design their own monsters that were on the loose in Philadelphia. They drew a picture of a monster, wrote a story about it, and created a "wanted" ad so people would be on the lookout. It was exactly the inspiration that Conrey needed. "Our ten-minute chat helped me get excited about the lesson. I had fun with the kids, and it made me more invested in the curriculum I was teaching."

Although Conrey's decision to ask another teacher for help may not sound unusual, research shows that it's quite rare among selfless givers. Selfless givers "feel uncomfortable receiving support," write Helgeson and colleague Heidi Fritz. Selfless givers are determined to be in the helper role, so they're reluctant to burden or inconvenience others. Helgeson and Fritz find that selfless givers receive far less support than otherish givers, which proves psychologically and physically costly. As burnout expert Christina Maslach and colleagues conclude, "there is now a consistent and strong body of evidence that a lack of social support is linked to burnout."

In contrast, otherish givers recognize the importance of protecting their own well-being. When they're on the brink of burnout, otherish givers seek help, which enables them to marshal the advice, assistance, and resources necessary to maintain their motivation and energy. Three decades of research show that receiving support from colleagues is a robust antidote to burnout. "Having a support network of teachers is huge," Conrey affirms.

But Overbrook didn't have a formal support network of teachers, so where did Conrey get her support network? She built one at Overbrook through the act of giving help.

For many years, experts believed that the stress response involved a choice: *fight or flight.* Since burnout means we lack the energy to fight, it's natural to choose flight, coping by avoiding the source of stress. Burnout experts Jonathon Halbesleben and Matthew Bowler studied professional firefighters over a two-year period. Sure enough, when the firefighters started to burn out, their performance ratings dropped. Burnout made them less concerned about achievement and status. Consequently, they invested less effort in their work, and their effectiveness suffered.

But surprisingly, in this study, burnout didn't decrease effort across the board. There was one place where firefighters actually *increased* their effort when they felt burned out: helping others. When the firefighters experienced signs of burnout, they were more likely to go out of their way to help colleagues with heavy workloads, share new knowledge with supervisors, give advice to newer colleagues, and even listen to colleagues' problems. Why would burnout increase their giving?

UCLA psychologist Shelley Taylor has discovered a stress response that differs from fight or flight. She calls it *tend and befriend.* "One of the most striking aspects of the human stress response is the tendency to affiliate—that is, to come together in groups to provide and receive joint protection in threatening times." Taylor's neuroscience research reveals that when we feel stressed, the brain's natural response is to release chemicals that drive us to bond. This is what the firefighters did: when they started to feel exhausted, they invested their limited energy in helping their colleagues. Intuitively, they recognized that giving would strengthen their relationships and build support (at least from matchers and givers). Although most givers are aware of this opportunity, it appears that only otherish givers actually take advantage of it.

Conrey Callahan built her support network by tending and befriending under stress. When she was at the pinnacle of exhaustion, she started mentoring TFA teachers and several of the younger teachers in her own school. One of the teachers Conrey mentored was Sarah. In the course of mentoring, one of the exercises that Conrey taught Sarah was the monster activity. Conrey had forgotten about it, and when she reached out for help, Sarah reminded her about it. The advice itself was helpful, but it also strengthened Conrey's sense of impact: she had given Sarah an activity that was a big hit with her own students.

Otherish givers build up a support network that they can access for help when they need it. This, along with chunking giving so that it's energizing, is what makes otherish givers less vulnerable to burnout than selfless givers. But how do otherish givers stack up against takers and matchers?

The Myth of Giver Burnout

Years ago, Dutch psychologists studied hundreds of health professionals. They tracked the amount of time and energy that the health professionals gave to patients, and asked them to report how burned out they felt. A year later, the psychologists measured giving and burnout again. Sure enough, the more the health professionals gave, the more burned out they became in the following year. Those who gave selflessly had the highest burnout rates: they contributed far more than they got, and it exhausted them. Those who acted like matchers and takers were far less burned out.

But strangely, in another study, the Dutch psychologists found evidence that some health care professionals seemed immune to burnout. Even when they gave a great deal of time and energy, they didn't exhaust themselves. These resilient health care professionals were otherish givers: they reported that they enjoyed helping other people and often went out of their way to do so, but weren't afraid to seek help when they needed it. The otherish givers had significantly lower burnout rates than the matchers and takers, who lacked the stamina to keep contributing. This study pointed to an unexpected possibility: although matchers and takers appear to be less vulnerable to burnout than selfless givers, the greatest resilience may belong to otherish givers.

Part of the reason for this is illuminated in fascinating work by Northwestern University psychologists Elizabeth Seeley and Wendi Gardner, who asked people to work on a difficult task that sapped their willpower. For example, imagine that you're very hungry, and you're staring at a plate of delicious chocolate chip cookies, but you have to resist the temptation to eat them. After using up their willpower in a task like this, participants squeezed a handgrip as long as they could. The typical participant was able to hold on for twenty-five seconds. But there was a group of people who were able to hold on 40 percent longer, lasting for thirty-five seconds.

The participants with unusually high stamina scored high on a questionnaire measuring "other-directedness." These other-directed people operated like givers. By consistently overriding their selfish impulses in order to help others, they had strengthened their psychological muscles, to the point where using willpower for painful tasks was no longer exhausting. In support of this idea, other studies have shown that givers accrue an advantage in controlling their thoughts, emotions, and behaviors. Over time, giving may build willpower like weightlifting builds muscles. Of course, we all know that when muscles are overused, they fatigue and sometimes even tear—this is what happens to selfless givers.

In Utah, a seventy-five-year-old man understands the resilience of otherish givers. His name is Jon Huntsman Sr., and his tiny photo from his company's annual report appeared in chapter 2, in juxtaposition with the full-size photo of Kenneth Lay (you might also recognize him as the father of former Utah governor and 2012 Republican presidential candidate Jon Huntsman Jr.). Back in 1990, the elder Huntsman was negotiating an acquisition with Charles Miller Smith, who was the president and CEO of a chemical company. During the negotiations, Smith's wife died. Huntsman empathized with Smith, so he decided not to push any further: "I decided the fine points of the last 20 percent of the deal would stand as they were proposed. I probably could have clawed another $200 million out of the deal, but it would have come at the expense of Charles' emotional state. The agreement as it stood was good enough."

Was a CEO's emotional state really worth $200 million to Huntsman? Believe it or not, this wasn't the first time Huntsman gave away a fortune during a negotiation. Just four years earlier, in 1986, he made a verbal agreement with a CEO named Emerson Kampen. Huntsman would sell 40 percent of a division of his company to Kampen's for $54 million. Due to legal delays, the contract wasn't written until six months later. By that time, Huntsman's profits had skyrocketed: that 40 percent of the division was now worth $250 million. Kampen called with a matcher's offer to split the difference, proposing to pay $152 million instead of the original $54 million. Huntsman was poised to bring in nearly triple the original agreement. But he said no. The $54 million was good enough. Kampen was incredulous: "That's not fair to you."

Huntsman believed in honoring his commitment to Kampen. Even though the lawyers hadn't drafted the original purchase agreement, he had shaken hands six months earlier on a verbal agreement. He signed for the $54 million, walking away from an extra $98 million. What type of businessman would make such irrational decisions?

In 1970, Huntsman started a chemical company that reigns today as the world's largest. He has been named Entrepreneur of the Year and earned more than a dozen honorary doctorates from universities around the world. He's a billionaire, one of the *Forbes* one thousand richest people in the world.

As his deal-making choices show, Huntsman is also a giver, and not just in business. Since 1985, he has been involved in serious philanthropy. He is one of just nineteen people in the world who have given at least $1 billion away. Huntsman has won major humanitarian awards for giving more than $350 million to found the world-class Huntsman Cancer Center, and made hefty donations to help earthquake victims in Armenia, support education, and fight domestic violence and homelessness. Of course, many rich people give away serious sums of money, but Huntsman demonstrates an uncommon intensity that sets him apart. In 2001, the chemical industry tanked, and he lost a sizable portion of his fortune. Most people would cut back on giving until they recovered. But Huntsman made an unconventional decision. He took out a personal loan, borrowing several million dollars to make good on his philanthropic commitments for the next three years.

Huntsman sounds like a classic example of someone who got rich and then decided to give back. But there's a different way of looking at Huntsman's success, one that might be impossible to believe if it weren't backed up by Huntsman's experience and by science. Maybe getting rich didn't turn him into a giver. What if we've mixed up cause and effect?

Huntsman believes that being a giver *actually made him rich*. In his giving pledge, Huntsman writes: "It has been clear to me since my earliest childhood memories that my reason for being was to help others. The desire to give back was the impetus for pursuing an education in business, for applying that education to founding what became a successful container company, and for using that experience to grow our differentiated chemicals corporation." As early as 1962, Huntsman told his wife that he "wanted to start his own business so he could make a difference" for people with cancer. Huntsman lost both of his parents to cancer, and had survived three bouts of cancer himself. Curing cancer is so deeply ingrained in Huntsman's fiber that he has even prioritized it above his political ideology. Although he worked in the Nixon White House and has been a long-time supporter of the Republican party, Huntsman has been known to favor Democratic candidates if they demonstrate a stronger commitment to curing cancer.

There's little doubt that Huntsman is a skilled businessman. But the very act of *giving money away* might have contributed to his fortune. In *Winners Never Cheat*, he writes, "Monetarily, the most satisfying moments in my life have not been the excitement of closing a great deal or the reaping of profits from it. They have been when I was able to help others in need . . . There's no denying that I am a deal junkie, but I also have developed an addiction for giving. The more one gives, the better one feels; and the better one feels about it, the easier it becomes to give."

This is an extension of the idea that otherish givers build willpower muscles, making it easy to give more, but is it possible that Huntsman actually made money by giving it away? Remarkably, there's evidence to support this claim. The economist Arthur Brooks tested the relationship between income and charitable giving. Using data from almost thirty thousand Americans in the year 2000, he controlled for every factor imaginable that would affect income and giving. He adjusted for education, age, race, religious involvement, political beliefs, and marital status. He also accounted for the number of times people volunteered. As expected, higher income led to higher giving. For every $1 in extra income, charitable giving went up by $0.14.*

But something much more interesting happened. For every $1 in extra charitable giving, income was $3.75 higher. Giving actually seemed to make people richer. For example, imagine that you and I are both earning $60,000 a year. I give $1,600 to charity; you give $2,500 to charity. Although you gave away $900 more than I did, according to the evidence, you'll be on track to earn $3,375 more than I will in the coming year. Surprising as it seems, people who give more go on to earn more.

Jon Huntsman Sr. may be on to something. Research shows that giving can boost happiness and meaning, motivating people to work harder and earn more money, even if the gift isn't on the colossal scale of Huntsman's. In a study by psychologists Elizabeth Dunn, Lara Aknin, and Michael Norton, people rated their happiness in the morning. Then, they received a windfall: an envelope with $20. They had to spend it by five P.M., and then they rated their happiness again. Would they be happier spending the money on themselves or on others?

Most people think they'd be happier spending the money on themselves, but the opposite is true. If you spend the money on

---

* There's a catch: as people get richer, they give more money in total, but they give smaller fractions of their annual income. In one study, psychologists demonstrated that merely thinking about socioeconomic status is enough to change the amount of charitable giving that we think is appropriate. When people thought about themselves as somewhere in the middle of the wealth ladder, they felt obligated to give 4.65 percent of their annual income to charity. But when they imagined themselves at the top of the ladder, they only reported an obligation to give 2.9 percent of their annual income to charity. Similar trends can be found in the real world: in the United States, households making less than $25,000 a year donate 4.2 percent of their income to charity. Households making more than $100,000 a year donate just 2.7 percent of their income to charity.

yourself, your happiness doesn't change. But if you spend the money on others, you actually report becoming significantly happier. This is otherish giving: you get to choose who you help, and it benefits you by improving your mood. Economists call it the warm glow of giving, and psychologists call it the helper's high. Recent neuroscience evidence shows that giving actually activates the reward and meaning centers in our brains, which send us pleasure and purpose signals when we act for the benefit of others.

These benefits are not limited to giving money; they also show up for giving time. One study of more than 2,800 Americans over age twenty-four showed that volunteering predicted increases in happiness, life satisfaction, and self-esteem—and decreases in depression— a year later. And for adults over sixty-five, those who volunteered saw a drop in depression over an eight-year period. Other studies show that elderly adults who volunteer or give support to others actually live longer. This is true even after controlling for their health and the amount of support they get from others. In one experiment, adults either gave massages to babies or received massages themselves. Postmassage, those who gave had lower levels of stress hormones— such as cortisol and epinephrine—than those who received. It seems that giving adds meaning to our lives, distracts us from our own problems, and helps us feel valued by others. As researchers Roy Baumeister, Kathleen Vohs, Jennifer Aaker, and Emily Garbinsky conclude in a national survey of Americans, "meaningfulness was associated with being a giver more than a taker."

There's a wealth of evidence that the ensuing happiness can motivate people to work harder, longer, smarter, and more effectively. Happiness can lead people to experience intense effort and long hours as less unpleasant and more enjoyable, set more challenging goals, and think more quickly, flexibly, and broadly about problems. One study even showed that when physicians were put in a happier mood, they made faster and more accurate diagnoses. Overall, on average, happier people earn more money, get higher performance ratings, make better decisions, negotiate sweeter deals, and contribute more to their organizations. Happiness alone accounts for about 10 percent of the variation between employees in job performance. By boosting happiness, giving might have motivated Jon Huntsman Sr. to work harder and smarter, helping him build up his fortune.

Huntsman is not the only influential businessperson who has come to view giving as a source of energy. In 2003, Virgin mogul Richard Branson set up a council called The Elders to fight conflict and promote peace, bringing together Nelson Mandela, Jimmy Carter, Kofi Annan, Desmond Tutu, and other leaders to alleviate suffering in Sudan, Cyprus, and Kenya. In 2004, Branson launched Virgin Unite, a nonprofit foundation that mobilizes people and resources to fight deadly diseases like AIDS and malaria, promote peace and justice, prevent climate change, and support entrepreneurs with microloans and new jobs in the developing world. In 2006, he pledged to donate all $3 billion of the profits from the Virgin airline and train businesses over the next decade to fight global warming. In 2007, he offered a $25 million prize for innovations to fight climate change. Was this string of events caused by a midlife crisis?

Actually, Branson was giving long before he became rich and famous. At age seventeen, a year after starting *Student* magazine and five full years before launching Virgin Records, Branson started his first charity. It was the Student Advisory Centre, a nonprofit organization that helped at-risk youth with a range of services. He made a list of problems that young people faced, from unwanted pregnancies to venereal disease, and convinced doctors to offer free or discounted services. He spent many nights on the phone at three A.M. consoling people who were contemplating suicide. Looking back, he notes that early in his career, he "had been interested in making money only to ensure *Student*'s continuing success and to fund the Student Advisory Centre." Today, giving continues to energize him. The "thing that gets me up in the morning is the idea of making a difference," Branson writes, "to help safeguard our future on this planet. Does that make me successful? It certainly makes me happy."

These energizing effects help to explain why otherish givers are fortified against burnout: through giving, they build up reserves of happiness and meaning that takers and matchers are less able to access. Selfless givers use up these reserves, exhausting themselves and often dropping to the bottom of the success ladder. By giving in ways that are energizing rather than exhausting, otherish givers are more likely to rise to the top. In two studies of employees in a wide range of jobs and organizations, psychologist David Mayer and I found that otherish employees made more sustainable contributions than the selfless givers, takers, or matchers. Employees who reported strong concern for benefiting others and creating a positive image for themselves were rated by supervisors as being the most helpful and taking the most initiative.

Ironically, because concern for their own interests sustains their energy, otherish givers actually give more than selfless givers. This is what the late Herbert Simon, winner of the Nobel Prize in economics, observed in the quote that opened this chapter. Otherish givers may appear less altruistic than selfless givers, but their resilience against burnout enables them to contribute more.

7

Chump Change

Overcoming the Doormat Effect

No good deed goes unpunished.
—attributed to Clare Boothe Luce, editor, playwright, and U.S. congresswoman

Lillian Bauer was a brilliant, hardworking manager at an elite consulting firm. She was recruited out of Harvard, and after leaving the firm to complete her MBA, her consulting firm lured her back. She was widely seen as a rising star, and she was on track to make partner far ahead of schedule, until word began to spread that she was too generous. Her promotion to partner was delayed for six months, and she received very direct feedback that she needed to say no more often to clients and colleagues. After a full year, she still had not made it.

Bauer was passionate about making a difference. She devoted several years to a nonprofit organization helping women launch and grow businesses. There, she introduced a microloan program, opening doors for low-income women to start their own companies. In one case, a woman needed a loan to open a salon, but was turned down by two banks. Bauer worked with her to strengthen her business plan and financial statements, and both banks ended up offering her loans at highly competitive rates. As a consultant, Bauer spent countless hours mentoring new employees, giving career advice to associates, and even helping junior colleagues strengthen their applications to business school. "I really want to help. If an hour of my time saves people ten hours or gives them an opportunity they otherwise wouldn't have, it's easy to make the tradeoff and give another hour of my time."

Bauer was extremely talented and driven, but she took giving so far that it was compromising her reputation and her productivity. "She never said no to anything," explained one consulting colleague. "She was so generous and giving with her time that she fell into the trap of being more of a pushover. It really delayed her promotion to partner." In a performance review, Bauer was told that she needed to be more selfish: she lacked the assertive edge that was expected of a consulting partner. She spent too much time developing those around her, and she was so committed to helping clients that she bent over backward to meet their requests. It was known that Bauer "wasn't as forceful in pushing clients as people felt she needed to be to make that partner hurdle, in those key moments where clients needed to hear a harsh message, or clients had been pushing an agenda in the wrong direction." For Bauer, being a giver became a career-limiting move.

In a study that mirrors Bauer's experience, management professors Diane Bergeron, Abbie Shipp, Ben Rosen, and Stacie Furst studied more than 3,600 consultants in a large professional services firm. The researchers coded giving behavior from company records of the weekly time that each consultant spent helping new hires, mentoring more junior consultants, and sharing knowledge or expertise with peers. After a year of tracking these giving behaviors every week, the researchers obtained data on each consultant's salary, advancement speed, and promotions.

The givers did worse on all three metrics. They had significantly lower salary increases, slower advancement, and lower promotion rates. The givers averaged 9 percent salary increases, compared with

10.5 percent and 11.5 percent for the takers and matchers, respectively. Less than 65 percent of the givers were promoted to a manager role, compared with 83 percent and 82 percent for the takers and matchers, respectively. And the givers who did get promoted had to wait longer, averaging twenty-six months to promotion, compared with less than twenty-four months for takers and matchers. This was a familiar pattern to Bauer: "If I err on one side, it's probably being too generous: putting others first, before myself."

Hundreds of miles east at Deloitte Consulting in New York City, Jason Geller was also on the fast track to partner. When he first started in consulting, Deloitte was just moving to e-mail and did not have a formalized knowledge management process—there was no system for storing and retrieving information that consultants gathered on specific industries and clients. Geller took the initiative to collect and share information. When he heard about a project, he would ask the team for its output. He kept a stack of articles on his nightstand, reading them in bed, and when he came across an interesting article, he would file it away. He conducted research on what Deloitte's competitors were doing. "I was a little bit of a geek."

Deloitte's knowledge management system became Jason Geller's brain, and his hard drive. His colleagues began calling it the J-Net, the Jason Network. When they had questions or needed information, he was the go-to guy. It was easier to ask him than to search for themselves, and he was always willing to share the knowledge from his brain or his growing database. No one asked him to create the J-Net; he just did it because it seemed like the right thing to do.

Since graduating from Cornell, Geller had spent his entire career at Deloitte, doing an MBA at Columbia along the way. He was grateful for the support that his mentors provided to him. A matcher would have paid it back, looking for ways to return the favor to his mentors. But as a giver, like Lillian Bauer, Geller wanted to pay it forward. "It becomes the natural way of doing things. You see that the folks who are successful are the ones who help others. I naturally fell into the practice of helping others. I saw that others created those opportunities for me, and I now work very hard to create them for other people." Geller made a standing offer to every new employee: he would help and mentor them in any way that he could.

The typical path to partner at Deloitte takes between twelve and fifteen years. Geller made it far ahead of schedule, in just nine years. At just thirty years old, he became one of the youngest partners in Deloitte history. Today, Geller is a partner in Deloitte's human capital consulting practice, where the business he leads globally and in the United States has been ranked number one in the marketplace. Yet a colleague describes him as a guy "who frequently shuns the spotlight in favor of his colleagues." As Deloitte's global and U.S. HR transformation practice leader, Geller has taken the J-Net to a new level and is a strong advocate for Deloitte's formal global knowledge management processes and technologies. With a mix of admiration and incredulity, one analyst notes that "although he is incredibly busy, he holds regular meetings with analysts so he can help them through any issues they may be facing at the time." Geller is reluctant to take credit for his accomplishments, but after some prodding, acknowledges that "being generous is what has made me successful here."

Although Lillian Bauer and Jason Geller are both givers, they found themselves on very different trajectories. Why did giving stall her career, while accelerating his?

The intuitive answer has to do with gender, but that's not the key differentiator—at least not in the conventional sense. Lillian Bauer fell into three major traps that plague many givers, male and female, in their dealings with other people: being too trusting, too empathetic, and too timid. In this chapter, my goal is to show you how successful givers like Jason Geller avoid these risks, and how givers like Lillian learn to overcome them by acting less selfless and more otherish. Becoming a doormat is the giver's worst nightmare, and I'll make the case that an otherish approach enables givers to escape the trap of being too trusting by becoming highly flexible and adaptable in their reciprocity styles. I'll also argue that an otherish style helps givers sidestep the land mines of being too empathetic and too timid by repurposing some skills that come naturally to them.

Sincerity Screening: Trusting Most of the People Most of the Time

In the opening chapter, we met an Australian financial adviser named Peter Audet, whose giver style paid off when he took a drive to visit a scrap metal client. But long before that, before he figured out how to be more otherish than selfless, Peter was ripped off by several takers. At twenty-two, he started his career as a financial adviser at a cutthroat company. It was his responsibility to aggressively build an insurance division for a business that primarily served retirement clients. Peter was working weekends to generate six-figure annual revenues, but received a tiny fraction of the revenues, taking home minimum wage of $400 per week. He stayed for nearly three years, and it was the most miserable time of his life. "My boss was greedy. He never recognized what you did, only what he could get from you." In appreciation of Peter's services, one of his insurance clients sent him a beautiful Christmas basket. His boss, a wealthy man who drove to work in a Mercedes-Benz, saw the basket and immediately took it home for himself: "I'm the boss, and it's mine."

Peter felt like he was drowning, and decided to strike off on his own as a financial adviser. In his first year alone, he quadrupled his salary. But five years later, he was manipulated by another taker. A friendly colleague, Brad, was not doing well at work. Brad landed another position that would start the following week, and he asked Peter for a favor. Would he buy Brad's clients on two days' notice so that Brad could afford to leave? As a giver, Peter trusted Brad and agreed on the spot. He purchased Brad's clients and began forging relationships with them, helping to solve their financial problems.

After a few months, Peter started to lose some of his clients. Strangely, they were all former clients of Brad's. It turned out that Brad was back in the business as a financial adviser, and he had called every one of the clients who he had sold to Peter. He just wanted to let them know he was back, and they were welcome to switch over to work with him again. Brad stole many of the clients back without paying Peter a dime for them. Peter lost around $10,000 in business.

Had Peter been able to identify Brad from the start as a taker, he might never have gone down that road. Trust is one reason that givers are so susceptible to the doormat effect: they tend to see the best in everyone, so they operate on the mistaken assumption that everyone is trustworthy. In one study, researchers tracked whether Americans had been victims of crimes such as fraud, con games, and identity theft. The givers were twice as likely to be victimized as the takers, often as a direct result of trusting takers. One giver was generous enough to cosign for a friend's car loan, and over a five-year period, the friend opened three credit cards in his identity, stealing more than $2,000.

To avoid getting scammed or exploited, it's critical to distinguish the genuine givers from the takers and fakers. Successful givers need to know who's likely to manipulate them so that they can protect themselves. Do we actually know takers when we see them? Many people think they can judge givers and takers in the blink of an eye. But in reality, they're wildly inaccurate. Blink again.

I don't mean to imply that we fail across the board in thin slicing. As Malcolm Gladwell revealed in *Blink*, many of our snap judgments of people are strikingly accurate. At a glance, we can often spot a passionate teacher, an extraverted salesperson, or a married couple in contempt. But we struggle mightily when guessing who's a genuine giver.

In one study, economists asked a group of Harvard students to predict the giving and taking behaviors of their close friends and of complete strangers. The friends and strangers received fifty tokens worth between ten and thirty cents each, and were asked to divide the tokens between themselves and the Harvard students. The Harvard students did no better in predicting how much their friends would give than they did in predicting the behavior of complete strangers. "They correctly expect that friends pass more tokens than strangers," the researchers write, "but they do not expect more tokens from generous friends compared to selfish friends." This is a crucial mistake, because the giving friends end up contributing quite a bit more than the takers.

When we try to zero in on a person's reciprocity signal, it's easy to be thrown off by plenty of noise. To judge givers, we often rely on personality cues, but it turns out these cues can be misleading. In half a century of research, psychologists have discovered a fundamental personality trait that distinguishes how people tend to appear in their social interactions. It's called agreeableness, and it's why Peter Audet was fooled by Brad. Like Brad, agreeable people tend to appear cooperative and polite—they seek harmony with others, coming across as warm, nice, and welcoming. Disagreeable people tend to be more competitive, critical, and tough—they're more comfortable with conflict, coming across as skeptical and challenging.*

We tend to stereotype agreeable people as givers, and disagreeable

---

* New research shows that these tendencies are heavily influenced by biological forces. In one study, psychologists used MRI to scan the brains of people who reported being agreeable versus disagreeable on a survey. The agreeable people had greater volume in the regions of the brain that process the thoughts, feelings, and motivations of others, such as the posterior cingulate cortex. According to behavioral geneticists, at least a third of agreeableness, and possibly more than half, is heritable—attributable to genes. Whether people have an agreeable or disagreeable personality seems to be at least partially hardwired.

people as takers. When a new contact appears affable, it's natural to conclude that he has good intentions. If he comes across as cold or confrontational, this seems like a sign that he doesn't care about what's in our best interests.* But in making these judgments, we're paying too much attention to the shell of a person's demeanor, overlooking the pearl—or clam—inside the shell. Giving and taking are based on our motives and values, and they're choices that we make regardless of whether our personalities trend agreeable or disagreeable. As Danny Shader, the serial entrepreneur from the opening chapter who initially walked away from David Hornik's term sheet, explains, "Whether you're nice or not nice is separate from whether you're self-focused or other-focused. They're independent, not opposites." When you combine outer appearances and inner intentions, agreeable givers and disagreeable takers are only two of the four combinations that exist in the world.

We often overlook that there are disagreeable givers: people who are rough and tough in demeanor, but ultimately generous with their time, expertise, and connections. As an example, Shader mentions the late Mike Homer, who ran marketing at Netscape. "He could be crusty as hell on the outside, but on the inside he was pure gold. When push came to shove, he always did the right thing, and he was incredibly loyal." Greg Sands, a Homer disciple and the managing director of a private equity firm, agrees. "Your fundamental concern is whether people are givers or takers, but you've got this

* Psychologists originally made the same mistake, including characteristics such as being altruistic within the broad trait of agreeableness. More recent research has shown that (a) compassion and politeness are two separate aspects of agreeableness, (b) the compassion dimension is more related to honesty and humility than to agreeableness, and (c) agreeableness can be distinguished from giver values. Throughout the book, I've taken care to focus primarily on studies that were explicitly designed to investigate giving, taking, or matching. At a few points, though, I have used studies of agreeableness to capture givers in places where survey items directly reference giving, like "I love to help others."

other axis, which is are they nice about it—is their fundamental demeanor welcoming? Homer had a hard edge. When he was locked onto a path, something that got in the way of that objective would just get swept away. But he had a big heart, and he wanted to be helpful. He was definitely off the charts on both [giving and disagreeableness]." Another one of Homer's former employees said that Homer "seemed like a taker, because he had incredibly high expectations and demands. But at the end of the day, he really cared about the people. One minute, he was giving me a tough time because his expectations weren't being met. The next day, he was helping me figure out what I wanted to do next in my career, what was the right next job for me."

The other counterintuitive combination of appearances and motives is the agreeable taker, otherwise known as a faker. Like Ken Lay at Enron, these people come across as pleasant and charming, but they're often aiming to get much more than they give. The ability to recognize agreeable takers as fakers is what protects givers against being exploited.

Although they don't always put their skills to good use, givers have an instinctive advantage in sincerity screening. Research suggests that in general, givers are more accurate judges of others than matchers and takers. Givers are more attentive to others' behaviors and more attuned to their thoughts and feelings, which makes it possible to pick up more clues—such as describing successes with first-person singular pronouns, like *I* and *me* instead of *us* and *we*. Givers also gain a sincerity screening advantage from habitually trusting others, which creates opportunities to see the wide range of behaviors of which other people are capable. Sometimes, givers get burned by takers. In other situations, givers find that their generosity is reciprocated or even exceeded. Over time, givers become sensitive to individual differences and shades of gray between the black-and-white boxes of agreeable and disagreeable.

But givers become doormats when they fail to use this fine-tuned knowledge of differences between veneers and motives. The inclination to give first and ask questions later often comes at the expense of sincerity screening. In consulting, Lillian Bauer made a habit of clearing her schedule for virtually anyone who asked, regardless of who they were. When a client asked for a supplementary analysis, even if it wasn't technically part of the project, she would do it, wanting to please the client. When a junior analyst needed advice, she would immediately open up time in her calendar, sacrificing her personal time.

At Deloitte, Jason Geller intuitively adopted an approach that closely resembles sincerity screening. Geller starts by offering help to every new hire, but in his initial conversations with them, he pays attention to who seems to be a giver versus a taker. "I can't proactively go and spend time with every single person in the practice globally, so I try to sense who's genuine and who's not. Some folks approach the conversation in terms of learning. Others come in and say, 'I want to get promoted to senior consultant. What should I do?'" Geller assumes these consultants are takers. "They focus on telling me what they're doing, with a thirty-minute agenda of things they want to update me on, because they want to make me aware. They're not really asking insightful questions; it's very superficial. We don't get deep enough for it to be really helpful for them."

Over time, as she sacrificed her own interests, Lillian Bauer began to recognize that some people operated like takers: "they're so self-focused that they will take what they can and move on, so I started being more systematic in how I helped other people." She started to pay more attention to who was asking and how they treated her, and made a list of reasons to say no. To continue giving but do so more efficiently, she wrote advice guides for engagement managers and associate partners, putting much of her knowledge on paper so she didn't end up repeating it to takers. "I found that was a more strategic way of being a giver," Bauer says.*

Once givers start to use their skills in sincerity screening to identify potential takers, they know when to put up their guard. But sometimes, this awareness sets in too late: givers have already become loyal to a taker. If givers are already trapped in exchanges where they feel concerned for a taker's interests, how do they protect themselves against the doormat effect?

Generous Tit for Tat: The Adaptable Giver

Several years after Brad stole his clients and his money, Peter Audet was working with a business partner named Rich. When they first paired up, Rich came across as highly agreeable: he was enthusiastic and friendly. But a colleague reflects that "although Rich looked like a giver because he acted supportive, he was really a taker. Peter was a giver, and Rich was sucking everything out of him." Rich was drawing a high salary, more than $300,000 a year, without contributing much to the financial success of the business. He was living on the Gold Coast of Australia, and he would spend his mornings on the beach, stroll into the office at ten A.M., and go to the pub at midday. "Brad gave me a pretty strong sense of what a taker looked like, and I realized that Rich was a big taker," Peter laments. "I was always doing extra work, and Rich was absolutely draining the business of money. He didn't really care about the staff or service to clients; he was starting to pollute the culture. He was taking advantage of me, trading off the back of my loyalty to him because we had built the business up from nothing."

Peter stayed timid until one Monday, when Rich announced that

---

* In this chapter, at the request of interviewees, I've disguised the identities of several key characters. Lillian Bauer is a pseudonym, as are Brad and Rich in Peter Audet's story, and Sameer Jain, a man you'll meet later.

he had bought a multimillion-dollar house on the Gold Coast. He needed $100,000, and he took it right out of the company account. At a board meeting that day, Rich left early to meet friends at the pub. This was the last straw for Peter; he knew Rich could no longer be trusted, so he promised the board that he would hold Rich accountable. But he had yet to formulate a plan—and he felt guilty and uncomfortable: "Rich was like my big brother." A colleague said, "It would have been hard for anybody, but I think it was harder because Peter is a giver. He knew what was at the other side of it for Rich, and he wanted to save him from it."

Peter was a victim of empathy, the powerful emotion that we experience when we imagine another person's distress. Empathy is a pervasive force behind giving behaviors, but it's also a major source of vulnerability. When Brad wasn't doing well and accepted a new job, Peter felt his pain, and bought his clients without hesitation. When he considered how Rich would feel about being ousted, Peter felt sorry for him, and didn't want to cut him out.

Peter was falling into an empathy trap that's visible in a classic negotiation study. Researchers brought people together in pairs to negotiate the purchase of electronics products such as TVs. Half of the negotiating pairs were strangers; the other half were dating couples. In each pair, one negotiator was the seller, and the other was the buyer. On average, who do you think would achieve more joint profits: the strangers or the dating couples?

I assumed that the dating couples would do better, because they would trust each other more, share more information, and discover opportunities for mutual gains.

But the dating couples did substantially *worse* than the strangers, achieving lower joint profits.

Before the negotiation, the researchers asked the dating couples how in love they were. The stronger their feelings of love, the worse they did.

The dating couples—especially the ones in love—operated like selfless givers. Their default approach was to empathize with their partners' needs and give in right away, regardless of their own interests. Concern for their partners had the effect of "short-circuiting efforts to discover integrative solutions in favor of more accessible but less mutually satisfactory outcomes," the researchers write, leading to a "'kid gloves' approach to problem solving." When researchers studied selfless givers at the bargaining table, the same pattern surfaced. People who agreed with statements like "I always place the needs of others above my own" were anxious about putting strain on the relationship, so they accommodated their counterparts by giving away value.

As with the dating couples in love, empathy had turned Peter into a doormat—until he discovered an alternative to empathy that's equally aligned with his natural strengths as a giver. Instead of contemplating Rich's feelings, Peter considered what Rich was thinking. This led to a powerful insight: Rich seemed interested in working on a new challenge, so Peter could appeal to Rich's self-interest. "You're clearly not enjoying running the business day-to-day," Peter told Rich, "so why don't you let me handle it? I think I'm old enough now that I'm ready for the heavy lifting." Rich agreed, expressing a desire to work on special projects in the entrepreneurial space to generate new revenue for the business. Peter supported the decision and started running board meetings.

Peter accomplished this maneuver by getting inside Rich's head, rather than his heart. Studies led by Columbia psychologist Adam Galinsky show that when we empathize at the bargaining table, focusing on our counterparts' emotions and feelings puts us at risk of giving away too much.* But when we engage in perspective taking,

---

* Away from the bargaining table, empathy isn't always as costly as it seems. In one study, veterinarians who empathized with their customers charged them

considering our counterparts' thoughts and interests, we're more likely to find ways to make deals that satisfy our counterparts without sacrificing our own interests. Peter never would have discovered his solution if he had continued to empathize with Rich. By shifting his focus from Rich's feelings to his thoughts, Peter was able to see the world through a taker's eyes and adjust his strategy accordingly.

Despite his success in drawing Rich into a role where he could do less harm, Peter couldn't quite let go of the desire to support Rich and help him succeed. At the same time, he knew there was still plenty of room for Rich to keep taking. Peter decided to trust but verify: he granted Rich the autonomy to work on special projects, but held him accountable for his results, asking him to report on his progress every ninety days. "I gave him the opportunity to measure his own contribution and for us to do the same." After six months, Rich had done very little. Peter conducted a formal analysis and wrote a board report. "When Rich's contribution ended up being zero, it was undeniably of his own doing. He was presented with a crude form of evidence of his own taking and lack of giving. The truth ultimately moved him on and set him free for me." Rich elected to leave and take his equity out of the business.

Peter was no longer a doormat; he had taken down a taker. Later, he learned that Rich had been even more of a taker than anyone realized: he had a large line of credit with the firm, and also owed the bank money. Peter had to write a check to settle because Rich was short. A year after Peter took over as managing director, Rich exited the firm. Fifteen months after Rich's departure, Peter's firm had turned around to achieve seven-figure profits, staff morale had skyrocketed, staff turnover had plummeted, and they were in

---

lower prices. However, after taking pricing out of the equation, the empathetic veterinarians had higher incomes, presumably because they attracted greater loyalty and more referrals from customers.

the running for firm of the year in the dealer group.

Once successful givers see the value of sincerity screening and begin to spot agreeable takers as potential fakers, they protect themselves by adjusting their behavior accordingly. Peter's experience offers a clue into how givers avoid getting burned: they become matchers in their exchanges with takers. It's wise to start out as a giver, since research shows that trust is hard to build but easy to destroy. But once a counterpart is clearly acting like a taker, it makes sense for givers to flex their reciprocity styles and shift to a matching strategy—as Peter did by requiring Rich to reciprocate by adding value to the business. "It's built into my nature now to not give takers much time, and certainly not waste my time with them," Peter says.

In one experiment, psychologists gave people the chance to work with partners who were either competitive or cooperative. The takers acted competitively regardless of who their partners were. The rest adapted to their partners; they were cooperative when working with cooperative partners, but once a partner was competitive, they matched their behavior, responding in a more competitive manner. Game theorists call this *tit for tat*, and it's a pure matcher strategy: start out cooperating, and stay cooperative unless your counterpart competes. When your counterpart competes, match the behavior by competing too. This is a wildly effective form of matching that has won many game theory tournaments. But tit for tat suffers from "a fatal flaw," writes Harvard mathematical biologist Martin Nowak, of "not being forgiving enough to stomach the occasional mishap."

Nowak has found that it can be more advantageous to alternate between giving and matching. In *generous tit for tat*, the rule is "never forget a good turn, but occasionally forgive a bad one." You start out cooperating and continue cooperating until your counterpart competes. When your counterpart competes, instead of always responding competitively, generous tit for tat usually means competing two thirds of the time, acting cooperatively in response to one of every three defections. "Generous tit for tat can easily wipe out tit for tat and defend itself against being exploited by defectors," Nowak writes. Generous tit for tat achieves a powerful balance of rewarding giving and discouraging taking, without being overly punitive. It comes with a risk: generous tit for tat encourages most people to act like givers, which opens the door for takers to "rise up again" by competing when everyone else is cooperating. But in a world where relationships and reputations are visible, it's increasingly difficult for takers to take advantage of givers. According to Nowak, "The generous strategy dominates for a very long time."

Generous tit for tat is an otherish strategy. Whereas selfless givers make the mistake of trusting others all the time, otherish givers start out with trust as the default assumption, but they're willing to adjust their reciprocity styles in exchanges with someone who appears to be a taker by action or reputation. Being otherish means that givers keep their own interests in the rearview mirror, taking care to trust but verify. When dealing with takers, shifting into matcher mode is a self-protective strategy. But one out of every three times, it may be wise to shift back into giver mode, granting so-called takers the opportunity to redeem themselves. This is what Peter Audet did with Rich by offering him the chance to earn his keep. Otherish givers carry the optimistic belief that Randy Pausch expressed in *The Last Lecture*: "Wait long enough, and people will surprise and impress you."

The value of generous tit for tat as an otherish approach was demonstrated by Abraham Lincoln in the Sampson story from the opening chapter. After Lincoln fell on his sword so that Lyman Trumbull could defeat James Shields in the Illinois Senate race, Trumbull came under fire for trying to sabotage Lincoln's career. Lincoln's wife, Mary Todd, said Trumbull had committed "selfish treachery" and she cut ties with Trumbull's wife, who had been one of her closest friends—Mary was a bridesmaid at the Trumbull wedding. Lincoln, however, was more inclined to forgive. He expressed faith to Trumbull: "Any effort to put enmity between you and me is as idle as the wind." At the same time, wanting to protect himself against defection, Lincoln warned Trumbull not to cross him: "While I have no more suspicion against you than I have of my best friend living, I am kept in a constant struggle against suggestions of this sort." Trumbull reciprocated, helping Lincoln in his next Senate bid.

In 1859, Chicago mayor John Wentworth accused Norman Judd of plotting against Lincoln to support Trumbull and advance his own political career. Whereas his wife never forgave Judd, Lincoln reminded Judd that "you did vote for Trumbull against me" but interpreted Judd's decision generously: "I think, and have said a thousand times, that was no injustice to me." Lincoln helped Judd mediate the conflict with Wentworth, but then asked for reciprocity: "it would hurt some for me to not get the Illinois delegation," Lincoln wrote. "Can you not help me a little in this matter, in your end of the vineyard?" Judd matched: he landed a major editorial supporting Lincoln in the *Chicago Tribune* the following week, secured the Republican Convention in Chicago where Lincoln had supporters, and made sure that Lincoln's detractors were seated in the back, limiting their influence. Although Lincoln's default was in line with a giver style, he recognized the value of occasional matching, and benefited from generous tit for tat. Lincoln's acute attention to others' perspectives gave him "the power to forecast with uncanny accuracy what his opponents were likely to do," explained his secretary's daughter, and use this forecast to "checkmate them."

Since Jason Geller first started mentoring new hires at Deloitte, he has adopted a version of generous tit for tat. At the end of the first meeting with a new hire, Geller makes an offer: "If this conversation was helpful, I'm happy to do it on a monthly basis." If the person agrees, Geller sets up a recurring monthly meeting in his calendar, with no end date. In addition to creating opportunities for Geller to give, the monthly meetings offer the side benefit of helping him understand who might be a taker. "Part of the value of the ongoing dialogue is you can tell pretty quickly who's faking it, because the good conversations and relationships build upon each other," Geller explains. "It's easy to fake it every six months, but not on a regular basis. That's part of why I encourage people to schedule that time. It's part of how you sort out who's genuine while making the biggest impact." Once Geller identifies a colleague as a taker, he keeps giving, but becomes more cautious in his approach. "I don't help them less, but the help starts to look different. I'll listen and engage, but we're not having a dialogue; there's not as much mentoring and coaching. It's not that I will consciously be less available to support them, but human nature leads you to invest your time where there is the biggest return—for both of us."

Initially, Lillian Bauer didn't vary her investment as a function of the requester's reciprocity style. Before she began sincerity screening, she was generous with every audience. That changed after she helped a family friend who sought her advice about landing a position at a top-tier consulting firm. Bauer responded in a characteristically generous fashion: she spent more than fifty hours coaching the candidate on nights and weekends and made connections for her at her own firm and several competing firms. The candidate ended up receiving offers from Bauer's firm and a competitor, and joined Bauer's firm. But then, despite the fact that Bauer and her colleagues had expended a great deal of time and energy recruiting her, the candidate requested a transfer to another office in a different country—in direct violation of the firm's recruiting guidelines. Bauer had been duped by an agreeable taker: "The discussions were very much around what was best for her and her only. The way she was talking about the decision made it clear this was all about her; she was obviously going to help herself." Having been taken advantage of, Bauer learned to be more cautious in dealing with takers. "After that point, it just completely changed the way I felt about her, and I wasn't willing to be as generous."

Through a combination of sincerity screening and generous tit for tat, Bauer was able to avoid becoming a doormat in advising and mentoring takers. But she hadn't overcome the obstacle of learning to challenge clients and say no to some of their requests, instead of being a pushover. "I was still saying yes to the client too much, instead of pushing back." What does it take for givers to become more assertive?

Assertiveness and the Advocacy Paradox

The men and women were equally qualified, but the men were earning substantially more money. Linda Babcock, an economist at Carnegie Mellon University, stared at the data in dismay. Although it was the twenty-first century, the male MBA graduates from her school had 7.6 percent higher salaries than their female counterparts. Carnegie Mellon is one of the world's finest technical institutions, boasting eighteen Nobel Prize winners, including seven in economics alone. When business students enroll for their MBAs at Carnegie Mellon, they are signing up for a serious quantitative challenge. The school offers degrees in computational finance, quantitative economics, and software engineering, and over 40 percent of all Carnegie Mellon MBAs accept jobs in finance. In such a quantitatively intense environment, the salary numbers suggested that women still face a glass ceiling. Babcock calculated that over a thirty-five-year career, this gap meant that each woman was losing an average of more than $1 million.

But the gender gap, it turns out, wasn't quite due to a glass ceiling. Men and women received similar starting offers, and the discrepancy emerged by the time they signed their final offers. Upon closer inspection, Babcock discovered a dramatic difference between men and women in the willingness to ask for more money. More than

half of the men—57 percent—tried to negotiate their starting salaries, compared with only 7 percent of the women. The men were
more than eight times as likely to negotiate as the women. The students who did negotiate (mostly men) improved their salaries by an
average of 7.4 percent, enough to account for the gender gap.

The discrepancy in willingness to negotiate wasn't limited to the
quantitative world of Carnegie Mellon MBAs. In another study, Babcock and her colleagues recruited people to play four rounds of
Boggle for a fee of somewhere between $3 and $10. When they finished, the researcher acted like a taker, handing them the minimum
of $3 and asking, "Is three dollars okay?" Once again, eight times as
many men as women asked for more money. The next study went
the same way, but the researcher handed them the minimum of $3
without asking if it was okay. None of the women asked for more
money, whereas 13 percent of the men took the initiative to ask for
more. With another group of participants, the researcher handed
over $3 and said, "The exact payment is negotiable." The majority of
the men (59 percent) seized the opportunity and asked for more,
compared with only 17 percent of the women. Overall, the men were
8.3 times more likely to ask for more money than the women. In
each case, the women were doormats, allowing takers to walk all
over them. Research shows that one of the main reasons that women
tend to negotiate less assertively than men is that they worry about
violating social expectations that they'll be warm and kind.*

* This raises a broader question: are women more likely to be givers than men?
Northwestern University psychologist Alice Eagly and her colleagues have sys-
tematically analyzed hundreds of studies on giving behaviors such as helping,
sharing, comforting, guiding, rescuing, and defending others. It turns out that
when we study their behaviors, men and women are equally likely to be givers.
They just give in different ways. On the one hand, in close relationships, women
tend to be more giving than men. On average, women are more likely than men
to donate organs to family members, assist coworkers, and mentor subordinates,
and female physicians tend to give greater emotional support to patients than

Yet women aren't the only ones who become pushovers at the bargaining table. The doormat effect is a curse that afflicts givers of both genders. In several experiments, male and female givers were willing to make large concessions just to reach an agreement that would make their counterparts happy, even if they had better options available. And in a series of studies led by Notre Dame professor Timothy Judge, nearly four thousand Americans filled out a survey on whether they were givers, indicating the degree to which they tended to be helpful, caring, and trusting. On average, the givers earned 14 percent lower income than their less giving counterparts, taking an annual pay hit of nearly $7,000. When the data were split by gender, the income penalty was three times greater for giver men than giver women. The female givers earned an average of 5.47 percent less money than their peers, for a difference of $1,828. The male givers earned an average of 18.31 percent less money than their peers, for a difference of $9,772.*

As we saw earlier in the chapter on powerless communication,

male physicians. On the other hand, when it comes to strangers, men are more likely to act like givers. On average, men are more likely than women to help in emergencies and risk their lives to save strangers. When women give more than men, it appears to be a function of motivation rather than ability. Research shows that women are better than men at reading other people's thoughts and feelings, but only when told that their empathy is being tested.

* This evidence sheds new light on the role of gender in the success of givers. Unfortunately, evidence suggests that giving is sometimes more rewarding for men than women. Whereas people are often surprised when men help, they tend to take it for granted when women give, which fits in with female gender role expectations. However, the research by Judge and colleagues complicates this picture by revealing that when men are too generous, they're punished more than women, incurring nearly triple the salary penalty—perhaps because they violate norms of masculinity. Rather than assuming that giving is a better deal for men than women, I believe that gender may be an amplifier of giver success and failure: giving benefits successful men more than women, but costs unsuccessful men more than women.

givers tend to be humble and uncomfortable asserting themselves directly. Studies in more controlled settings have shown that in zero-sum situations, givers frequently shy away from advocating for their own interests: when negotiating their salaries, they make more modest requests than matchers and takers, and end up accepting less favorable outcomes. This reluctance to be assertive is especially likely to afflict agreeable givers, who pay a price in their pocketbooks.*

At a professional services firm, a man who I'll call Sameer Jain was a giver who consistently fell victim to the doormat effect. Sameer was ranked at the top of his class and the top 10 percent of all employees in the northeast United States at his firm, and dedicated much of his time to helping colleagues and mentoring junior

* Although there's consistent evidence that a lack of assertiveness is one reason for the giver pay disadvantage, there's a second factor at play. Givers often choose lower-paying careers: they're willing to make less of a living in order to make more of a difference. One recent study replicated the basic finding that givers earn lower incomes even after accounting for the occupations in which they work, but this reduced the disadvantage—suggesting that part of the difference is due to givers' accepting lower-paying jobs. To illustrate, Cornell economist Robert Frank found that employees in the most socially responsible occupations earned annual salaries of approximately 30 percent less than those in the middle and 44 percent less than those at the bottom of the social responsibility spectrum. Private-sector employees earned annual salaries averaging 21 percent higher than government employees, who in turn were 32 percent above nonprofit employees. Guess who's more likely to end up in government and nonprofit jobs? The givers. In one amusing study, Frank asked economics students to consider doing the exact same job in two different organizations: one with strong giver values and one . . . less so. The students reported that they would accept 50 percent lower salaries to work as an advertising copywriter for the American Cancer Society than for Camel cigarettes, 17 percent lower salaries to work as an accountant at an art museum than at a petrochemical company or as a recruiter at the Peace Corps than Exxon Mobil, and 33 percent lower salaries as a lawyer for the Sierra Club than for the National Rifle Association. Interestingly, men were less willing to sacrifice their salaries than women. Of course, whether the participants would show these preferences in their actual behavior is another matter—but I'm willing to bet that selfless givers are more likely to do so than otherish givers.

employees. Despite being a star performer, he watched his friends at other firms get promoted faster and earn more income, and he never negotiated his salary or asked for a raise. On several occasions, he watched assertive peers who were no better performers negotiate raises and promotions, sailing past him in the corporate hierarchy. "I did not push hard enough to make that happen for myself. I didn't want to make others uncomfortable or overstep my bounds."

Growing up in India, Sameer was a pushover, which made him the butt of jokes in his family. His father came from a background in poverty, and learned to be a hard-nosed negotiator who bargained for everything, clawing his family up to the middle class. Sameer grew up shielded, protected from having to assert himself. His sub-missiveness bothered his wife, who was a tough negotiator. When they first started dating, Sameer was about to sign a lease on an apartment. His wife intervened, negotiated on his behalf, and reduced the rent by $600 a year. He was impressed, but also embar-rassed. Since then, whenever they make a purchase, he has turned to his wife to negotiate, knowing that he would be a doormat. "To be honest, I've been ashamed of this for a long time," he admits.

After he left the professional services firm, Sameer completed an MBA and received a job offer from a *Fortune* 500 medical technology company, his ideal employer. He wasn't entirely satisfied with the terms of the offer, but as usual, he was reluctant to negotiate. "I felt awkward. I like my boss, and I didn't want to make him uncomfort-able." Weakening Sameer's position further, the economy had just crashed, and his peers were all signing without negotiating.

But something was different this time. By a couple months later, Sameer had negotiated increases in his total compensation to the tune of more than $70,000. He had undergone a chump change, trans-forming from his traditional doormat status into a more assertive, more successful negotiator. "My wife was stunned, and she compli-mented my persistence and effectiveness as a negotiator," he says.

"For her to see me as a good negotiator is the ultimate validation." What was it that drove Sameer to step up to the plate?

The answer can be found in an ingenious experiment conducted by Linda Babcock and her colleagues. The participants were 176 senior executives from private and public organizations, with titles ranging from CEO and COO to president, general manager, and chairman. The executives all started with the same information: an employee in a software company was being promoted, and they were negotiating compensation for the new position. The male executives playing the role of the employee landed an average of $146,000, 3 percent higher than the women's average of $141,000. But with a single sentence, Babcock and colleagues helped the female executives boost their averages to $167,000, outdoing the men by 14 percent.

All it took was to tell them they were playing a different role. Instead of imagining that they were the employee, the female executives were asked to imagine that they were the employee's mentor. Now the women were agents advocating for someone else. Interestingly, they didn't set higher goals, but they were willing to push harder to achieve their goals, which led them to better outcomes. In a similar study, researchers Emily Amanatullah and Michael Morris asked men and women to negotiate the terms of an attractive job offer. Half were instructed to imagine that they had received the offer themselves and negotiate accordingly. The other half were instructed to imagine that they had referred a friend for the job and were now responsible for negotiating on behalf of the friend. Once again, all of the participants set similar goals, irrespective of whether they were male or female, or negotiating for themselves or a friend.

But their actual behavior in the negotiations varied strikingly. Regardless of whether they were negotiating for themselves or others, the men requested starting salaries averaging $49,000. The women followed a different path. When they were negotiating for themselves, they requested starting salaries averaging only $42,000—16.7 percent lower than the men.

This discrepancy vanished when the women negotiated on behalf of a friend. As advocates, women did just as well as the men, requesting an average of $49,000. In another study, Amanatullah and Morris found the same results with experienced executives negotiating: male executives landed the same salaries regardless of whether they were negotiating for themselves or others, whereas female executives did much better when negotiating for others than themselves. And Vanderbilt professors Bruce Barry and Ray Friedman found that in short-term, single-issue negotiations, givers do worse than takers, because they're willing to give larger slices of the pie to their counterparts. But this disadvantage disappears entirely when the givers set high goals and stick to them—which is easier for givers to do when advocating for someone else.

Advocating for others was the key to Sameer's chump change. When he shied away from negotiating with his initial employer, Sameer was thinking about his own interests. With the *Fortune* 500 medical technology company, he put himself in a different frame of mind: he was representing his family's interests. Although he might be a doormat when he was responsible for himself, being a giver meant that he didn't want to let other people down. "I used it as a psychological weapon against myself, to motivate myself," Sameer says. "The solution was thinking about myself as an agent, an advocate for my family. As a giver, I feel guilty about pushing too much, but the minute I start thinking, 'I'm hurting my family, who's depending on me for this,' I don't feel guilty about pushing for that side."

By thinking of himself as an agent representing his family, Sameer summoned the resolve to make an initial request for a higher salary and tuition reimbursement. This was an otherish strategy. On the one hand, he was doing what givers do naturally: advocating for other people's interests. On the other hand, he intentionally advocated for his family, whose interests were closely aligned with his own. At the same time, he wasn't pushing so far as to become a taker: he sought a balance in meeting his family's interests and his company's. "My value system means that I'm not going to do anything that's wrong or unfair," Sameer explains. "I'm not going to try to gouge anyone, but I am going to push to the point that's right and fair."

When Sameer first contacted his new boss to negotiate, he asked for a salary increase and reimbursement of his MBA tuition. This matched what other firms were offering, but the boss came back with disappointing news from HR: they weren't able to grant either request. At that point, Sameer felt the urge to back down. He wanted to be a giver toward his boss, and he was worried that getting more money would harm his boss's performance or compromise his budget. But Sameer had massive debt from student loans, and he felt responsible for his family first. He asked again, convincing his boss to lobby HR for the bump in his salary and signing bonus. He ended up getting a $5,000 salary increase and a $5,000 signing bonus increase. By that time, his $10,000 signing bonus had expired. Sameer asked for that too, and got it. His boss assured him that this was the best he could do.

Sameer was already up $20,000 in the first year alone, not to mention the dividends that the base salary increase would accrue, but he wasn't done yet. He still wasn't receiving tuition reimbursement, so he was determined to find another way to support his family. He had plenty of free time during his last semester of school, so he negotiated a consulting arrangement to work for the company part-time. The company agreed to pay him $135 per hour, which would net Sameer another $50,000 in the span of a few months. At that point, he signed the contract, having upped his total compensation by more than $70,000. "Being able to keep pushing, a large part of that was being an agent," Sameer says. "If I don't push now, what's going to happen when I get another promotion? I'm going to be that guy who has three kids and gets pushed around. Thinking of myself as an agent motivated me to keep going. It gave me some extra cojones."

Although advocating for his family helped him succeed, Sameer was still concerned about how it would affect his reputation at the firm and his relationship with his boss. When the negotiation was finished, his boss shared a surprising sentiment: he admired Sameer's assertiveness. "It was part of why my boss wanted me," Sameer says. "He respected that I wasn't going to be pushed around anymore." Givers, particularly agreeable ones, often overestimate the degree to which assertiveness might be off-putting to others. But Sameer didn't just earn respect by virtue of negotiating; his boss was impressed with how he negotiated. When HR initially rejected Sameer's request, he explained his family's circumstances. "I don't just have to worry about paying rent now. I have a family to support and loans to repay. Can you make this more palatable for me?" By asking on behalf of his family, instead of himself, Sameer was maintaining an image as a giver. He showed that he was willing to advocate for others, which sent a positive signal about how hard he would work when representing the company's interests.

Babcock and colleagues call this a *relational account*—an explanation for a request that highlights concern for the interests of others, not only oneself. When women ask for a higher salary, they run the risk of violating expectations that they will be "other-oriented and caring, giving rather than taking in character," Babcock writes with Hannah Riley Bowles. Whereas women may be uniquely worried that assertiveness will violate gender norms, givers of both sexes worry about violating their own reciprocity preferences. If they push too hard, they'll feel like takers, rather than givers. But when givers are advocating for someone else, pushing is closely aligned with their values of protecting and promoting the interests of others: givers can chalk it up to caring. And by offering relational accounts, givers do more than just think of themselves as agents advocating for others;

they present themselves as agents advocating for others, which is a powerful way to maintain their self-images and social images as givers.

This reasoning proved relevant to Lillian Bauer when she decided to stop letting clients treat her like a doormat. "I want to be generous, and I build trust with clients, but that doesn't mean they can walk all over me," Bauer notes. To decline requests from clients that fell outside the scope of a project, she used a combination of advocacy and relational accounts. Starting with advocacy, Bauer began to think about herself as an agent for the consultants on her team. "Givers have a protective side. In negotiating with a client, I feel a lot of responsibility for my team, and it makes me more willing to draw a hard line." Then, she developed a habit of articulating this responsibility to her clients: "When a client makes an unreasonable request, I explain that it's going to stretch my team, or kill them working crazy hours. The client knows I will bend over backward to do what's right for them, so when I do push back, it has a lot more impact: there's a good reason for it."

Pushing Past Pushover

Lillian's progress struck a chord with me. As a freshman in college, I accepted a job selling advertisements for the Let's Go travel guides. Written and produced entirely by Harvard students, the Let's Go guides were billed as the bible of the budget traveler, rivaling Lonely Planet, Frommer's, and Rick Steves' as the go-to resource for getting around a foreign country on the cheap. On my first day, my manager handed me a list of clients and said, "These people spent about $300,000 last year on ads in the Let's Go books. Just call them up and convince them to advertise again." Then she turned around and walked away.

As I realized that I wouldn't get any training, I began to panic. I had no product knowledge and no relevant experience, and I had never left North America. I was only eighteen years old, and I had no business making sales pitches to senior vice presidents at major international companies.*

I mustered up the courage to call one of Let's Go's longtime advertisers, a man named Steven who ran a travel agency. The moment he started talking, it was clear he was furious. "At first, I was glad to see that my agency was written up in the books, separate from my ad," he snarled, "until I saw that outdated contact information was listed. So your readers can reach me, I've had to pay hundreds of dollars to maintain old postal addresses and e-mail accounts." I gently explained that advertising and editorial are separate departments; I could ensure the accuracy of his ads, but I had no influence over the content of the books themselves. Steven didn't care; he demanded an advertising discount to make up for the editorial error and threatened not to renew his ad if I didn't comply. Feeling bad for him, I granted him a 10 percent discount. This violated a Let's Go policy that appeared in my contract, prohibiting all discounts that didn't appear in our media kit, and it was a preview of more mistakes to come.

After contacting several dozen clients, I had given three more discounts and signed very few contracts, which became mortifying when I learned that Let's Go had a 95 percent client renewal rate. Along with bringing in no revenue, when a client demanded a refund on the previous year's ad, I caved, becoming the first employee to give away money that was already on the books. In empathizing with clients and trying to meet their needs in any way possible, I was helping them at my own expense—not to mention my company's. I was a disaster, and I was ready to quit.

It wasn't the first time I had been a giver to a fault. When I was

---

* Only later did I learn that my manager hired me because my predecessor had quit three weeks into the job, and she was desperate to find a replacement. The position had been open for twenty-two days, and I was the sole candidate.

fourteen, I decided to become a springboard diver. I was determined to master the art of hurling myself into the air, doing somersaults and twists, and entering the water gracefully without a splash. Never mind that I could hardly jump, flip, or twist, I was terrified to try new dives, and my teammates called out my lack of flexibility by nick-naming me Frankenstein. One day, my coach brought a metronome to practice in the hopes of improving my timing. After several hours of effort, he declared me incapable of rhythm.

For the next four years, I trained six hours a day. Eventually, I became a two-time state finalist, a two-time junior Olympic national qualifier, and an All-American diver. I would go on to compete at the NCAA varsity level at Harvard. But along the way, I sacrificed my own success. Several months before the biggest meet of my life, I volunteered to coach two of my competitors. I taught them new dives, critiqued their form, and revealed the secret of the rip entry, showing them how to disappear into the water at the end of a dive.

They returned the favor by beating me at the state championships, by just a handful of points.

At Let's Go, I was once again benefiting others at a personal cost. Although I was helping my clients save money, I was a pushover, losing revenues for the company and sacrificing my own commission. But the following week, I happened to meet a new assistant manager at Let's Go whose position was created as a result of the advertising revenue that my predecessor generated. The job made it possible for her to pay for school. It was the inspiration that I needed: I realized that my colleagues were depending on me. As a student, I didn't have a wife and children yet, but I could see myself as an agent on behalf of college students in search of jobs that would defray the cost of tuition and provide meaningful work experiences. I might be a doormat when lobbying solely for my own interests, but when I was representing the interests of students, I was willing to fight to protect them.

Before a heated negotiation with a merciless French hotelier who demanded a discount, I thought about how the revenue could support job creation, which gave me the resolve to dig in my heels. I added a relational account: if I gave him a discount, it would only be fair to offer the same to our other clients, and I had a responsibility to be consistent. He ended up paying the full price.

After four months, I had set company records by bringing in more than $600,000 in revenue, nearly doubling my predecessor's tally, and landing more than $230,000 from cold calls to new prospects. I sold the largest advertising package in company history, and our president announced at a banquet that I was "one of the finest advertising associates ever to come through" the company. At age nineteen, I was promoted to director of advertising sales, which put me in charge of a budget above $1 million and tasked me with hiring, training, and motivating my own staff.

Right after I was promoted, the Internet bubble collapsed. More than a dozen clients went out of business before our advertising season even started, and six of our ten biggest clients informed me that their advertising budgets had been slashed, so they wouldn't be able to renew. When all was said and done, Let's Go lost twenty-two loyal clients and 43 percent of the total budget from the previous year. The worst blow came when our largest client called. It was Michael, the vice president of the student travel agency that had purchased the record-setting package the previous year. "I'm very sorry to tell you this, because we love your product and value this relationship." Michael took a deep breath. "But due to budget constraints and a declining travel market, I'm not sure if we can afford to advertise this year at all. To even consider it, we'll need a major discount."

Knowing that many jobs depended on revenue from Michael's company, I became an advocate and pushed back. Because his rivals were pulling their ads, I told Michael, it was an opportunity to gain a leg up on the competition—and what better time to invest than during a recession? He said he would check with his boss and get back to me. The following week, he called with bad news: he had authorization to advertise in our books only if he could have the same package as the prior year, and only with a 70 percent discount. This would slash his expenditure of just under $120,000 to below $40,000.

While I was trying to figure out how much of a discount we could afford, I went to coach a diving practice. Sitting on the pool deck, it dawned on me that there was a major difference between diving and Let's Go. Individual sports involved zero-sum contests where helping competitors win meant that I would be more likely to lose. In business, though, win-win was possible; my clients' interests didn't have to be at odds with my own. When I began to contemplate Michael's interests, I realized that he might value products to give away for free in his store. I learned from colleagues that our publishing contract gave Let's Go the rights to sell or license any content that didn't exceed twenty pages, so I offered him sponsorship of a new product: twenty-page Let's Go travel booklets that he could hand out to customers. Customers would appreciate the free travel tips and might stay longer in the store or be more likely to return. Since the funds would come from his distribution budget rather than his advertising budget, he was able to consider the possibility. When I gave further thought to Michael's interests, I realized that the booklets would be more valuable to him if he could sponsor them exclusively, rather than featuring other companies' ads. We agreed on a mutually beneficial deal for exclusive sponsorship, and he ended up spending more than $140,000, topping my own previous record for the largest ad package in company history.

Whereas advocacy and relational accounts enabled me to become more assertive in win-lose negotiations, it was perspective taking that helped me expand the pie and succeed in win-win negotiations. Ultimately, despite the dot-com bust, this approach led more than half of our renewal clients to increase their ad packages. Our team brought in more than $550,000 in profits, making it possible to increase the size of our staff and introduce new marketing initiatives. After months of hounding delinquent clients to send their payments, I became the only manager in recent history to bring in 100 percent of accounts receivable, leaving no bad debt. I was elected to the company's board of directors and earned the manager of the year award for leadership, commitment, and business acumen. The lessons I learned at Let's Go stuck with me, and I decided to spend the rest of my career teaching other givers what I had discovered about overcoming the doormat effect.

For a number of years, researchers have known that successful negotiators tend to operate in an otherish fashion. In a comprehensive analysis of twenty-eight different studies led by Dutch psychologist Carsten De Dreu, the best negotiators weren't takers or selfless givers. The takers focused on claiming value: they saw negotiations as zero-sum, win-lose contests and didn't trust their opponents, so they bargained aggressively, overlooking opportunities to create value through developing an understanding of their counterparts' interests. The selfless givers made too many concessions, benefiting their counterparts at a personal cost. The most effective negotiators were otherish: they reported high concern for their own interests *and* high concern for their counterparts' interests. By looking for opportunities to benefit others and themselves, otherish givers are able to think in more complex ways and identify win-win solutions that both takers and selfless givers miss. Instead of just giving away value like selfless givers, otherish givers create value first. By the time they give slices of pie away, the entire pie is big enough that there's plenty left to claim for themselves: they can give more *and* take more.

This notion of expanding the pie captures a turning point in Lillian Bauer's career. Although she had learned to push back with clients and place boundaries on the time she spent mentoring and helping takers, she wasn't willing to let go of helping givers and matchers. When junior associates who didn't seem like takers needed help, she still gave in a selfless manner, sacrificing inordinate amounts of her time regardless of her own schedule and demands.

Jason Geller adopted a more otherish approach: he found a way to expand the amount of giving that he could accomplish without increasing the demands on his time. Geller engaged others in sharing the workload, creating opportunities for them to become givers, while keeping himself from becoming overloaded. As a senior manager, when junior analysts asked him for help, Geller would suggest a lunch, and invite a couple newer managers to come along. This opened the door for the managers to have access to him, and for them to provide mentoring to the junior analysts. "It's a great way for them to build the support of folks more junior to them," he says. Instead of doing all of the giving himself, he was able to connect junior analysts with multiple mentors, who provided a broader base of knowledge and advice.

After being told she was too generous, Bauer adopted an approach that resembled Geller's. She started doing group mentoring sessions instead of only one-on-ones:

> I asked myself, "Am I really the only person who can help in this particular instance?" I tried not to think about myself as the only resource I was optimizing, and started connecting people to help each other. Now, I'm quite explicit with my mentees. I tell them, "People did this for me, and you need to do this for other people. There is an expectation that when you receive that kind of generosity from people, you need to pay it forward."

By deciding not to carry the burden alone, Bauer expanded the pie, enabling her giving to have a broader impact while protecting her own time. "If you have a natural mix of givers, takers, and matchers in your company," Bauer says, "you can do a lot to magnify the giver tendency, suppress the more aggressive taker tendencies, and shift the matchers toward giving. There's an energy and a satisfaction that you get out of it. In its own way, it's addictive."

Instead of assuming that they're doomed to become doormats, successful givers recognize that their everyday choices shape the results they achieve in competitive, confrontational situations. The dangers lie less in giving itself, and more in the rigidity of sticking with a single reciprocity style across all interactions and relationships. As the psychologist Brian Little puts it, even if a style like giving is our first nature, our ability to prosper depends on developing enough comfort with a matching approach that it becomes second nature. Although many successful givers start from the default of trusting others' intentions, they're also careful to scan their environments to screen for potential takers, always ready to shift from feeling a taker's emotions to analyzing a taker's thoughts, and flex from giving unconditionally to a more measured approach of generous tit for tat. And when they feel inclined to back down, successful givers are prepared to draw reserves of assertiveness from their commitments to the people who matter to them.

For Lillian Bauer, these shifts in strategy catalyzed a chump change. As Bauer learned to leverage her natural strengths in advocating for others and reading other people's motives, she adapted her behavior to invest in those on whom she could have the greatest influence and encouraged them to give as well. The cumulative effect was that she transformed from a doormat into a successful giver. Even though her generosity initially slowed her rise to partner, she ended up getting there ahead of schedule. Lillian Bauer was one of the first members of her consulting class to make partner.

8

The Scrooge Shift

*Why a Soccer Team, a Fingerprint, and a Name
Can Tilt Us in the Other Direction*

> *How selfish soever man may be supposed, there are evidently some
> principles in his nature which interest him in the fortunes of others,
> and render their happiness necessary to him, although he derives
> nothing from it except the pleasure of seeing it.*
>
> —Adam Smith, father of economics

In 1993, a man named Craig Newmark left IBM after seventeen years to take a computer security position at Charles Schwab in San Francisco. As a single guy new to the Bay Area, he was looking for ways to spice up his social life. In early 1995, he started e-mailing friends to share information about local arts and technology events. Word of mouth spread, and people began to expand the postings beyond events to feature job openings, apartments, and miscellaneous items for sale. By June, the e-mail list had grown to 240 people. It was too large for direct e-mail, so Craig moved it to a listserv. In 1996, a website was born, and it was called Craigslist. By the end of 2011, there were Craigslist sites in more than seven hundred locations around the world. In the United States alone, roughly fifty million people visit Craigslist each month, making Craigslist one of the ten most popular websites in the country—and one of the forty most visited in the world.

Craigslist flourished by appealing to our basic matcher instincts. It facilitates transactions in which buyers and sellers can agree on a fair price, exchanging goods and services for what they're worth. Fundamentally, Craigslist is about trading value in direct exchanges between people, creating a matcher's preferred even balance of give and take. "We're not altruistic," Newmark writes. "From one perspective, we're like a flea market."

Could a system like this function based entirely on giving, instead of matching?

In 2003, an Ohio native by the name of Deron Beal decided to find out. Just like Craig Newmark, Beal was in a new city where he lacked information, so he started an e-mail list of friends. Following the lead from Craigslist, Beal was aiming to create Internet-based local communities of exchange for anyone to access, connecting people who wanted goods with people who were ready to part with them. But in a radical departure from the typical Craigslist exchange, Beal set an unusual ground rule: no currency or trading allowed. The network was called Freecycle, and all goods had to be given away for free.

The idea for Freecycle was sparked when Beal developed and ran a recycling program for businesses at a nonprofit organization called Rise in Tucson, Arizona. Local businesses began to give Beal used items that were still in good condition but weren't recyclable, like computers and desks. In the hopes of giving the items away to people who needed them, Beal spent hours on the phone offering them to charities, but made little progress. At the same time, he had a bed that he wanted to give away, but thrift shops wouldn't accept it. He realized that he might be able to solve both of these problems with an online community that matched givers and receivers more efficiently.

Beal sent an initial e-mail announcing Freecycle to about forty friends, inviting them to join and spread the word. When some of the earliest Freecycle members started posting items to give away, Beal was caught off guard. One woman offered to give away a partially used bottle of hair dye, which would expire in a matter of hours. "It needs to be used really soon," she wrote, "so if anyone has an urge to go darker, tonight is the night." A Texas man posted a more desirable item—fishing tackle—but had a string attached. He would only give it away to someone from whom fishing tackle had been stolen. "As a kid thirty-four years ago, I stole a tackle box. There's no way I can find the person and make it right, so I'm trying to do the next best thing." With some people finding matcher loopholes in the system, and others trying to give away junk, Freecycle seemed like a lost cause.

But Beal believed that "one person's trash really is another's treasure." And some people gave away actual treasure on Freecycle that they could have easily sold on Craigslist. One person donated a camera in excellent condition worth at least $200; others gave away good computers, flat-screen TVs, baby car seats, pianos, vacuum cleaners, and exercise equipment. When Freecycle started in May 2003, there were thirty members. Within a year, Freecycle had grown at an astonishing rate: there were more than 100,000 members in 360 cities worldwide. By March 2005, Freecycle had increased tenfold in membership, reaching a million members.

Recently, social scientists Robb Willer, Frank Flynn, and Sonya Zak decided to study what drives people to participate in exchange systems. They were striving to get to the bottom of a vigorous debate among social scientists, many of whom believed that the types of direct exchanges that take place on Craigslist were the optimal way of exchanging resources. By allowing people to trade value back and forth, a system like Craigslist capitalizes on the fact that most people are matchers. But some experts anticipated the rapid growth of systems like Freecycle, where members give to one person and receive from another, never trading value back and forth with the same person. These researchers were convinced that although such a generalized reciprocity system relies on people to be givers and can be exploited by takers, it could be just as productive in facilitating the exchange of goods and services as direct matching.

The intuitive explanation is that the two types of systems attract different types of people. Perhaps matchers were drawn to Craigslist, whereas givers flocked to Freecycle.* As Deron Beal told me, "If there were only takers, there would be no Freecycle." But Willer's team found that this wasn't the whole story.

Although Freecycle grew in part by attracting people who already leaned strongly in the giver direction, it accomplished something much more impressive. Somehow, Freecycle managed to encourage matchers and takers to act like givers. To figure out how Freecycle works, Willer's team studied random samples of members at both Craigslist and Freecycle. They collected surveys from more than a thousand members of the two exchange organizations from dozens of communities around the United States, measuring reciprocity styles by asking members to answer a series of questions about whether they generally preferred to maximize their own gains or contribute to others. The givers had donated an average of twenty-one items on Freecycle. The takers could have given nothing, but they had given away an average of more than nine items each on Freecycle.

Interestingly, in fact, people often join Freecycle to take, not give. "People usually hear about Freecycle as a way to get free stuff. Your average person will join thinking, 'I can get something for nothing,'" Beal says. "But a paradigm shift kicks in. We had a big wave of new parents who needed help in hard times. They received strollers, car seats, cribs, and high chairs. Later, instead of selling them on Craigslist, they started giving them away."

---

* Many Craigslist pages do have a section for giving away free items, but its popularity is dwarfed by that of the buying and selling pages.

What drives people to join a group with the intention of taking, but then end up giving?

The answer to this question opens up another way that givers avoid the bottom of the success ladder. When dealing with individuals, it's sensible for givers to protect themselves by engaging in sincerity screening and acting primarily like matchers in exchanges with takers. But in group settings, there's a different way for givers to make sure that they're not being exploited: get everyone in the group to act more like givers. The strategy was foreshadowed by Jason Geller and Lillian Bauer, who directly asked their mentees to pay it forward in mentoring groups of more junior colleagues. Earlier, Adam Rifkin, the Silicon Valley giver who was named *Fortune*'s best networker, did the same thing in his entire network. He invited the people who benefited from his giving to help other people in his web of relationships, and a giving norm evolved. As I noted in the opening chapter, people rarely have a single reciprocity style that they apply uniformly to every domain of their lives. If a group develops a norm of giving, members will uphold the norm and give, even if they're more inclined to be takers or matchers elsewhere. This reduces the risks of giving: when everyone contributes, the pie is larger, and givers are no longer stuck contributing far more than they get.

What is it about groups that can tilt members in the giver direction? At the end of this chapter, I'll introduce you to a powerful activity that some of the world's leading companies and business schools have started using to motivate giving among takers and matchers, as well as givers. But first, by unpacking Freecycle's success in motivating matchers and takers to give, we can gain a deeper understanding of what individuals and organizations can do to foster greater levels of giving. The starting point is to ask why people give in the first place.

The Altruism Debate

For nearly forty years, two of the world's most distinguished psychologists have locked horns over whether the decision to give can be purely altruistic, or whether it's always ultimately selfish. Rather than debate philosophy, each has come to battle wielding a deadlier weapon: the psychological experiment.

The defendant of pure altruism is C. Daniel Batson, who believes that we engage in truly selfless giving when we feel empathy for another person in need. The greater the need, and the stronger our attachment to the person experiencing it, the more we empathize. When we empathize with a person, we focus our energy and attention on helping him or her—not because it will make us feel good but because we genuinely care. Batson believes that although some people feel empathy more intensely and frequently than others, virtually all humans have the capacity for empathy—even the most disagreeable of takers. As Adam Smith put it centuries ago: "the emotion which we feel for the misery of others . . . is by no means confined to the virtuous and humane, though they perhaps may feel it with the most exquisite sensibility. The greatest ruffian, the most hardened violator of the laws of society, is not altogether without it."

The devil's advocate is Robert Cialdini, who argues that there's no such thing as pure altruism. He believes that human beings are frequently generous, giving, and caring. But he doesn't think these behaviors are entirely altruistic in origin. He believes that when others hurt, we hurt—and this motivates us to help. Cialdini's first challenge to Batson's claims was that when empathy leads us to help, it's not because our ultimate goal is to benefit the other person. He proposed that when others are in need, we feel distressed, sad, or guilty. To reduce our own negative feelings, we help. Cialdini accumulated an impressive body of studies suggesting that when people feel distressed, guilty, or sad toward another person in need, they help.

Batson's rebuttal: it's true that people sometimes help to reduce negative feelings, but this isn't the only reason. And negative feelings don't always lead to helping. When we feel distressed, sad, or guilty, our ultimate goal is to reduce these negative feelings. In some cases, helping is the strategy that we choose. But in many cases, we can reduce our negative feelings in other ways, such as distracting ourselves or escaping the situation altogether. Batson figured out a clever way to tease apart whether empathy drives us to help because we want to reduce another person's distress or our own distress. If the goal is to reduce our own distress, we should choose whatever course of action makes us feel better. If the goal is to reduce another person's distress, we should help even when it's costly and other courses of action would make us feel good.

In one experiment, Batson and colleagues gave people a choice: watch a woman receive electric shocks or leave the experiment to avoid the distress. Not surprisingly, 75 percent left. But when they felt empathy for the woman, only 14 percent left; the other 86 percent stayed and offered to take the shocks in her place. And of the people who stayed to help, the ones who empathized the most strongly were willing to endure four times as many shocks as those who felt less empathy. Batson and colleagues demonstrated this pattern in more than half a dozen experiments. Even when people can reduce their negative feelings by escaping the situation, if they're feeling empathy, they stay and help anyway, at a personal cost of time and pain. On the basis of this evidence, Batson concluded that reducing bad feelings is not the only reason people help, and a comprehensive analysis of eighty-five different studies backed him up.

But Cialdini, one of the greatest social thinkers of our time, wasn't done yet. He acknowledged that empathy can drive helping. Feelings of concern and compassion certainly motivate us to act for the benefit of others at a personal cost. But he wasn't convinced that this reflects pure altruism. He argued that when we empathize with a victim in need, we become so emotionally attached that we experience a sense of oneness with the victim. We merge the victim into our sense of self. We see more of ourselves in the victim. And this is why we help: we're really helping ourselves. Quoting Adam Smith again, "By the imagination we place ourselves in his situation, we conceive ourselves enduring all the same torments, we enter as it were into his body, and become in some measure the same person with him, and thence form some idea of his sensations, and even feel something."

Cialdini and colleagues conducted numerous experiments supporting this idea. Empathy leads to a sense of oneness, or self-other overlap, and this leads to greater helping. Batson's team came back with another rebuttal: that *is* altruism. If we empathize with other people to the point of merging our own identities with theirs, we care about them as much as we care about ourselves. Because we no longer place our interests above theirs, helping them is purely altruistic.

Stalemate.

Both camps agree that empathy leads to helping. Both camps agree that a sense of oneness is a key reason why. But they fundamentally differ about whether oneness is selfish or altruistic. I believe there's a middle ground here, and it's one that Deron Beal discovered early on. When he started Freecycle, he wanted to keep used goods out of landfills by giving them away to people who wanted them. But he also had some personal interests at stake. In his recycling program, he had a warehouse full of stuff he couldn't use or recycle, and his boss wanted the warehouse emptied. In addition, Beal was hoping to get rid of an old mattress that he owned. None of his friends needed it, and it was too big to throw away. To dump it, he would need to borrow a truck and drive the mattress to a landfill, where he would be charged for disposal. Beal realized it would be easier and cheaper if he could just give it away to someone on Freecycle.

This is why many takers and matchers started giving on Freecycle. It's an efficient way to get rid of things they don't want and probably can't sell on Craigslist. But soon, Beal knows from personal experience, people who initially give things away for selfish reasons begin to care about the people they're helping. When the recipient arranged to pick up his mattress, Beal was thrilled. "I thought I was getting away with giving a mattress away, that I was the one benefiting," he says. "But when the person showed up at my door and thanked me, I felt good. It was only partially a selfish act: I was helping someone else in a way that made me happy. I felt so darn good about it that I started giving away other items."

After a decade of research, I've come to the conclusion that Beal's experience is the norm rather than the exception. Oneness is otherish. Most of the time that we give, it's based on a cocktail of mixed motives to benefit others and ourselves. Takers and matchers may be most likely to give when they feel they can advance others' interests and their own at the same time. As the primatologist Frans de Waal writes in *The Age of Empathy*, "The selfish/unselfish divide may be a red herring. Why try to extract the self from the other, or the other from the self, if the merging of the two is the secret behind our cooperative nature?"

Consider Wikipedia, the online encyclopedia written for free by upwards of three million volunteers, with more than a hundred thousand of them contributing regularly. When asked why they write for Wikipedia, hardly any volunteers reported being involved for self-serving reasons, such as to make new contacts, build their reputations, reduce loneliness, or feel valued and needed. But the relatively altruistic value of helping others wasn't the sole factor they emphasized either. Wikipedia contributors aren't necessarily givers across the different domains of their lives, but they're volunteering their time to exhaustively summarize and cross-reference Wikipedia entries. Why? In a survey, two reasons dominated all others: they thought it was fun and they believed information should be free. For many volunteers, writing Wikipedia entries is otherish: it provides personal enjoyment and benefits others.

Beal believes the otherish structure of Freecycle is one of the major reasons that it grew so fast. Giving away items that we don't need, and benefiting others in the process, is the gift economy equivalent of Adam Rifkin's five-minute favors: low cost to oneself coupled with potentially high benefit to others. It's noteworthy that Freecycle's formal mission statement highlights two sets of benefits: members can contribute to others and gain for themselves. The mission is to "build a worldwide gifting movement that reduces waste, saves precious resources & eases the burden on our landfills while enabling our members to benefit from the strength of a larger community."

Beyond this otherish structure, there's a central feature of a Freecycle community that motivates people to start giving. A clue to the mechanism lies in the story of a French consultant who struggled for years to earn the trust of a potential client—until he recognized the power of a sense of community.

From Enemies to Allies

During the 2008 global financial crisis, one of the many companies to suffer was a French firm that I'll call Nouveau. Nouveau was headquartered in a small city in the middle of France that boasted a beloved soccer team. The founders had chosen the city as their headquarters in an effort to restore the city's glory, but the population was shrinking and profits were falling, and there was pressure to relocate to a larger city. Nouveau's executives decided to save headquarters with a dramatic reorganization. Seeking outside assistance, the CFO issued a request for proposals to consulting firms. Nouveau was open to working with whichever firm presented the best proposal, with one exception: one particular consulting firm could not be trusted.

This firm had been working with Nouveau's chief competitor for years. Nouveau's top brass worried that inside information could be leaked accidentally—or even stolen by a taker.

The suspect consulting firm's lead partner, who I'll call Phillippe, was aware of the distrust from the Nouveau executives. Phillippe's firm had submitted proposals to Nouveau in the past, and they were always rejected. The consultants had repeatedly explained the firm's strict confidentiality policies, but the Nouveau executives didn't buy it. Eventually, the consultants concluded that it was a waste of time to continue making proposals. But Phillippe was genuinely interested in contributing to Nouveau's success, so he led his team in preparing and submitting a proposal for the reorganization. Then they sat down to brainstorm: how can we prove to Nouveau that we're trustworthy?

Phillippe's firm was the last to pitch to Nouveau. At the pitch meeting, Phillippe arrived at Nouveau's headquarters with five consultants in tow. They were escorted into a large room where ten Nouveau executives sat across from them. Phillippe's team presented the proposal, and the Nouveau executives were unmoved. "We like your proposal," one executive said, "but we can't trust you. Why should we enter into a relationship with you? How can we be sure that you will put our interests first?" Phillippe reminded them of his firm's confidentiality policies and code of honor, reinforcing that its reputation hinged on upholding the highest standards for clients, but his promise fell on deaf ears.

Phillippe had run out of logical arguments, so he resorted to the only other ammunition that he had. He reached into his briefcase and pulled out the blue scarf of the city's famed soccer club. Donning the scarf as a symbol of hometown pride, he made a plea: "We've been trying to convince you for many years that our confidentiality policies can be trusted. Since we're not managing to say that with words, we'd like to show our commitment in a different way." The five members of Phillippe's team followed suit, putting the soccer scarves around their necks.

The Nouveau executives were surprised. They asked which partner would take the lead on the project. Phillippe stepped up: "I am going to take the lead, and we will begin our work over the August break. I can commit to this because your headquarters is next to my home."

A few hours later, Phillippe's firm landed the project.

The Nouveau executives had not known that Phillippe was from their city. "This was a reorganization task," Phillippe explains, "and having someone care about this city, and the people living in it, was a plus for the employees and the company. It was a bit of common ground."

Common ground is a major influence on giving behaviors. In one experiment, psychologists in the United Kingdom recruited fans of the Manchester United soccer team for a study. When walking from one building to another, the soccer fans saw a runner slip on a grass bank, where he fell holding his ankle and screaming in pain. Would they help him?

It depended on the T-shirt that he was wearing. When he wore a plain T-shirt, only 33 percent helped. When he wore a Manchester United T-shirt, 92 percent helped. Yale psychologist Jack Dovidio calls this "activating a common identity." When people share an identity with another person, giving to that person takes on an otherish quality. If we help people who belong to our group, we're also helping ourselves, as we're making the group better off.*

* When he wore the T-shirt of a rival soccer team, Liverpool FC, 30 percent helped, which raises the question of whether it's possible to get people to help a rival. Before the staged emergency, the fans had written about why Manchester United was their favorite team, how long they had supported the team, how often they watched the team play, and how they felt when the team won and lost. The fans were thinking about themselves as Manchester United fans, so the vast

A common identity was a key active ingredient behind the rapid growth of Freecycle, and the unusually high levels of giving. When Berkeley professor Robb Willer's team compared Craigslist and Freecycle members, they were interested in the degree to which each group experienced identification and cohesion. The more members identified, the more they saw Craigslist or Freecycle as an important part of their self-images, as reflecting their core values. The more cohesion members reported, the more they felt part of a meaningful Craigslist or Freecycle community. Would members experience greater identification and cohesion with Craigslist or Freecycle?

The answer depends on how much a member has received from the site. For members who received or bought few items, there were no differences in identification and cohesion between Craigslist and Freecycle. People were equally attached and connected to both sites. But for members who received or bought many items, there were stark differences: members reported substantially greater identification and cohesion with Freecycle than Craigslist. This was true even after accounting for members' tendencies toward giving: regardless of whether they were givers or not, members who participated frequently felt more attached to Freecycle than to Craigslist. Why

---

majority of them didn't want to help their enemy. But the psychologists had a trick up their sleeves. In another version of the study, instead of writing about why they loved Manchester United, the fans wrote about why they were soccer fans, what it meant to them, and what they had in common with other fans. When the runner twisted his ankle, the fans were still much more likely to help if he was wearing a Manchester United T-shirt (80 percent) than a plain T-shirt (22 percent). But when he was wearing the T-shirt of their rival, Liverpool FC, 70 percent helped. When we look at a rival as a fellow soccer fan, rather than as an enemy, we can identify with him. Oftentimes, we fail to identify with people because we're thinking about ourselves—or them—in terms that are too specific and narrow. If we look more broadly at commonalities between us, it becomes much easier to see giving as otherish.

would people feel more identified and connected with a community where they give freely rather than matching evenly?

Willer's team argues that for two central reasons receiving is a fundamentally different experience in generalized giving and direct matching systems. The first distinction lies in the terms of the exchange. In direct matching, the exchange is an economic transaction. When members buy an item on Craigslist, they know that sellers are typically trying to maximize their own gains with little concern for buyers' interests. In contrast, in generalized giving, givers aren't getting anything tangible back from the recipients. When members receive an item on Freecycle, they're accepting a gift from a giver with no strings attached. According to Willer's team, this "suggests that the giver is motivated to act in the interest of the recipient rather than in his or her own self-interest," which "communicates a regard for the recipient beyond the instrumental value attached to the item itself." In comparison with an economic transaction, a gift is value-laden.

The second distinction has to do with who's responsible for the benefits you receive. When you buy on Craigslist, if you receive an item at a good price, you can chalk it up to your savvy as a negotiator or the kindness (or naïveté) of an individual seller. You're exchanging back and forth with another individual; you're not getting anything from the Craigslist community. "As a result, participants in direct exchange will be less inclined to identify with the group because they will be less likely to derive the emotional experience of group membership," Willer's team writes. In generalized giving, on the other hand, the community is the source of the gifts you receive. An effective system of generalized giving typically involves cycles of exchange with the following structure: person A gives to person B, who gives to person C. When Freecycle members receive multiple items from different people, they attribute the benefits to the whole group, not to individual members.

Together, these two forces facilitate the development of a bond with Freecycle. Instead of buying an item from another person, people feel that they're receiving gifts from a community. The gratitude and goodwill generated means that they begin to identify with the community, seeing themselves as Freecycle members. Once this identification happens, people are willing to give freely to anyone who shares the Freecycle identity. This extends their willingness to give across the whole Freecycle community, spurring members to offer items that they no longer need in response to requests when they can help. By giving away things they don't want, takers can feel like they're not losing anything of value, yet maintain the norm of giving so they can still get free stuff when they want it. For matchers, because there's no way to pay it back, paying it forward is the next best thing—especially since they're helping people just like themselves. In a classic experiment, when people received help from one peer, they were more likely to give help to another peer, matching by following the norm of social responsibility. This is what happened with the parents who gave away baby supplies: they restored their sense of a reciprocal, even exchange by donating items they no longer needed to fellow parents in similar situations.

People are motivated to give to others when they identify as part of a common community. But not all individuals and groups are equally likely to attract this type of identification. There's something else about the Freecycle community that fosters identification—and it's a factor well understood by Adam Rifkin.

The Search for Optimal Distinctiveness

When I first met Adam Rifkin, I asked him to tell me about the most interesting contacts in his network. "One of my favorite people," he replied, "is Adam Rifkin."

He wasn't talking about himself. Adam Rifkin has developed a strong connection with another man named Adam Rifkin—a

Hollywood writer, director, producer, and actor who has been a major contributor to films such as *Detroit Rock City* and *He-Man*. To avoid confusion, I'll call him Hollywood Adam, referring to his endearing doppelgänger as Panda Adam.

In 1992, when Hollywood Adam was just getting his start, Panda Adam moved to Los Angeles to start his doctoral program at Caltech. People would accidentally call Panda Adam when they were trying to reach Hollywood Adam. Panda Adam wanted to get in touch with Hollywood Adam to clear up the confusion, so he put his phone number on the Internet. For three years, no one called. In 1996, Hollywood Adam was in New York, and a friend showed him Panda Adam's website. "I knew nothing about the Internet, and I was impressed with what he'd created. I'd been mistaken for him a number of times, so I called him right away."

It was morning on the East Coast, and just after dawn on the West Coast. The piercing sound of a ringing phone woke a sleeping Panda Adam.

Panda Adam (groggily): "Hello?"

Hollywood Adam: "Adam Rifkin, this is Adam Rifkin."

Panda Adam: "I've been waiting my whole life for this call."

On the surface, they didn't have much in common. As far as they could tell, they weren't related. Panda grew up in New York; Hollywood grew up in Chicago. Panda was a software engineer; Hollywood was in film. But when they met face-to-face, they felt an instant bond. "Hollywood Adam is a fascinating character," says Panda Adam. "His career in Hollywood and mine in Silicon Valley have had more parallels than I would have guessed. Any time somebody asks me for a connection in Hollywood, he's usually the person I start with. Hollywood Adam has made countless introductions to help people I know. Many people in Hollywood are narcissistic and self-centered, but Hollywood Adam is as good-natured and kind as they come. We kind of have the same philosophy."

"Panda Adam is a great guy," says Hollywood Adam. "We have a similar sense of humor. We help each other without keeping score. Neither one of us ever gives it any thought; we just do what's helpful." Panda Adam was the person who introduced Hollywood Adam to Twitter. When Hollywood Adam did a series for Showtime called *Look*, Panda Adam invited him up to northern California to do screenings at YouTube and Twitter. Why did the two Adam Rifkins identify so strongly with each other?

If you're thinking it's a name similarity effect, the data suggest that you're right—at least partially. Brett Pelham, a psychologist at the University at Buffalo, noticed that we seem to prefer people, places, and things that remind us of ourselves. Because we associate our names so strongly with our identities, we might be attracted to major decisions that remind us of our names. In an effort to demonstrate this, Pelham and his colleagues have conducted a mind-boggling, controversial set of studies.

Across five different studies, they found that people are unusually likely to end up living in places that resemble their first names. In one study, Pelham's team searched the forty biggest cities in the United States for the one hundred most common first names that shared their first three letters with these cities. Then, they matched up names in terms of how popular they were in different age groups. It turns out that people named Jack are *four times* more likely than people named Phillip to live in Jacksonville, even though the names are equally common. (The Phils have apparently retreated to Philadelphia, where they outnumber the Jacks.) And it's not that they're named after these places; people are more likely to *move* to places that resemble their own names (Georgia is twice as likely to move to Georgia as chance would predict).

It works for careers too: in 1990, Dennis was the fortieth most common male first name in the United States. Jerry was the thirty-ninth, and Walter was forty-first.

There were 270 dentists in the United States named Jerry.

There were 257 dentists in the United States named Walter.

How many dentists were named Dennis?

Statistically, there should have been somewhere between 257 and 270.

In reality, there were 482.

If your name was Dennis, you were almost twice as likely to become a dentist as if you had the equally common name of Jerry or Walter. Other studies show that people with the last name Lawyer are more likely to become lawyers than doctors, at rates 44 percent higher than chance; the opposite is true for people named Doctor, at 38 percent greater than chance rates. The attraction also holds for products and people that we associate with ourselves. Pelham and colleagues have found that people prefer chocolates, crackers, and teas that include the letters of their own names—and that they're more attracted to potential dates who have similar initials, even though they insist that this similarity doesn't influence their attraction. And evidence shows that similarity can influence whom we decide to help. Researchers Jeff Galak, Deborah Small, and Andrew Stephen studied more than 289,000 loans to more than 23,000 borrowers on Kiva, a microfinance website where people can give loans as small as $25 to help people in the developing world escape poverty and start businesses. People were more likely to give microloans to borrowers who shared their first initials or their occupations.*

---

* There are plenty of alternative explanations for many of these findings. Wharton professor Uri Simonsohn has scrutinized the data, and although he believes that name similarity *can* influence our decisions, he argues persuasively that many of the existing studies have been biased by other factors. For example, he finds that people named Dennis are overrepresented among lawyers, not only dentists. But this doesn't explain why randomized, controlled experiments show that people help others with similar names, buy products that match their initials, and are attracted to dates who share their initials—and it doesn't account for some recent studies on how names can sabotage success. Psychologists have

It appears that similarity to the self adds a bit of grease to the attraction process: people are just a bit more enthusiastic, friendly, and open-minded when they meet someone who reminds them of themselves. This is what happened to the two Adam Rifkins when they first met. They initially clicked based on a superficial similarity, which opened the door for them to connect based on real similarities—and start helping each other. This is not unusual; the web is now full of "Googlegangers," or people with the same name who have formed online groups.

But the bond between the two Adam Rifkins goes beyond the fact that they have the same name. To illustrate, imagine that you show up for a study along with a college student. A researcher takes your fingerprints, under the guise of studying whether they reveal anything about your personality. You both fill out a personality questionnaire. As you're getting ready to leave, the student pulls out a paper from her backpack. "For an English class that I'm taking, I need to find someone I don't know to critique my essay. I wonder if you could read this eight-page essay for me and give me one page of written

---

found that on average, people whose names start with *A* and *B* get better grades and are accepted to higher-ranked law schools than people whose names start with *C* and *D*—and that professional baseball players whose names start with *K*, the symbol for strikeouts, strike out 9 percent more often than their peers. The speculation here is that people are more comfortable with negative outcomes that subtly remind them of themselves. Other evidence lends tentative support to this idea: athletes, doctors, and lawyers whose first names start with *D* die sooner than those with other initials. Professional baseball players with positive initials (A.C.E., J.O.Y., W.O.W.) live an average of thirteen years longer than players with negative initials (B.U.M., P.I.G., D.U.D.). And in California between 1969 and 1995, compared with neutral initials, women with positive initials lived an average of 3.4 years longer, men with positive initials lived an average of 4.5 years longer, and men with negative initials died an average of 2.8 years earlier. Consistent with the idea that initials affect how we take care of ourselves, people with positive initials have lower accident and suicide rates, which are higher for people with negative initials.

feedback on whether my arguments are persuasive and why? I need the written feedback by this time tomorrow." Would you help her?

You were just in the control group in a study led by the psychologist Jerry Burger, where 48 percent of participants helped. But other participants were led to believe that they had something in common with the student making the request. After they filled out the questionnaire, the researcher examined a fingerprint evaluation sheet and remarked, "This is interesting. You both have Type E fingerprints."

Now, would you be more likely to help?

It depends on how the similarity was framed. Half of the time, the researcher mentioned that Type E fingerprints are common: about 80 percent of the population has them. The other half of the time, the researcher mentioned that Type E fingerprints are very rare: only about 2 percent of the population has them.

When the similarity was common, 55 percent of participants helped—hardly more than the control group. But when the similarity was rare, 82 percent of participants helped. It was not just any commonality that drove people to act like givers. It was an uncommon commonality. In Pelham's studies, name-similarity effects on where we live, what careers we choose, and whom we marry are stronger for people with rare names than common names. We gravitate toward people, places, and products with which we share an uncommon commonality. This is the bond that the two Adam Rifkins felt when they first connected. Adam Rifkin is a rare name, and the uncommon commonality may have greased the attraction process. Indeed, Pelham's research shows that the more unique your name is, the more likely you are to identify with places that resemble your name.

To explain why uncommon commonalities are so transformative, the psychologist Marilynn Brewer developed an influential theory. On the one hand, we want to fit in: we strive for connection, cohesiveness, community, belonging, inclusion, and affiliation with others. On the other hand, we want to stand out: we search for uniqueness, differentiation, and individuality. As we navigate the social world, these two motives are often in conflict. The more strongly we affiliate with a group, the greater our risk of losing our sense of uniqueness. The more we work to distinguish ourselves from others, the greater our risk of losing our sense of belongingness.

How do we resolve this conflict? The solution is to be the same and different at the same time. Brewer calls it the principle of *optimal distinctiveness*: we look for ways to fit in and stand out. A popular way to achieve optimal distinctiveness is to join a unique group. Being part of a group with shared interests, identities, goals, values, skills, characteristics, or experiences gives us a sense of connection and belonging. At the same time, being part of a group that is clearly distinct from other groups gives us a sense of uniqueness. Studies show that people identify more strongly with individuals and groups that share unique similarities. The more rare a group, value, interest, skill, or experience is, the more likely it is to facilitate a bond. And research indicates that people are happier in groups that provide optimal distinctiveness, giving a sense of both inclusion and uniqueness. These are the groups in which we take the most pride, and feel the most cohesive and valued.

Freecycle initially provided a sense of optimal distinctiveness through its emphasis on protecting the environment. The central goal was different from most recycling movements: instead of reprocessing old materials into new ones, members found recipients who wanted goods that couldn't be reprocessed, keeping them out of landfills. This common purpose created a shared identity within the Freecycle community, fostering a sense of connection across diverse ideologies. The original group of Freecycle volunteers in Tucson included a liberal Democrat who was passionate about environmental sustainability, a conservative Republican who didn't believe in waste, and a Libertarian who wanted to empower people to do things themselves, rather than relying on governmental support. Over time, as membership expanded and diversified, each Freecycle community provided an outlet for people to customize giving to their own interests. In New York, for example, a local group made a habit of shutting down a city block for Freecycle gifting events.

By fostering a common identity and opportunities for unique self-expression, Freecycle was able to mobilize a giving system based on generalized reciprocity: you give to help others in the community, and you know that someone in the community will give to you. But Willer's team finds that there's a catch: such a system depends on a "critical mass of exchange benefits," which "creates positive sentiments toward the group, sentiments that help fuel further contributions." In other words, people only identify with a generalized giving group after they receive enough benefits to feel like the group is helping them. With Freecycle, this outcome was by no means guaranteed; after all, if the givers on the site had been overwhelmed by takers looking for a free ride, the whole thing might never have gotten off the ground. How did Freecycle accumulate that initial critical mass of giving and discourage free riding?

Why Superman Backfires and People Conserve Electricity

When Freecycle first launched, one of the early members was a ninety-eight-year-old man. He collected parts to fix up bicycles and gave them to local children. He was an "incredible role model," Deron Beal recalls. Tucson citizens were able to identify with the man as a fellow resident. When they saw him give, he was a member of their unique community, so they felt more compelled to follow his example. New York University psychologist Jonathan Haidt refers to this as *elevation*, the warm feeling of being moved by others' acts of giving, which can "seem to push a mental 'reset button,' wiping out feelings of cynicism and replacing them with . . . a sense of moral inspiration." When elevated, Haidt and psychologist Sara Algoe write, "we feel as though we have become (for a moment) less selfish, and we want to act accordingly."

But it was more than just common identity that made this elderly man such an elevating role model. Consider an experiment by psychologists Leif Nelson and Michael Norton, who randomly assigned people to list either ten features of a superhero or ten features of Superman. When invited to sign up as community service volunteers, the group that listed superhero features was nearly twice as likely to volunteer as the Superman group. Three months later, Nelson and Norton invited both groups to a meeting to kick off their volunteering. The people who had written about a superhero were four times more likely to show up than the people who had written about Superman. Thinking about a superhero three months earlier supported giving. In comparison, thinking about Superman discouraged giving. Why?

When people think about the general attributes of superheroes, they generate a list of desirable characteristics that they can relate to themselves. In the study, for example, people wrote about how superheroes are helpful and responsible, and they wanted to express these giver values, so they volunteered. But when people think specifically about Superman, what comes to mind is a set of impossible standards, like those popularized in the TV series *The Adventures of Superman:* "faster than a speeding bullet, more powerful than a locomotive, able to leap tall buildings in a single bound." No one can be that strong or heroic, so why bother trying?

On Freecycle, givers modeled a standard that seemed attainable. When members saw a ninety-eight-year-old man building bikes for kids, they knew they could do something too. When members saw people giving away items like clothes and old electronics, they felt it would be easy for them to do the same. The small acts of giving that started on Freecycle made it easy and acceptable for other people to give small amounts. Indeed, Cialdini finds that people donate more money to charity when the phrase "even a penny will help" is added to a request. Interestingly, this phrase increases the number of people who give without necessarily decreasing the amount that they give. Legitimizing small contributions draws in takers, making it difficult and embarrassing for them to say no, without dramatically reducing the amount donated by givers.

Although most people joined Freecycle to get free stuff, this doesn't mean that taking was their primary reciprocity style. When people join a group, they look for cues about appropriate behavior. When new Freecycle members saw similar others modeling low-cost acts of giving, it became natural for them to follow suit. By making giving visible, Freecycle made it easy for people to see the norm.

It's a powerful lesson, even more so when we realize how much the visibility of giving can affect reciprocity styles. In many domains of life, people end up taking because they don't have access to information about what others are doing. Just a few months after Freecycle got off the ground, Cialdini worked with a team of psychologists to survey more than eight hundred Californians about their energy consumption. They asked the Californians how important the following factors were in shaping their decisions to save energy:

- It saves money
- It protects the environment
- It benefits society
- A lot of other people are doing it

The Californians consistently reported that the most important factor was protecting the environment. Benefiting society was second, saving money was third, and following the lead of other people was last. Cialdini's team wanted to see whether people were right about their own motivations, so they designed an experiment.

They visited nearly four hundred homes in San Marcos, California, and randomly assigned them to receive one of four different types of door hangers:

Save money by conserving energy: According to researchers at Cal State San Marcos, you could save up to $54 per month by using fans instead of air conditioning to keep cool in the summer.

Protect the environment by conserving energy: According to researchers at Cal State San Marcos, you can prevent the release of up to 262 lbs. of greenhouse gases per month by using fans instead of air conditioning to keep cool this summer.

Do your part to conserve energy for *future generations*: According to researchers at Cal State San Marcos, you can reduce your monthly demand for electricity by 29% using fans instead of air conditioning to keep cool this summer.

Join your neighbors in conserving energy: In a recent survey of households in your community, researchers at Cal State San Marcos found that 77% of San Marcos residents often use fans instead of air conditioning to keep cool in the summer.

Cialdini's team conducted door-to-door interviews at each household, without knowing which door hangers they had. When asked how motivating the door hangers were, the residents whose hangers emphasized joining their neighbors reported the lowest motivation. They reported 18 percent lower desires to conserve energy than residents with the protect-the-environment hangers, 13 percent lower than residents with the future-generations hangers, and 6 percent lower than residents with the save-money hangers.

But when Cialdini's team looked at the residents' energy bills to see what people actually did, they found something surprising: the residents were wrong about what motivated them. During the following two months, the residents whose door hangers emphasized joining their neighbors actually conserved the *most* energy. On average, the "join your neighbors" hanger led to between 5 and 9 percent fewer daily kilowatt-hours of energy used than the other three hangers—which were all equally ineffective. Knowing that other people were conserving energy was the best way to get residents to follow suit.

But perhaps it was the people who were already conserving electricity in each neighborhood who responded most visibly, picking up the slack for the electricity takers. To find out whether sharing information about their neighbors' conservation efforts could motivate conservation among people who were consuming high levels of electricity, Cialdini's team ran another experiment with nearly three hundred households in California. This time, they gave residents door hangers that provided feedback on how their electricity consumption compared with similar households in their neighborhood over the past week or two. These door hangers provided feedback on whether residents were consuming less (giving) or more (taking) than their neighbors.

Over the next few weeks, the electricity takers significantly reduced their energy consumption, by an average of 1.22 kilowatt-hours per day. Seeing that they were taking more than the average in their neighborhood motivated them to match the average, decreasing their energy consumption.* But this only works when

---

* Ironically, the message backfired for the people who were conserving energy in a giver fashion. Once they saw they were below the norm for electricity consumption, they felt licensed to take more, and actually increased their consumption by an average of 0.89 kilowatt-hours per day. The psychologists were able to prevent this unintended consequence by drawing a ☺ next to the information that households were consuming less than average. Apparently, this small signal of social approval was enough to motivate people to continue acting like givers.

people are compared with their neighbors. As Cialdini's team explains:

> The key factor was which other people—other Californians, other people in their city, or other residents in their specific community. Consistent with the idea that people are most influenced by similar others, the power of social norms grew stronger the closer and more similar the group was to the residents: The decision to conserve was most powerfully influenced by those people who were most similar to the decision makers—the residents of their own community.

Inspired by this evidence, the company Opower sent home energy report letters to 600,000 households, randomly assigning about half of them to see their energy use in comparison with that of their neighbors. Once again, it was the takers—those consuming the most—who conserved the most after seeing how much they were taking. Overall, just showing people how they were doing relative to the local norm caused a dramatic improvement in energy conservation. The amount of energy saved by this feedback was equivalent to the amount of energy that would be saved if the price of electricity increased by up to 28 percent.

People often take because they don't realize that they're deviating from the norm. In these situations, showing them the norm is often enough to motivate them to give—especially if they have matcher instincts. Part of the beauty of Freecycle is that members have constant access to the norm. Every time a member offers to give something away, it's transparent: others can see how frequent giving is, and they want to follow suit. Because Freecycle is organized in local communities, members are seeing giving by their neighbors, which provides feedback on how their own giving stacks up relative to the local norm. Whether people tend to be givers, takers, or matchers, they don't want to violate the standards set by their neighbors, so they match.

Today, according to Yahoo!, only two environmental terms in the world are searched more often than *Freecycle*: *global warming* and *recycling*. By the summer of 2012, Freecycle had more than nine million members in over 110 countries, expanding at a rate of eight thousand members every week. Many people still join with a taker mentality, hoping to get as much free stuff as possible. But receiving benefits from a group of local citizens who serve as role models for small acts of giving continues to create a common identity in Freecycle communities, nudging many members in the giver direction. Together, the nine million Freecycle members give away more than thirty thousand items a day weighing nearly a thousand tons. If you piled together the goods given away in the past year, they'd be fourteen times taller than Mount Everest. As Charles Darwin once wrote, a tribe with many people acting like givers, who "were always ready to aid one another, and to sacrifice themselves for the common good, would be victorious over most other tribes; and this would be natural selection."

When I learned about the success of Freecycle, I began to wonder if these principles could play out in everyday life, in an organization without an environmental focus. What would it take to create and sustain a giving system in a company or a school?

The Reciprocity Ring

When I joined the faculty at Wharton, the world's oldest collegiate business school, I decided to try a giving experiment in my classroom. I announced that we would be running an exercise called the Reciprocity Ring, which was developed by University of Michigan sociologist Wayne Baker and his wife Cheryl at Humax. Each student would make a request to the class, and the rest of the class would try to use their knowledge, resources, and connections to help fulfill the request. The request could be anything meaningful in their professional or personal lives, ranging from job leads to travel tips.

In a matter of minutes, I was facing a line of students—some cynical, others anxious. One student pronounced that the exercise wouldn't work, because there aren't any givers at Wharton: givers study medicine or social work, not business. Another admitted that he would love advice from more experienced peers on strengthening his candidacy for consulting jobs, but he knew they wouldn't help him, since they were competing with him for these positions.

Soon, these students watched in disbelief as their peers began to use their networks to help one another. A junior named Alex announced that he loved amusement parks, and he came to Wharton in the hopes of one day running Six Flags. He wasn't sure how to get started—could anyone help him break into the industry? A classmate, Andrew, raised his hand and said he had a weak tie to the former CEO of Six Flags. Andrew went out on a limb to connect them, and a few weeks later, Alex received invaluable career advice from the ex-CEO. A senior named Michelle confided that she had a friend whose growth was stunted due to health problems, and couldn't find clothes that fit. A fellow senior, Jessica, had an uncle in the fashion business, and she contacted him for help. Three months later, custom garments arrived at the doorstep of Michelle's friend.

Wayne Baker has led Reciprocity Rings at many companies, from GM to Bristol-Myers Squibb. Oftentimes, he brings leaders and managers together from competing companies in the same industry and invites them to make requests and help one another. In one session, a pharmaceutical executive was about to pay an outside vendor $50,000 to synthesize a strain of the PCS alkaloid. The executive asked if anyone could help find a cheaper alternative. One of the group members happened to have slack capacity in his lab, and was able to do it for free.

The Reciprocity Ring can be an extremely powerful experience. Bud Ahearn, a group president at CH2M HILL, noted that leaders in his company "are strong endorsers, not only because of the hundreds of thousands of annual dollar value, but because of the remarkable potential to advance the quality of our 'whole' lives." Baker has asked executives to estimate the dollar value and time saved in participating for two and a half hours. Thirty people in an engineering and architectural consulting firm estimated savings exceeding $250,000 and fifty days. Fifteen people in a global pharmaceutical firm estimated savings of more than $90,000 and sixty-seven days.

Personally, after running the Reciprocity Ring with leaders, managers, and employees from companies such as IBM, Citigroup, Estée Lauder, UPS, Novartis, and Boeing, I've been amazed by the requests that have been fulfilled—from landing a coveted job at Google to finding a mentor to receiving autographed memorabilia from a child's favorite professional football player. But before this happens, just as my Wharton students did, many participants question whether others will actually give them the help that they need. Each time, I respond by asking whether they might be underestimating the givers in their midst.

In a study by researchers Frank Flynn and Vanessa Bohns, people learned that they would be approaching strangers in New York City and asking them to a fill out a survey. The participants estimated that only one out of every four people would say yes. In reality, when the participants went out and asked, one out of every two said yes. In another study in New York City, when participants approached strangers and asked them to borrow a cell phone, they expected 30 percent to say yes, but 48 percent did. When people approached strangers, said they were lost and asked to be walked to a nearby gym, they expected 14 percent to do it, but 43 percent did. And when people needed to raise thousands of dollars for charity, they expected that they would need to solicit donations from an average of 210 people to meet their fund-raising goals, anticipating an average donation under $50. They actually hit their goals after approaching half as many people—on average, it only required 122 people, whose donations were over $60 each.

Why do we underestimate the number of people who are willing to give? According to Flynn and Bohns, when we try to predict others' reactions, we focus on the costs of saying yes, overlooking the costs of saying no. It's uncomfortable, guilt-provoking, and embarrassing to turn down a small request for help. And psychological research points to another factor—equally powerful, and deeply rooted in American culture—that causes people to believe there aren't many givers around them.

Workplaces and schools are often designed to be zero-sum environments, with forced rankings and required grading curves that pit group members against one another in win-lose contests. In these settings, it's only natural to assume that peers will lean in the taker direction, so people hold back on giving. This reduces the actual amount of giving that occurs, leading people to underestimate the number of people who are interested in giving. Over time, because giving appears to be uncommon, people with giver values begin to feel that they're in the minority.

As a result, even when they do engage in giving behaviors, people worry that they'll isolate themselves socially if they violate the norm, so they disguise their giving behind purely self-interested motives. As early as 1835, after visiting the United States from France, the social philosopher Alexis de Tocqueville wrote that Americans "enjoy explaining almost every act of their lives on the principle of self-interest." He saw Americans "help one another" and "freely give part of their time and wealth for the good of the state," but was struck by the fact that "Americans are hardly prepared to admit" that these acts were driven by a genuine desire to help others. "I think that in this way they often do themselves less than justice," he wrote. A century and a half later, the Princeton sociologist Robert Wuthnow interviewed a wide range of Americans who chose helping professions, from cardiologists to rescue workers. When he asked them to explain why they did good deeds, they referenced self-interested reasons, such as "I liked the people I was working with" or "It gets me out of the house." They didn't want to admit that they were genuinely helpful, kind, generous, caring, or compassionate. "We have social norms against sounding too charitable," Wuthnow writes, such that "we call people who go around acting too charitable 'bleeding hearts,' 'do-gooders.'"

In my experience, this is what happens in many businesses and universities: plenty of people hold giver values, but suppress or disguise them under the mistaken assumption that their peers don't share these values. As the psychologists David Krech and Richard Crutchfield explained many years ago, this creates a situation where "no one believes, but everyone thinks that everyone believes." Consider a 2011 survey of Harvard freshmen: they consistently reported that compassion was one of their top values, but near the bottom of Harvard's values. If many people personally believe in giving, but assume that others don't, the whole norm in a group or a company can shift away from giving. "Ideas can have profound effects even when they are false—when they are nothing more than ideology," writes the psychologist Barry Schwartz. "These effects can arise because sometimes when people act on the basis of ideology, they inadvertently arrange the very conditions that bring reality into correspondence with the ideology." When people assume that others aren't givers, they act and speak in ways that discourage others from giving, creating a self-fulfilling prophecy.

As a structured form of giving, the Reciprocity Ring is designed to disrupt this self-fulfilling prophecy. The first step is to make sure that people ask for help. Research shows that at work, the vast majority of giving that occurs between people is in response to direct requests for help. In one study, managers described times when they gave and received help. Of all the giving exchanges that occurred, roughly 90 percent were initiated by the recipient asking for help. Yet when we have a need, we're often reluctant to ask for help. Much of the time, we're embarrassed: we don't want to look incompetent or needy, and we don't want to burden others. As one Wharton dean explains, "The students call it Game Face: they feel pressured to look successful all the time. There can't be any chinks in their armor, and opening up would make them vulnerable."

In the Reciprocity Ring, because everyone is making a request, there's little reason to be embarrassed. By making requests explicit and specific, participants provide potential givers with clear direction about how to contribute effectively. As in Freecycle, the Reciprocity Ring often starts with givers stepping up as role models for contributions. But in every Reciprocity Ring, there are likely to be many matchers and some people who prefer to operate as takers. For a generalized giving system to achieve sustainable effectiveness, as in Freecycle, these matchers and takers need to contribute. Otherwise, the givers will end up helping everyone while receiving little in return, placing themselves at risk for getting burned or burning out. Do matchers and takers step up?

Because people often present meaningful requests in Reciprocity Rings, many matchers are drawn in by empathy. When I heard a powerful CEO's voice tremble as he sought advice and connections to fight a rare form of cancer, the empathy in the room was palpable. "I was surprised by how much I wanted to help," one financial services executive confides. "My job requires me to be very task-focused and financially oriented. I didn't expect to care that much, especially about a stranger I'd never met. But I really felt for his need, and wanted to do whatever I could to contribute and fulfill his request."

Even when they don't empathize, matchers still end up making plenty of contributions. It's very difficult to act like a pure matcher in the Reciprocity Ring, since it's unlikely that the people you help will be the same people who can help fulfill your request. So the easiest way to be a matcher is to try to contribute the same amount that other people do. The Reciprocity Ring creates a miniature version of Panda Adam Rifkin's network: participants are encouraged to do five-minute favors for anyone else in the group. To make sure that every request is granted, participants need to make multiple contributions, even to people who haven't helped them directly. By giving more than they take, participants amplify the odds that everyone in the group will have their requests fulfilled, much like Panda Adam setting a pay-it-forward norm in his network.

But what about the takers? Many audiences are concerned that takers will capitalize on the opportunity to get help without contributing in return. To examine this risk, Wayne Baker and I surveyed more than a hundred people about their giver and taker values. Then they participated in the Reciprocity Ring, and we counted the number of contributions they made. As expected, the givers made significantly more contributions than the takers. The givers averaged four contributions each.

Surprisingly, though, the takers were still quite generous, averaging three contributions each. Despite valuing power and achievement far more than helping others, the takers gave three times more than they got. The Reciprocity Ring created a context that encouraged takers to act like givers, and the key lies in making giving public. Takers know that in a public setting, they'll gain reputational benefits for being generous in sharing their knowledge, resources, and connections. If they don't contribute, they look stingy and selfish, and they won't get much help with their own requests. "Being altruistic is often seen as 'good,' and being greedy or selfish is not," writes Duke behavioral economist Dan Ariely with two colleagues, so giving is "a way to signal to others that one is good."

Research shows that givers usually contribute regardless of

whether it's public or private, but takers are more likely to contribute when it's public. In one study, when others could see their results, takers contributed a large number of ideas during brainstorming. But when their results were hidden, takers added less value. Other studies reveal that takers go green to be seen: they prefer luxurious products over green products when their decisions are private, but shift to green products when their decisions are public, hoping to earn status for protecting the environment. I saw a similar trend among Wharton students: each week in class, I opened the floor for a few students to present requests and invited the whole class to contribute. One November morning, five students made requests, and I was stunned to see a student who had described himself as a taker offer to help four of them. Once his reputation among his peers depended on giving, he contributed. By making contributions visible, the Reciprocity Ring sets up an opportunity for people of any reciprocity style to be otherish: they can do good and look good at the same time.

Identity Shifts and Reciprocity Reversals

This raises a fundamental question: does a generalized giving system like Freecycle or the Reciprocity Ring motivate takers to become better fakers, or can it actually turn takers into givers? In some ways, I'd say the motives don't matter: it's the behavior itself that counts. If takers are acting in ways that benefit others, even if the motives are primarily selfish rather than selfless or otherish, they're making contributions that sustain generalized giving as a form of exchange.

That said, if we ignore motives altogether, we overlook the risk that takers will decrease their giving as soon as they're out of the spotlight. In one study conducted by Chinese researchers, more than three hundred bank tellers were considered for a promotion. The managers rated how frequently each bank teller had engaged in giving behaviors like helping others with heavy workloads and volunteering for tasks that weren't required as part of their jobs. Based on giving behavior, the managers promoted seventy of the bank tellers.

Over the next three months, the managers came to regret promoting more than half of the tellers. Of the seventy tellers who were promoted, thirty-three were genuine givers: they sustained their giving after the promotion. The other thirty-seven tellers declined rapidly in their giving. They were fakers: in the three months before the promotion, they knew they were being watched, so they went out of their way to help others. But after they got promoted, they reduced their giving by an average of 23 percent each.

What would it take to nudge people in the giving direction? When Harvard dean Thomas Dingman saw that Harvard students valued compassion but thought others didn't, he decided to do something about it. For the first time in the university's four centuries, Harvard freshmen were invited to sign a pledge to serve society. The pledge concluded: "As we begin at Harvard, we commit to upholding the values of the College and to making the entryway and Yard a place where all can thrive and where the exercise of kindness holds a place on a par with intellectual attainment."

Believing in the power of a public commitment, Dingman decided to go one step beyond inviting students to sign the pledge. To encourage students to follow through, their signatures would be framed in the hallways of campus dorms. A storm of objections quickly emerged, most notably from Harry Lewis, a computer science professor and the former dean of Harvard College. "An appeal for kindness is entirely appropriate," Lewis responded. "I agree that the exercise of personal kindness in this community is too often wanting," he wrote on his blog, but "for Harvard to 'invite' people to pledge to kindness is unwise, and sets a terrible precedent."

Is Lewis right?

In a series of experiments led by NYU psychologist Peter

Gollwitzer, people who went public with their intentions to engage in an identity-relevant behavior were significantly *less likely* to engage in the behavior than people who kept their intentions private. When people made their identity plans known to others, they were able to claim the identity without actually following through on the behavior. By signing the kindness pledge, Harvard students would be able to establish an image as givers without needing to act like givers.

Dingman quickly dropped the idea of posting signatures publicly. But even then, evidence suggests that privately signing a kindness pledge might backfire. In one experiment, Northwestern University psychologists randomly assigned people to write about themselves using either giver terms like *caring*, *generous*, and *kind* or neutral terms like *book*, *keys*, and *house*. After the participants filled out another questionnaire, a researcher asked them if they wanted to donate money to a charity of their choosing. Those who wrote about themselves as givers donated an average of two and a half times *less* money than those who wrote about themselves with neutral words. "I'm a giving person," they told themselves, "so I don't have to donate this time." The kindness pledge might have a similar effect on Harvard students. When they sign the pledge, they establish credentials as givers, which may grant them a psychological license to give less—or take more.

When we're trying to influence someone, we often adopt an approach that mirrors the Harvard pledge: we start by changing their attitudes, hoping that their behaviors are likely to march in the same direction. If we get people to sign a statement that they'll act like givers, they'll come to believe that giving is important, and then they'll give. But according to a rich body of psychological detective work, this reasoning is backward. Influence is far more powerful in the opposite direction: change people's behaviors first, and their attitudes often follow. To turn takers into givers, it's often necessary to convince them to start giving. Over time, if the conditions are right, they'll come to see themselves as givers.

This didn't happen to the bank tellers in China: even after three months of helping colleagues, once they got promoted, they stopped giving. Over the past thirty-five years, research launched by Batson and his colleagues shows that when people give, if they can attribute it to an external reason like a promotion, they don't start to think of themselves as givers. But when people repeatedly make the personal choice to give to others, they start to internalize giving as part of their identities. For some people, this happens through an active process of cognitive dissonance: once I've made the voluntary decision to give, I can't change the behavior, so the easiest way to stay consistent and avoid hypocrisy is to decide that I'm a giver. For other people, the internalization process is one of learning from observing their own behaviors. To paraphrase the writer E. M. Forster, "How do I know who I am until I see what I do?"

In support of this idea, studies of volunteering show that even when people join a volunteer organization to advance their own careers, the longer they serve and the more time they give, the more they begin to view the volunteering role as an important aspect of their identities. Once that happens, they start to experience a common identity with the people they're helping, and they become givers in that role. Research documents a similar process inside companies: as people make voluntary decisions to help colleagues and customers beyond the scope of their jobs, they come to see themselves as organizational citizens.*

---

* Interestingly, even though people of any reciprocity style can internalize a giving identity, there's still a difference between givers and takers. In one study at a *Fortune* 500 retail company with colleagues Jane Dutton and Brent Rosso, I found that when people gave to help coworkers, they were more likely to see themselves as helpful, generous, and caring people. This is the pattern that emerges for true givers: repeated acts of voluntary helping contribute to the

Part of the wisdom behind Freecycle and the Reciprocity Ring is that both of these generalized giving systems encourage giving while maintaining a sense of free choice. Although there's a strong norm of giving, it's entirely up to each participant to decide what to give and whom to help. When my Wharton class went through the Reciprocity Ring, as different students chose their own ways to give and peers to help, a distinctive common identity began to develop. "This is a unique group of people at Wharton that cares about each other," one student said. Although the students were competing for the same jobs in management consulting and investment banking, they started helping one another prepare for interviews, sharing tips and offering advice. After the class ended, a group of students took the initiative to start an alumni listserv so that they could continue helping one another. According to one student, "because of the emphasis on the benefit of giving and helping in our shared community, I'd be far more comfortable and likely to ask for (and probably receive) help from a random member of the alumni group than my other groups."

At the end of the semester, the cynical student who had questioned whether there were any givers at Wharton quietly approached me. "Somehow," he said, "everyone in the class became intrinsically motivated to give, and it transcends the class itself."

---

development of a giver identity in general. For takers, though, the giver identity that develops may not translate to other roles or organizations. They might become a giver on Freecycle, but when they join another organization, they shift back to taking until they internalize that organization's identity. As we saw earlier, the more the organization provides a sense of optimal distinctiveness, the faster that identification tends to occur.

9

Out of the Shadows

Some people, when they do someone a favor, are always looking for a chance
to call it in. And some aren't, but they're still aware of it—still regard it as
a debt. But others don't even do that. They're like a vine that produces
grapes without looking for anything in return . . . after helping others . . .
They just go on to something else . . . We should be like that.

—Marcus Aurelius, Roman emperor

A number of years ago, an imposing figure made his mark on the sports world. Well over six feet tall and two hundred pounds, Derek Sorenson was a tough, aggressive competitor who struck fear into the hearts of his opponents. He led his NCAA team to a national championship and went on to play in the pros. After his career was cut short by an injury, he was courted by the finest professional teams in his sport to become a contract negotiator. He would be wheeling and dealing with players and agents in the hopes of building a world-class team.

To sharpen his bargaining skills, Derek enrolled in a negotiation course at a leading business school. During each class session, he had the chance to practice negotiating in a variety of roles, ranging from a pharmaceutical executive trying to buy a manufacturing plant to a condo developer in a heated dispute with a carpenter. In one of his earliest negotiations, Derek bought a property as a real estate investment, and in top taker form, he persuaded the listing agent to sell at a price that went directly against her client's interests.

On an icy winter evening, Derek played the role of one of four fishermen who ran competing businesses. They were overfishing to the point that the resource would become extinct, and they sat down to discuss how they should handle the dilemma. One negotiator suggested that they should split the maximum total fishing in four equal parts. Another proposed a different way of matching based on equity rather than equality: since some of them were running larger operations than others, they should each reduce their fishing by 50 percent. They all agreed that this was a fair solution, and the meeting was adjourned. Now, it was up to each negotiator to make an individual decision about whether to honor the agreement and how much to fish.

Two of the negotiators stuck to their commitments, reducing their fishing by 50 percent. The third operated like a giver: she reduced her fishing by 65 percent. The group was all set to keep the resource intact, but Derek chose not to reduce his fishing at all. He took as much as he could, actually increasing his fishing total and decimating the other three entrepreneurs. Before the group met, Derek had the lowest profits of the four. After he took far more than his share of the harvest, his profits were 70 percent higher than the giver's and 31 percent higher than those of the other two. When confronted by his colleagues, Derek responded, "I wanted to win the negotiations and destroy my competitors."

Just a few months later, Derek began a meteoric rise in his career. He was hired by a professional sports team and established a reputation as a dominant negotiator, playing a key role in assembling a team that went on to win a world championship. Derek was promoted in an unusually short period of time and recognized as one of the one hundred most powerful people in his sport—while still in his thirties.

When Derek first started working for his team as a professional negotiator, his job was to manage the budget, identify top prospects, and negotiate contracts with agents to sign new players and keep existing players. Since resources were tight, bargaining like a taker would work to his advantage. Derek began to search for underrated talent, and stumbled upon a gem of a player in the minor leagues. He sat down with the player's agent to negotiate a contract. True to form, Derek made a lowball offer. The agent was frustrated: several comparable players were earning higher salaries. The agent accused Derek of pushing him around and demanded more money, but Derek ignored the demands and didn't budge. Eventually, the agent gave in and agreed to Derek's terms. It was a win for Derek, saving his team thousands of dollars.

But when Derek went home that night, he had an uneasy feeling. "I could just feel through the conversation that he was pretty upset. He brought up a couple points on comparable players, and in the heat of things, I probably wasn't listening too much. He was going away with a bad taste in his mouth." Derek decided he didn't want to end the exchange with the agent on a sour note. So he tore up the contract and met the agent's original request, giving him thousands of extra dollars for the player.

Was this a wise decision? Derek was costing his team money, and potentially creating a precedent for doing so in other negotiations. Besides, the deal was settled. The agent had agreed to the lowball offer and Derek had achieved his goal. Going back on it hardly seemed like a smart move.

Actually, it was much smarter than it first appeared. When Vanderbilt researchers Bruce Barry and Ray Friedman studied negotiations, they had a hunch that sharper negotiators would get better results, as they could gather and analyze more information, keep track of multiple issues, and generate hidden solutions. In one study, Barry and Friedman obtained data on the intelligence of nearly a hundred MBA students. They measured intelligence using each student's score on the GMAT, a rigorous test that is widely used in business school admissions to measure quantitative, verbal, and analytical abilities. The participants negotiated in pairs, playing either the developer of a new mall or the representative of a potential store to anchor the mall. After they finished negotiating, they submitted their final agreements, and two experts assessed the value of the deal to each party.

As expected, the joint gains were highest when both parties were very intelligent. Barry and Friedman broke down each party's gains, expecting to find that the smarter negotiators got better deals for themselves. But they didn't. The brightest negotiators got better deals *for their counterparts*.

"The smarter negotiator appears to be able to understand his or her opponents' true interests and thus to provide them with better deals at little cost to him- or herself," Barry and Friedman write. The more intelligent you are, the more you help your counterpart succeed. This is exactly what Derek did when he gave the agent more money for the minor league player. He was giving in an otherish way that was low cost to him but high benefit to the agent and the player. A few thousand dollars was small potatoes to his team, but very significant to the player.

What drove Derek to shift in the giver direction? Shortly before the negotiation with the agent, Derek had gained a window into something that mattered deeply to him: his reputation. At the end of the negotiation course, every participant submitted votes for negotiation awards. Derek received zero votes for Most Cooperative, zero for Most Creative, and zero for Most Ethical. In fact, there was only one award for which he received any votes. For this particular award, Derek received the vast majority of the votes. He was the landslide winner for Most Ruthless.

But Derek achieved something more memorable that week. He became the only student in business school history to be voted the

Most Ruthless negotiator *in a class that he never took*. At the same time that he was enrolled in his course, another negotiation class was under way. None of these students in the other class ever sat across the bargaining table from Derek. Some of them had never met him. Yet his reputation spread so quickly that they voted for him as Most Ruthless anyway.

Derek was negotiating the way any reasonable person would in a taker's world. As a professional athlete, he had learned that if he didn't claim as much value as possible, he was at risk for becoming a doormat. "It was the team against the player. The team was always trying to take money out of my pocket, so I viewed a negotiation to be a combative process, which produced a winner and a loser," Derek says. "I had to try to take more and more." After being anointed the Most Ruthless negotiator by his peers—and a group of strangers—Derek began to reflect on his reciprocity style at the bargaining table. "While I gained a short-term benefit by taking, in the long run I paid. My relationship with a colleague was ruined, and it caused the demise of my reputation," he said. In the negotiation with the agent, when he ripped up the contract and gave the agent more money, "It built goodwill. The agent was extremely appreciative," Derek reflects. "When the player came up for free agency, the agent gave me a call. Looking back on it now, I'm really glad I did it. It's definitely improved our relationship, and helped out our organization. Maybe Most Ruthless is maturing."

Actually, I believe maturing is the wrong way to describe Derek's transformation. Maturation implies a process of growth and development, but in a sense, Derek was actually taking a step backward to express core values that he had embraced for years away from the bargaining table. Long before he ever negotiated like a taker, his peers perceived him as a generous, helpful person who would make time for anyone who asked. He spent countless hours providing advice to colleagues who were interested in sports management careers and mentoring young athletes who aspired to follow in his footsteps. Growing up, he was elected captain of virtually every team on which he played, from elementary school through high school, all the way through college. He even became captain as a rookie on his first professional team—players twice his age respected his commitment to putting the team's interests ahead of his own.

At the bargaining table, Derek's transition wasn't about learning a new set of values. It was about developing the confidence and courage to express an old set of values in a new domain. I believe this is true for most people who operate like matchers professionally, and my hope is that others like Derek won't wait for a Most Ruthless award to start finding ways to act in the interest of others at work. For Derek these days, a signature form of giving is helping opposing teams gather information about players. Even though they're competing in a zero-sum sport, he shares knowledge to help rival teams make good decisions about players who have been on his team in the past. "On the field, I want to beat up opposing teams. But off the field, I'm always trying to help them out."

Today, Derek attributes his success in building a championship-winning professional sports team to his shift from taking toward giving. Yet he still worries about what will happen if people outside his inner circle find out about his shift in the giver direction. In fact, Derek Sorenson is a pseudonym: before sharing his story, he asked me to disguise his identity. "I don't want it to get out there that I've given more money than I needed to a player," he says.

These fears persist among many successful givers, but they're not insurmountable. Consider Sherryann Plesse, the financial services executive from the opening chapter who hid the fact that kindness and compassion emerged as her top strengths. When I originally asked her to tell her story, like Derek, she only agreed under the condition that she would remain anonymous. Six months later, she changed her mind. "I've started an underground campaign of givers coming out of the closet," she said. "Being a giver has contributed to my personal and professional success. It's liberating to talk about it. I'm not afraid anymore."

What changed her mind? When Sherryann first recognized her giver attributes, she was focused on the risks: people expected her to be tough and results-oriented, and might see giving as a sign of weakness. But when she started taking a close look around her company, she was struck by the realization that all of her professional role models were givers. Suddenly, her frame of reference shifted: instead of just seeing givers at the bottom, she recognized a surprising number of givers at the top. This isn't what we usually notice when we glance up at the horizon at successful people. By and large, because of their tendencies toward powerful speech and claiming credit, successful takers tend to dominate the spotlight. But if you start paying attention to reciprocity styles in your own workplace, I have a hunch that you'll discover plenty of givers achieving the success to which you aspire.

Personally, the successful people whom I admire most are givers, and I feel that it's my responsibility to try and pass along what I've learned from them. When I arrived at Wharton, my charge was to teach some of the world's finest analytic minds to become better leaders, managers, and negotiators. I decided to introduce them to reciprocity styles, posing the question that animated the introduction to this book: who do you think ends up at the bottom of the success ladder?

The verdict was nearly unanimous: givers. When I asked who rises to the top, the students were evenly split between matchers and takers. So I chose to teach them something that struck them as heretical. "You might be underestimating the success of givers," I told them. It's true that some people who consistently help others without expecting anything in return are the ones who fall to the bottom.

But this same orientation toward giving, with a few adjustments, can also enable people to rise to the top. "Focus attention and energy on making a difference in the lives of others, and success might follow as a by-product." I knew I was fighting an uphill battle, so I decided to prove them wrong.

This book is that proof.

Although many of us hold strong giver values, we're often reluctant to express them at work. But the growth of teamwork, service jobs, and social media has opened up new opportunities for givers to develop relationships and reputations that accelerate and amplify their success. We've covered evidence that givers can rise to the top across a stunningly diverse range of occupations, from engineering to medicine to sales. And remember when Peter Audet, the Australian financial adviser, seemed to be wasting hours of his time by driving out to help a poor scrap metal worker manage his money? The client turned out to be the wealthy owner of a scrap metal business, resulting in major gains for Peter's firm—but the story doesn't end there.

Peter learned that the scrap metal owner was too busy running the business to take a vacation, and he wanted to help. A few months later, another client expressed that she wasn't happy in her job as a manager at an auto body shop. Peter recommended her to the scrap metal owner, who had a need for her skills, and it turned out that she lived five minutes away from the scrap metal yard. She started work three weeks later, and the client took his wife on their first vacation in years. "Both of these clients are happy and grateful that I think about their whole lives, not just their investments," Peter says. "The more I help out, the more successful I become. But I measure success in what it has done for the people around me. That is the real accolade."

In the mind of a giver, the definition of success itself takes on a distinctive meaning. Whereas takers view success as attaining results that are superior to others' and matchers see success in terms of balancing individual accomplishments with fairness to others, givers are inclined to follow Peter's lead, characterizing success as individual achievements that have a positive impact on others. They see success in terms of making significant, lasting contributions to a broad range of people. Taking this definition of success seriously might require dramatic changes in the way that organizations hire, evaluate, reward, and promote people. It would mean paying attention not only to the productivity of individual people but also to the ripple effects of this productivity on others. If we broadened our image of success to include contributions to others along with individual accomplishments, people might be motivated to tilt their professional reciprocity styles toward giving. If success required benefiting others, it's possible that takers and matchers would be more inclined to find otherish ways to advance personal and collective interests simultaneously.

The connection between individual and collective success underlies every story of successful givers in this book. As an entrepreneur, Adam Rifkin built his network of influential people by trying to help everyone he met, launching successful companies and enabling thousands of colleagues to find jobs, develop skills, and start productive businesses along the way. As a venture capitalist, David Hornik invested in lucrative companies and fortified his reputation by helping aspiring entrepreneurs create better pitches and gain funding for their start-ups. As a comedy writer, George Meyer earned Emmys and established a reputation as the funniest writer in Hollywood while elevating the effectiveness of and opening doors for the people who collaborated with him on *Army Man* and *The Simpsons*.

In the classroom, C. J. Skender earned dozens of teaching awards while inspiring a new generation of students, seeing their potential and motivating them to achieve this potential, and Conrey Callahan sustained her energy and was nominated for a national teaching award after she started a nonprofit to help underprivileged children prepare for college. In health care, Kildare Escoto and Nancy Phelps rose to the top of their company's sales revenue charts by striving to help patients. In consulting, Jason Geller and Lillian Bauer made partner early by virtue of the contributions that they made through mentoring and developing others, which in turn enriched the knowledge of junior colleagues. In politics, Abraham Lincoln became president—and built a legacy as one of the greatest leaders in world history—by helping his rivals earn coveted political positions.

This is what I find most magnetic about successful givers: they get to the top without cutting others down, finding ways of expanding the pie that benefit themselves and the people around them. Whereas success is zero-sum in a group of takers, in groups of givers, it may be true that the whole is greater than the sum of the parts. As Simon Sinek writes, "Givers advance the world. Takers advance themselves and hold the world back."

Armed with this knowledge, I've seen some people become more strategic matchers, helping others in the hopes of developing the relationships and reputations necessary to advance their own success. Can people succeed through instrumental giving, where the primary intent is getting? At the beginning of the book, I suggested that in the long term, the answer might be no.

There's a fine line between giving and clever matching, and this line blurs depending on whether we define reciprocity styles by the actions themselves, the motives behind them, or some combination of the two. It's a deep philosophical question, and it's easy to identify with a range of views on how strategic matchers should be evaluated. On the one hand, even if the motives are mixed, helping behaviors often add value to others, increasing the total amount of giving in a social system. On the other hand, as we saw with Ken Lay, our behaviors leak traces of our motives. If recipients and witnesses of our giving begin to question whether the motives are self-serving, they're less likely to respond with gratitude or elevation. When strategic matchers engage in disingenuous efforts to help others primarily for personal gain, they may be hoisted by their own petard: fellow matchers may withhold help, spread negative reputational information, or find other ways to impose a taker tax.

To avoid these consequences, would-be matchers may be best served by giving in ways that they find enjoyable, to recipients whose well-being matters to them. That way, even if they don't reap direct or karmic rewards, matchers will be operating in a giver's mind-set, leading their motives to appear—and become—more pure. Ultimately, by repeatedly making the choice to act in the interest of others, strategic matchers may find themselves developing giver identities, resulting in a gradual drift in style toward the giving end of the reciprocity spectrum.

We spend the majority of our waking hours at work. This means that what we do at work becomes a fundamental part of who we are. If we reserve giver values for our personal lives, what will be missing in our professional lives? By shifting ever so slightly in the giver direction, we might find our waking hours marked by greater success, richer meaning, and more lasting impact.

ACTIONS FOR IMPACT

If you're interested in applying the principles in this book to your work or your life, I've compiled a set of practical actions that you can take. Many of these actions are based on the strategies and habits of successful givers, and in each case, I've provided resources and tools for evaluating, organizing, or expanding giving. Some of the steps focus on incorporating more giving into your daily behaviors; others emphasize ways that you can fine-tune your giving, locate fellow givers, or engage others in giving.

1. *Test Your Giver Quotient*. We often live in a feedback vacuum, deprived of knowledge about how our actions affect others. So that you can track your impact and assess your self-awareness, I've designed a series of free online tools. Visit www.giveandtake.com to take a free survey that tests your giver quotient. Along with filling out your own survey, you can invite people in your network to rate your reciprocity style, and you'll receive data on how often you're seen as a giver, taker, and matcher.

2. *Run a Reciprocity Ring*. What could be achieved in your organization—and what giving norms would develop—if groups of people got together weekly for twenty minutes to make requests and help one another fulfill them? For more information on how to start a Reciprocity Ring in your organization, visit Cheryl and Wayne Baker's company, Humax (www.humaxnetworks.com), which offers a suite of social networking tools for individuals and organizations. They've created materials to run a Reciprocity Ring in person and a Ripplleffect tool for running it online. People typically come together

in groups of fifteen to thirty. Each person presents a request to the group members, who make contributions: they use their knowledge, resources, and connections to help fulfill the request.

3. *Help Other People Craft Their Jobs—or Craft Yours to Incorporate More Giving.* People often end up working on tasks that aren't perfectly aligned with their interests and skills. A powerful way to give is to help others work on tasks that are more interesting, meaningful, or developmental. In 2011, a vice president named Jay at a large multinational retailer sent e-mails to each of his employees announcing a top-secret mission, with details to be shared on a need-to-know basis in one-on-one meetings. When employees arrived individually for the meetings, Jay unveiled the confidential project. He asked them what they would enjoy doing that might also be of interest to other people. He inquired about their hobbies and personal interests, and what they would love to spend more time doing at the company. He then sent them out into the company to pursue their mission with three rules: it has to (1) appeal to at least one other person, (2) be low or no cost, and (3) be initiated by you.

Throughout the year, Jay checked in to see how the secret missions were going. About two thirds of his employees had made some effort toward making their visions a reality, and roughly half of those employees succeeded in launching them. One of Jay's favorite missions resulted in a book club where employees read books and discussed topics that were of personal interest and relevance to their jobs. "People had permission to do all of that stuff before I ever asked that question," Jay reflects. "But somehow, asking that question in my role gives people permission to pursue their interests in a way they didn't have before. It's planting seeds, with some percentage of them turning into real initiatives." These seeds have bloomed for many of his employees, and for Jay as well: in 2012, he was selected to become the vice president of HR for a major division of his company, where he's responsible for more than 45,000 employees.

In the secret missions, Jay encouraged his employees to engage in job crafting, a concept introduced by Amy Wrzesniewski and Jane Dutton, management professors at Yale and the University of Michigan, respectively. Job crafting involves innovating around a job description, creatively adding and customizing tasks and responsibilities to match personal interests and values. A natural concern is that people might craft their jobs in ways that fail to contribute to their organizations. To address this question, Amy, Justin Berg, and I partnered with Jennifer Kurkoski and Brian Welle, who run a people and innovation lab at Google. In a study across the United States and Europe, we randomly assigned Google employees working in sales, finance, operations, accounting, marketing, and human resources to a job-crafting workshop. The employees created a map of how they'd like to modify their tasks, crafting a more ideal but still realistic vision of their jobs that aligned with their interests and values.

Six weeks later, their managers and coworkers rated them as significantly happier *and* more effective. Many Google employees found ways to spend more time on tasks that they found interesting or meaningful; some delegated unpleasant tasks; and others were able to customize their jobs to incorporate new knowledge and skills that they wanted to develop. All told, Google employees found their work more enjoyable and were motivated to perform better, and in some cases, these gains lasted for six months. Job crafting worked across reciprocity styles: givers, takers, and matchers all became more effective. The givers saw job crafting as an opportunity to expand their impact, so they generated ways to add more value to other people and the company, such as mentoring junior colleagues, creating better products for clients, and improving training for new hires. The matchers were grateful for the opportunity to pursue more meaningful and interesting work, and reciprocated by working harder. Even the takers recognized that to advance their own careers, they needed to craft their jobs in ways that would benefit the company as well as themselves.

To help people craft their jobs, Justin, Amy, and Jane have developed a tool called the Job Crafting Exercise. It's what we used to conduct the Google workshops, and it involves creating a "before sketch" of how you currently allocate your time and energy, and then developing a visual "after diagram" of how you'd like to modify your job. The booklets can be ordered online (www.jobcrafting.org) and completed in teams or individually to help friends and colleagues make meaningful modifications to their jobs.

4. *Start a Love Machine.* In many organizations, givers go unrecognized. To combat this problem, organizations are introducing peer recognition programs to reward people for giving in ways that leaders and managers rarely see. A Mercer study found that in 2001, about 25 percent of large companies had peer recognition programs, and by 2006, this number had grown to 35 percent—including celebrated companies like Google, Southwest Airlines, and Zappos.

A fascinating approach called the Love Machine was developed at Linden Lab, the company behind the virtual world Second Life. In a high-technology company, many employees aim to protect their time for themselves and guard information closely, instead of sharing their time and knowledge with colleagues. The Love Machine was designed to overcome this tendency by enabling employees to send a Love message when they appreciated help from a colleague. The Love messages were visible to others, rewarding and recognizing giving by linking it to status and reputations. One insider viewed it as a way to get "tech geeks to compete to see who could be the most helpful." Love helped to "boost awareness of people who did tasks that were sometimes overlooked. Our support staff, for instance, often received the most Love," says Chris Colosi, a former Linden manager. "Once you introduce a certain percentage of takers into your system, you need to think about what effect an incentive will have, but I enjoyed the idea of Love for tasks that were outside of someone's job description or requirements."

To try out the Love Machine in your organization, look up a new electronic tool called SendLove. It's available from LoveMachine (www.lovemachineinc.com), a new start-up that asks you to start by choosing a recognition period. Team members can send each other short messages recognizing giving, and the messages are all publicly visible.

5. *Embrace the Five-Minute Favor.* If you visit a 106 Miles Meetup (www.meetup.com/106miles), you might see Panda Adam Rifkin in top form. He's a master of the five-minute favor, and you can follow Panda's lead by asking people what they need and looking for ways to help at a minimal personal cost. Rifkin's two favorite offers are to give honest feedback and make an introduction. For example, here's a simple exercise to get started as a connector. Start by going through your Rolodex, LinkedIn, or Facebook network. Identify pairs of people who share an uncommon commonality. Then, pick one pair a week and introduce them by e-mail. To gather feedback on the quality of your introductions and make them more powerful, visit https://intros.to, an excellent resource created by givers Robyn Scott and Alex Lovell-Troy. Rifkin also recommends reconnecting with dormant ties—not to get something, but to give. Once a month, reach out to one person with whom you haven't spoken in years. Find out what they're working on and ask if there are ways that you can be helpful. On a related note, you can learn more about David Hornik's approach to giving by visiting Venture Blog (www.venture-blog.com/).

6. *Practice Powerless Communication, but Become an Advocate.* Developing greater comfort and skill with powerless communication requires a change in habits—from talking to listening, self-promoting to advice-seeking, and advocating to inquiring. Jim Quigley, a senior partner at Deloitte who previously served as CEO, decided

to work on his powerless communication. He set a goal in meetings to talk no more than 20 percent of the time. "One of my objectives is listening. Many times, you can have bigger impact if you know what to ask, rather than knowing what to say. I don't learn anything when I'm speaking. I learn a lot when I'm listening," Quigley told me. As he shifted from answers toward questions, Quigley found himself gaining a deeper understanding of other people's needs. "It doesn't come naturally to everyone, but it's a habit, and you can form that habit." For more on the power of powerless communication, visit the blogs by Susan Cain (www.thepowerofintroverts.com) and Jennifer Kahnweiler (www.theintrovertedleaderblog.com).

At the same time, it's important to make sure that powerless communication doesn't come at the expense of assertiveness when advocating for others' interests and our own. GetRaised is a free resource that offers advice on negotiating salary increases. According to cofounder Matt Wallaert, the average pay increase is $6,726, provided that you're underpaid. About half of male users succeed in getting a raise—compared with three quarters of female users (https://getraised.com).

7. *Join a Community of Givers*. To find other givers, join a Freecycle community to give away goods and see what other people need (www.freecycle.org). Another inspiring community of givers is ServiceSpace (www.servicespace.org), the home of a series of Giftivism initiatives started by Nipun Mehta. Headquartered in Berkeley, California, ServiceSpace has over 400,000 members and sends over fifty million e-mails a year. Yet they still operate by three rules: "no staff, no fundraising, and no strings attached." Through ServiceSpace, Nipun has created a platform for people to increase their giver quotients, divided into three categories: gift economy projects, inspirational content, and volunteer and nonprofit support. One of the gift economy projects is Karma Kitchen, where the menu has no prices. When the bill arrives, it reads $0.00 and contains just

two sentences: "Your meal was a gift from someone who came before you. To keep the chain of gifts alive, we invite you to pay it forward for those who dine after you." Another gift economy project is HelpOthers.org, which collects stories of people playing giver tag: do something anonymously for someone else, and leave a smile card inviting them to pay it forward.

Nipun describes how one woman at a *Fortune* 500 company went to get a drink from the vending machine, and put extra change in with a note: "Your drink has been paid for by someone you don't know. Spread the love." Then, she brought in doughnuts and left another smile card behind. "A guy noticed this trend, and he decides to send an e-mail to the whole building," Nipun says, laughing. "The guy writes, 'I've been trying to track them down for a long time, and I think it's between floors two and three.' Now everybody's on alert for kindness, and a bunch of people start doing it." On the Service-Space website, you can order smile cards, help support nonprofit causes, subscribe to the weekly newsletter, or read a thought-provoking list of ways to give, such as paying the toll for the person behind you or thanking people for helping you by writing a complimentary note to their boss. "The more you give, the more you want to do it—as do others around you. It's like going to the gym," Nipun says. "If you've been working out your kindness muscles, you get stronger at it."

Another impressive initiative is HopeMob, billed as the place "where generous strangers unite to bring immediate hope to people with pressing needs all over the world" (http://hopemob.org). For ideas about how to organize your own group of people to perform random acts of kindness, see the initiatives under way at Extreme Kindness in Canada (http://extremekindness.com) and The Kindness Offensive in the UK (http://thekindnessoffensive.com). The Kindness Offensive is a group of people who strive to be aggressively helpful, organizing some of the grandest random acts of kindness in human history. They've provided a toy for every child in a hospital in London, given away half a million pancakes, distributed tons of give-aways at festivals around Britain, provided free medical supplies and housing support to families in need and hosted tea parties for elderly people, obtained an electric guitar for a ten-year-old boy, and landed free front-row seats and behind-the-scenes training at the Moscow Circus for a father hoping to surprise his daughter. It may be no coincidence that the founder's name is David Goodfellow.

You might also be intrigued by BNI (www.bni.com), Ivan Misner's business networking organization with the motto of "Givers gain," as well as the Go-Giver Community (www.thegogiver.com/community)—a group of people who read *The Go-Giver* fable by Bob Burg and John David Mann, and decided that giving would be a powerful way to live their professional lives.

8. *Launch a Personal Generosity Experiment.* If you'd rather give on your own, try the GOOD thirty-day challenge (www.good.is/post/the-good-30-day-challenge-become-a-good-citizen). Each day for a month, GOOD suggests a different way to give. For more examples of random acts of kindness, check out Sasha Dichter's thirty-day generosity experiment (http://sashadichter.wordpress.com) and Ryan Garcia's year of daily random acts of kindness (www.366randomacts.org). Dichter, the chief innovation officer at the Acumen Fund, embarked on a monthlong generosity experiment in which he said yes to every request for help that he received. Garcia, a sales executive at ZocDoc, is performing one random act of kindness every day for an entire year and keeping a blog about his experience, from stepping up as a mentor to thanking a customer service representative. As we saw in chapter 6, this generosity experiment is likely to be most psychologically rewarding if you spend somewhere between two and eleven hours a week on it, and if you distribute it into larger chunks—multiple acts once a week, instead of one act every day.

9. *Help Fund a Project.* Many people are seeking financial support

for their projects. On Kickstarter (www.kickstarter.com), known as the world's largest funding platform for creative projects, you can find people looking for help in designing and launching movies, books, video games, music, plays, paintings, and other products and services. On Kiva (www.kiva.org), you can identify opportunities to make microloans of $25 or more to entrepreneurs in the developing world. Both sites give you the chance to see and follow the progress of the people you help.

10. *Seek Help More Often.* If you want other people to be givers, one of the easiest steps is to ask. When you ask for help, you're not always imposing a burden. Some people are givers, and by asking for help, you're creating an opportunity for them to express their values and feel valued. By asking for a five-minute favor, you impose a relatively small burden—and if you ask a matcher, you can count on having an opportunity to reciprocate. Wayne and Cheryl Baker note that people can "Start the spark of reciprocity by making requests as well as helping others. Help generously and without thought of return; but also ask often for what you need."

ACKNOWLEDGMENTS

The seeds for this book were planted by my grandparents, Florence and Paul Borock, who tirelessly invested their time and energy in others without expecting anything in return. Growing up, my curiosity about psychology and fascination with the quality of work life were sparked by my parents, Susan and Mark. My diving coach, Eric Best, showed me that psychology was a major force behind success, introduced me to the power of giving in developing others, and encouraged me to pursue a career that combined psychology and writing. I found that career thanks to Brian Little, whose wisdom and generosity changed the course of my life. Brian embodies the very best of the human condition, and it is due to his depth of knowledge, commitment to students, and ability to captivate an audience that I became a professor. As I began to study organizational psychology, I benefited tremendously from the mentoring of Jane Dutton, Sue Ashford, Richard Hackman, Ellen Langer, and Rick Price. In particular, Jane has challenged me to think more deeply and encouraged me to reach more broadly in striving to do research that makes a difference.

They say it takes an army to write a book, and mine was no exception: I felt very lucky to work with an army of givers whose fingerprints grace each page. Leading the charge was Richard Pine at InkWell, who exemplifies every quality that an author could possibly want in an agent. Richard has a true gift for seeing the potential in ideas and people, and is uniquely skilled and passionate in connecting them in powerful ways that use the written word to make the world a better place. From helping me find my voice in writing for a popular audience and championing the topic, to offering keen insights about the substance and identifying successful givers in our midst, Richard has had an indelible impact on this book and my life.

The other major creative force behind this book was editor extraordinaire Kevin Doughten. Among his many contributions, it is noteworthy that it was Kevin who put George Meyer on my radar and recognized that a unique feature of giver success lies in lifting others up. Kevin knows from personal experience, as this is the influence of his success on his authors. His perceptive, comprehensive feedback sharpened the structure, strengthened the arguments, and enriched the stories and studies—and motivated me to rewrite three chapters from scratch. Along with shaping every sentence in the book, Kevin's guidance has fundamentally altered the way that I approach writing more generally.

At Viking, Rick Kot has gone far above and beyond the call of duty in offering his ingenuity, discerning eye, social capital, and stewardship. I feel fortunate to benefit from his support and the editorial, publicity, and marketing contributions of Catherine Boyd, Nick Bromley, Peter Chatzky, Risa Chubinsky, Carolyn Coleburn, Winnie De Moya, Andrew Duncan, Clare Ferraro, Alexis Hurley, Whitney Peeling, Lindsay Prevette, Britney Ross, Jeff Schell, Nancy Sheppard, Michael Sigle, Dennis Swaim, and Jeannette Williams, and the givers at Napa Group, LLC.

When I first contemplated the possibility of writing this book, many colleagues provided sage advice. I am especially grateful to Jennifer Aaker, Teresa Amabile, Dan Ariely, Susan Cain, Noah Goldstein, Barry Schwartz, Marty Seligman, Richard Shell, Bob Sutton, and Dan Pink—who not only shared invaluable insights, but also came up with the title. The idea for the book itself was inspired by a discussion with Jeff Zaslow and brought to life through dialogue with Justin Berg, whose vision and expertise immensely improved the form and function.

For discerning feedback on drafts, I thank Andy Bernstein, Ann Dang, Katherine Dean, Gabe Farkas, Alex Fishman, Alyssa Gelkopf, Kelsey Hilbrich, Katie Imielska, Mansi Jain, Valentino Kim, Phil Levine, Patrice Lin, Nick LoBuglio, Michelle Lu, Sara Luchian, Lindsay Miller, Starry Peng, Andrew Roberts, Danielle Rode, Suruchi Srikanth, Joe Tennant, Ryan Villanueva, Guy Viner, Becky Wald, Teresa Wang, Catherine Wei, and Tommy Yin. For leads on stories and connections to interviewees, I sincerely appreciate the help of Cameron Anderson, Dane Barnes, Renee Bell, Tal Ben-Shahar, Jesse Beyroutey, Grace Chen, Chris Colosi, Angela Duckworth, Bill Fisse, Juliet Geldi, Tom Gerrity, Leah Haimson, Dave Heckman, Dara Kritzer, Adam Lashinsky, Laurence Lemaire, Matt Maroone, Cade Massey, Dave Mazza, Chris Myers, Meredith Myers, Jean Oelwang, Bob Post, Jon Rifkind, Gavin Riggall, Claire Robertson-Kraft, Scott Rosner, Bobbi Silten, Matt Stevens, Brandon Stuut, Jeff Thompson, Mike Useem, Jerry Wind, Amy Wrzesniewski, George Zeng, and the extraordinary anonymous givers at Riley Productions (www.rileyprods.com).

For sharing their wisdom, knowledge, and experiences in interviews, along with the people quoted in the book, I thank Antoine Andrews, Peter Avis, Bernie Banks, Colleen Barrett, Margaux Bergen, Bob Brooks, Rano Burkhanova, Jim Canales, Virginia Canino, Bob Capers, Brian Chu, Bob Coghlan, Matt Conti, Mario DiTrapani, Atul Dubey, Nicole DuPre, Marc Elliott, Scilla Elworthy, Mark Fallon, Mike Feinberg, Christy Flanagan, Mike Fossaceca, Anna Gauthier, Jeremy Gilley, Kathy Gubanich, Michelle Gyles-McDonnough, Kristen Holden, Beak Howell, Tom Jeary, Diane and Paul Jones, Rick Jones, Melanie Katzman, Colin Kelton, Richard Lack, Larry Lavery, Eric Lipton, Theresa Loth, Nic Lumpp, Dan Lyons, Sergio Magistri, Susan Mathews, Tim McConnell, David McMullen, Debby McWhinney, Rick Miller, Roy Neff, Randi

Nielsen, Scott O'Neil, Jenna Osborne, Charles Pensig, Bob Post, Larry Powell, Kate Richey, Manfred Rietsch, Jon Rifkind, Larry Roberts, Clare Sanderson, Rebecca Schreuder, Bill Sherman, Scott Sherman, John Simon, Ron Skotarczak, Marijn Spillebeen, David Stewart, Craig Stock, Suzanne Sutter, Pat Sweeney, Vivek Tiwary, Vickie Tolliver, Ashley Valentine, Tony Wells, Matthew Wilkins, Yair Yoram, Jochen Zeitz, and Fatima Zorzato.

Rachel Carpenter and Erica Connelly provided a wealth of innovative ideas for spreading the word about this book, and organized a productive ideation session in which Alison Bloom-Feshbach, Zoe Epstein, Sean Griffin, Adria Hou, Katherine Howell, Ian Martinez, Scott McNulty, Annie Meyer, and Becky Wald were kind enough to participate and contribute. For spending a week keeping giver journals, I appreciate the help of Josh Berman, Charles Birnbaum, Adam Compain, Keenan Cottone, Ben Francois, Jean Lee, Josh Lipman, Charlie Mercer, Phil Neff, Mary Pettit, Matt Pohlson, Kiley Robbins, Chris Sergeant, Kara Shamy, Charlene Su, and Nina Varghese.

Many other friends, colleagues, students, and family members helped to brainstorm about the framing and content of the book, including Sam Abzug, David Adelman, Bob Adler, Sebastian Aguilar, Tanner Almond, Michael Althoff, Dan Baker, Rangel Barbosa, Dominique Basile, Deepa Bhat, Bill Boroughf, Andrew Brodsky, Anita Butani, Lewis Chung, Constantinos Coutifaris, Cody Dashiell-Earp, Kathryn Dekas, Alex Edmans, Mehdi El Hajoui, Mark Elliott, Jerrod Engelberg, Dafna Eylon, Jackie Fleishman, Michelle Gaster, Christina Gilyutin, Guiherme Giserman, Ross Glasser, Matt Goracy, Brett Lavery Gregorka, Dan Gruber, Sheynna Hakim, Howard Heevner, Greg Hennessy, Dave Hofmann, Victoria Holekamp, Rick Horgan, John Hsu, David Jaffe, Amanda Jefferson, Nechemya Kagedan, Melissa Kamin, Jonathan Karmel, Ely Key, Jeff Kiderman, Anu Kohli, Ben Krutzinna, Amin Lakhani, Chester Lee, Amanda Liberatore, Nicole Lim, Lindsey Mathews Padrino, Amy Matsuno, Lauren Miller, Zach

Miller, Josephine Mogelof, Lauren Moloney-Egnatios, David Moltz, Brian Nemiroff, Celeste Ng, Dan Oppedisano, Matt Pohlson, Georges Potworowski, Derrick Preston, Vyas Ramanan, David Rider, David Roberts, Jeremy Rosner, Juan Pablo Saldarriaga, Frances Schendle, Christine Schmidt, Margot Lee Schmorak, Ari Shwayder, Kurt Smith, Scott Sonenshein, Mike Taormina, Palmer Truelson, Jonathan Tugman, Eric Tulla, Mike Van Pelt, Jamie Wallis, Michael Wolf, Rani Yadav, Lauren Yaffe, Andrew Yahkind, and Ashley Yuki.

For their encouragement over the years, I thank Traci; Florie; my grandparents Marion and Jay Grant; my in-laws, Adrienne and Neal Sweet; and the Impact Lab. Most of all, I could not have written this book without the support of my wife, Allison. She has devoted countless hours to brainstorming, reading, discussing, and searching, and words cannot describe how much her love means to me. Every time I sat down to write, I drew on the example she sets. When it comes to giving in the family domain, she is the ultimate role model. Our children, Joanna, Elena, and Henry, are the greatest sources of joy and meaning in my life. I am incredibly proud of them, and I hope this book will offer their generation a new perspective on what it means to succeed.

REFERENCES

Chapter 1: Good Returns

1 **Opening quote:** Samuel L. Clemens (aka Mark Twain), "At the Dinner to Joseph H. Choate, November 16, 1901," in *Speeches at the Lotos Club*, ed. J. Elderkin, C. S. Lord, and H. N. Fraser (New York: Lotos Club, 1911), 38.

1 **Story of David Hornik and Danny Shader:** Personal interviews with David Hornik (January 30 and March 12, 2012) and Danny Shader (February 13, 2012).

4 **preferences for reciprocity:** Edward W. Miles, John D. Hatfield, and Richard C. Huseman, "The Equity Sensitivity Construct: Potential Implications for Worker Performance," *Journal of Management* 15 (1989): 581–588.

6 **most people act like givers in close relationships:** Margaret S. Clark and Judson Mills, "The Difference between Communal and Exchange Relationships: What It Is and Is Not," *Personality and Social Psychology Bulletin* 19 (1993): 684–691.

6n **people engage in a mix of giving, taking, and matching:** Alan P. Fiske, *Structures of Social Life: The Four Elementary Forms of Human Relations* (New York: Free Press, 1991).

7 **world of engineering:** Francis J. Flynn, "How Much Should I Give and How Often? The Effects of Generosity and Frequency of Favor Exchange on Social Status and Productivity," *Academy of Management Journal* 46 (2003): 539–553.

7 **medical students in Belgium:** Filip Lievens, Deniz S. Ones, and Stephan Dilchert, "Personality Scale Validities Increase Throughout Medical School," *Journal of Applied Psychology* 94 (2009): 1514–1535.

7 **salespeople in North Carolina:** Adam M. Grant and Dane Barnes, "Predicting Sales Revenue" (working paper, 2011).

8 **givers earn 14 percent less money:** Timothy A. Judge, Beth A. Livingston, and Charlice Hurst, "Do Nice Guys—and Gals—Really Finish Last? The Joint Effects of Sex and Agreeableness on Income," *Journal of Personality and Social Psychology* 102 (2012): 390–407.

8 **twice the risk of becoming victims of crimes:** Robert J. Homant, "Risky Altruism as a Predictor of Criminal Victimization," *Criminal Justice and Behavior* 37 (2010): 1195–1216.

8 **judged as 22 percent less powerful and dominant:** Nir Halevy, Eileen Y. Chou, Taya R. Cohen, and Robert W. Livingston, "Status Conferral in Intergroup Social Dilemmas: Behavioral Antecedents and Consequences of Prestige and Dominance," *Journal of Personality and Social Psychology* 102 (2012): 351–366.

11 **envy successful takers:** Eugene Kim and Theresa M. Glomb, "Get Smarty Pants: Cognitive Ability, Personality, and Victimization," *Journal of Applied Psychology* 95 (2010): 889–901.

12 **"It's easier to win":** Personal interview with Randy Komisar (March 30, 2012).

12 **"Politics":** Bill Clinton, *Giving: How Each of Us Can Change the World* (New York: Random House, 2007), ix.

12 **My account of Abraham Lincoln's rise is based primarily on the riveting book by Doris Kearns Goodwin,** *Team of Rivals: The Political Genius of Abraham Lincoln* (New York: Simon & Schuster, 2006).

16 **more popular than any other politician:** Max J. Skidmore, *Presidential Performance: A Comprehensive Review* (Jefferson, NC: McFarland & Co., 2004).

16 **experts in history, political science, and psychology rated the presidents:** Steven J. Rubenzer and Thomas R. Faschingbauer, *Personality, Character, and Leadership in the White House: Psychologists Assess the Presidents* (Dulles, VA: Brassey's, 2004), 223.

18 **"valuable in a marathon":** Personal interview with Chip Conley (February 24, 2012).

18 **"no longer have to choose":** Personal interview with Bobbi Silten (February 9, 2012).

18 **companies regularly use teams:** Paul Osterman, "Work Reorganization in an Era of Restructuring: Trends in Diffusion and Effects on Employee Welfare," *Industrial and Labor Relations Review* 53 (2000): 179–196; and Duncan Gallie, Ying Zhou, Alan Felstead, and Francis

Green, "Teamwork, Skill Development and Employee Welfare," *British Journal of Industrial Relations* 50 (2012): 23–46.

19 **service sector continues to expand:** Adam M. Grant and Sharon K. Parker, "Redesigning Work Design Theories: The Rise of Relational and Proactive Perspectives," *Academy of Management Annals* 3 (2009): 317–375.

21 **financial advisers:** Personal interviews with Steve Jones (July 13, 2011) and Peter Audet (December 12, 2011 and January 19, 2012).

23 **One of his studies:** Shalom H. Schwartz and Anat Bardi, "Value Hierarchies across Cultures: Taking a Similarities Perspective," *Journal of Cross-Cultural Psychology* 32 (2001): 268–290.

25 **afraid to admit it:** Personal interview with Sherryann Plesse (October 21, 2011).

26 **pressured to lean in the taker direction:** Dale T. Miller, "The Norm of Self-Interest," *American Psychologist* 54 (1999): 1053–1060.

26 **putting on a business suit:** see Jeffrey Sanchez-Burks, "Protestant Relational Ideology: The Cognitive Underpinnings and Organizational Implications of an American Anomaly," *Research in Organizational Behavior* 26 (2005): 267–308; and "Protestant Relational Ideology and (In)Attention to Relational Cues in Work Settings," *Journal of Personality and Social Psychology* 83 (2002): 919–929.

26 **fear of exploitation by takers:** Robert H. Frank, *Passions Within Reason: The Strategic Role of the Emotions* (New York: W. W. Norton, 1988), xi.

Chapter 2: The Peacock and the Panda

31 **Opening quote:** Coretta Scott King, *The Words of Martin Luther King, Jr.* (New York: Newmarket Press, 2008), 17.

32 **Enron:** Bethany McLean and Peter Elkind, *The Smartest Guys in the Room: The Amazing Rise and Scandalous Fall of Enron* (New York: Portfolio, 2004); Mimi Swartz and Sherron Watkins, *Power Failure: The Inside Story of the Collapse of Enron* (New York: Crown, 2004); and Judy Keen, "Bush, Lay Kept Emotional Distance," *USA Today*, February 26, 2002.

34 **networks come with three major advantages:** Brian Uzzi and Shannon Dunlap, "How to Build Your Network," *Harvard Business*

Review December (2005): 53–60; and Ronald Burt, *Structural Holes: The Social Structure of Competition* (Cambridge, MA: Harvard University Press, 1995).

36 **LinkedIn founder:** Reid Hoffman, "Connections with Integrity," *strategy+business*, May 29, 2012.

37 **"kissing up, kicking down":** Roos Vonk, "The Slime Effect: Suspicion and Dislike of Likable Behavior Towards Superiors," *Journal of Personality and Social Psychology* 74 (1998): 849–864.

37 **glowing first impressions of takers:** Mitja D. Back, Stefan C. Schmukle, and Boris Egloff, "Why Are Narcissists So Charming at First Sight? Decoding the Narcissism-Popularity Link at Zero Acquaintance," *Journal of Personality and Social Psychology* 98 (2010): 132–145.

37 **feel entitled to pursue self-serving goals:** Serena Chen, Annette Y. Lee-Chai, and John A. Bargh, "Relationship Orientation as a Moderator of the Effects of Social Power," *Journal of Personality and Social Psychology* 80 (2001): 173–187; and Katherine A. DeCelles, D. Scott DeRue, Joshua D. Margolis, and Tara L. Ceranic, "Does Power Corrupt or Enable? When and Why Power Facilitates Self-Interested Behavior," *Journal of Applied Psychology* 97 (2012): 681–689.

38n **ultimatum games:** Daniel Kahneman, Jack L. Knetsch, and Richard H. Thaler, "Fairness and the Assumptions of Economics," *Journal of Business* 59 (1986): S285–S300.

38 **"karma police":** Gretchen Rubin, "Giving Deserved Praise," *Psychology Today*, May 15, 2012, accessed April 11, 2013, www.psychologytoday.com/blog/the-happiness-project/201205/giving-deserved-praise.

39 **sharing reputational information:** Matthew Feinberg, Joey Cheng, and Robb Willer, "Gossip as an Effective and Low-Cost Form of Punishment," *Behavioral and Brain Sciences* 35 (2012): 25; and Matthew Feinberg, Robb Willer, Jennifer Stellar, and Dacher Keltner, "The Virtues of Gossip: Reputational Information Sharing as Prosocial Behavior," *Journal of Personality and Social Psychology* 102 (2012): 1015–1030.

39 **"can't pursue the benefits of networks":** Wayne E. Baker, *Achieving Success Through Social Capital: Tapping Hidden Resources in Your Personal and Business Networks* (San Francisco: Jossey-Bass, 2000), 19.

40 **CEOs in computer hardware and software companies:** Arijit Chatterjee and Donald C. Hambrick, "It's All about Me: Narcissistic Chief Executive Officers and Their Effects on Company Strategy and Perfor-

mance," *Administrative Science Quarterly* 52 (2007): 351–386.

42n **"technology firms led by givers have higher returns on assets":** Suzanne J. Peterson, Benjamin M. Galvin, and Donald Lange, "CEO Servant Leadership: Exploring Executive Characteristics and Firm Performance," *Personnel Psychology* 65 (2012): 565–594.

44 **"network ties are the conduits":** Benjamin S. Crosier, Gregory D. Webster, and Haley M. Dillon, "Wired to Connect: Evolutionary Psychology and Social Networks," *Review of General Psychology* 16 (2012): 230–239.

45 **Facebook profiles:** Laura E. Buffardi and W. Keith Campbell, "Narcissism and Social Networking Websites," *Personality and Social Psychology Bulletin* 34 (2008): 1303–1314.

45 **social media to catch takers:** Personal interview with Howard Lee (December 11, 2011).

47 **"Adam Rifkin":** Personal interviews with Adam Rifkin (January 28, 2012), Jessica Shambora (February 9, 2012), Raymond Rouf (February 16, 2012), and Eghosa Omoigui (March 14, 2012); visit to 106 Miles (May 9, 2012); Brian Norgard conversation (http://namesake.com/conversation/brian/like-welcome-ifindkarma-namesake-community); Adam Rifkin's website (http://ifindkarma.com/) and Graham Spencer's websites (www.gspencer.net).

47 **more LinkedIn connections:** Jessica Shambora, "*Fortune*'s Best Networker," *Fortune*, February 9, 2011, accessed January 26, 2012, http://tech.fortune.cnn.com/2011/02/09/fortunes-best-networker/.

50 **norm of reciprocity:** Robert B. Cialdini, *Influence: The Psychology of Persuasion* (New York: HarperBusiness, 2006).

50 **"It's better to give before you receive":** Keith Ferrazzi and Tahl Raz, *Never Eat Alone: And Other Secrets to Success, One Relationship at a Time* (New York: Crown Business, 2005), 22.

51 **"hopes of getting something in return":** Personal interview with Dan Weinstein (January 26, 2012).

52 **"How can I help":** Guy Kawasaki interview with Warren Cass, accessed May 14, 2012, www.youtube.com/watch?feature=player_embedded&v=_OsWvp2X8gk.

54 **"weak ties":** Mark Granovetter, "The Strength of Weak Ties: A Network Theory Revisited," *Sociological Theory* 1 (1983): 201–233.

56 *pronoia:* Fred H. Goldner, "Pronoia," *Social Problems* 30 (1982): 82–91;

and personal interview with Brian Little (January 24, 2011).

58 **dormant ties:** Daniel Z. Levin, Jorge Walter, and J. Keith Murnighan, "Dormant Ties: The Value of Reconnecting," *Organization Science* 22 (2011): 923–939; and "The Power of Reconnection: How Dormant Ties Can Surprise You," *MIT Sloan Management Review* 52 (2011): 45–50.

61 **energy through networks:** Rob Cross, Wayne Baker, and Andrew Parker, "What Creates Energy in Organizations?" *MIT Sloan Management Review* 44 (2003): 51–56.

64 **"someone else will do something for me down the road":** Robert Putnam, *Bowling Alone: The Collapse and Revival of American Community* (New York: Simon & Schuster, 2000), 21.

65 **giving can be contagious:** James H. Fowler and Nicholas A. Christakis, "Cooperative Behavior Cascades in Human Social Networks," *PNAS* 107 (2010): 5334–5338.

66 **consistent givers:** J. Mark Weber and J. Keith Murnighan, "Suckers or Saviors? Consistent Contributors in Social Dilemmas," *Journal of Personality and Social Psychology* 95 (2008) 1340–1353.

67 **professional engineers:** Francis J. Flynn, "How Much Should I Give and How Often? The Effects of Generosity and Frequency of Favor Exchange on Social Status and Productivity," *Academy of Management Journal* 46 (2003): 539–553.

Chapter 3: The Ripple Effect

70 **Opening quote:** John Andrew Holmes, *Wisdom in Small Doses* (Lincoln, NE: The University Publishing Company, 1927).

71 **George Meyer:** David Owen, "Taking Humor Seriously: George Meyer, the Funniest Man behind the Funniest Show on TV," *New Yorker*, March 13, 2000; Simon Vozick-Levinson, "For *Simpsons* Writer Meyer, Comedy Is No Laughing Matter," *Harvard Crimson*, June 4, 2003; Eric Spitznagel, "George Meyer," *Believer*, September 2004; Mike Sacks, *And Here's the Kicker: Conversations with 21 Top Humor Writers on Their Craft* (Cincinnati: Writers Digest Books, 2009); and personal interviews with Meyer (June 21, 2012), Tim Long (June 22, 2012), Carolyn Omine (June 27, 2012), and Don Payne (July 12, 2012).

73 **geniuses and genius makers:** Liz Wiseman and Greg McKeown,

Multipliers: How the Best Leaders Make Everyone Smarter (New York: HarperBusiness, 2010).

73 **highly creative people:** Donald W. MacKinnon, "The Nature and Nurture of Creative Talent," *American Psychologist* 17 (1962): 484–495; and "Personality and the Realization of Creative Potential," *American Psychologist* 20 (1965): 273–281.

74 **creative scientists:** Gregory Feist, "A Structural Model of Scientific Eminence," *Psychological Science* 4 (1993): 366–371; and "A Meta-Analysis of Personality in Scientific and Artistic Creativity," *Personality and Social Psychology Review* 2 (1998): 290–309.

77 **Frank Lloyd Wright:** Roger Friedland and Harold Zellman, *The Fellowship: The Untold Story of Frank Lloyd Wright and the Taliesin Fellowship* (New York: HarperCollins, 2007), 138; Ed de St. Aubin, "Truth Against the World: A Psychobiographical Exploration of Generativity in the Life of Frank Lloyd Wright," in *Generativity and Adult Development: How and Why We Care for the Next Generation,* ed. Dan P. McAdams and Ed de St. Aubin (Washington, DC: American Psychological Association, 1998), 402 and 408; Christopher Hawthorne, "At Wright's Taliesin, Maybe the Walls Can Talk," *Los Angeles Times,* September 3, 2006; and Brendan Gill, *Many Masks: A Life of Frank Lloyd Wright* (New York: De Capo Press, 1998), 334.

80 **Edgar Tafel:** Joan Altabe, "Fallingwater Is Falling Apart," *Gadfly Online,* February 18, 2002; see also Hugh Pearman, "How Many Wrights Make a Wrong?" *Sunday Times Magazine,* June 12, 2005.

80 **cardiac surgeons:** Robert Huckman and Gary Pisano, "The Firm Specificity of Individual Performance: Evidence from Cardiac Surgery," *Management Science* 52 (2006): 473–488.

81 **Star analysts:** Boris Groysberg, Linda-Eling Lee, and Ashish Nanda, "Can They Take It with Them? The Portability of Star Knowledge Workers' Performance," *Management Science* 54 (2008): 1213–1230; and Boris Groysberg and Linda-Eling Lee, "The Effect of Colleague Quality on Top Performance: The Case of Security Analysts," *Journal of Organizational Behavior* 29 (2008): 1123–1144.

84 **interdependence as a sign of weakness:** MarYam G. Hamedani, Hazel R. Markus, and Alyssa S. Fu, "My Nation, My Self: Divergent Framings of America Influence American Selves," *Personality and Social Psychology Bulletin* 37 (2011): 350–364.

85 **this makes their groups better off:** Nathan P. Podsakoff, Steven W. Whiting, Philip M. Podsakoff , and Brian D. Blume, "Individual- and Organizational-Level Consequences of Organizational Citizenship Behaviors: A Meta-Analysis," *Journal of Applied Psychology* 94 (2009): 122–141; and Philip M. Podsakoff , Scott B. MacKenzie, Julie B. Paine, and Daniel G. Bachrach, "Organizational Citizenship Behaviors: A Critical Review of the Theoretical and Empirical Literature and Suggestions for Future Research," *Journal of Management* 26 (2000): 513–563.

85 **expedition behavior:** Personal interviews with Jeff Ashby (July 9, 2012) and John Kanengieter (July 13, 2012).

86–87 **no longer have a target on their backs:** Eugene Kim and Theresa M. Glomb, "Get Smarty Pants: Cognitive Ability, Personality, and Victimization," *Journal of Applied Psychology* 95 (2010): 889–901.

87 **revealed his skills:** Sabrina Deutsch Salamon and Yuval Deutsch, "OCB as a Handicap: An Evolutionary Psychological Perspective," *Journal of Organizational Behavior* 27 (2006): 185–199.

87 *idiosyncrasy credits:* Edwin P. Hollander, "Conformity, Status, and Idiosyncrasy Credit," *Psychological Review* 65 (1958): 117–127; see also Charlie L. Hardy and Mark Van Vugt, "Nice Guys Finish First: The Competitive Altruism Hypothesis," *Personality and Social Psychology Bulletin* 32 (2006): 1402–1413.

87 **Berkeley sociologist:** Robb Willer, "Groups Reward Individual Sacrifice: The Status Solution to the Collective Action Problem," *American Sociological Review* 74 (2009): 23–43.

88 **givers get extra credit:** Adam M. Grant, Sharon Parker, and Catherine Collins, "Getting Credit for Proactive Behavior: Supervisor Reactions Depend on What You Value and How You Feel," *Personnel Psychology* 62 (2009): 31–55.

90 **study of Slovenian companies:** Matej Cerne, Christina Nerstad, Anders Dysvik, and Miha Škerlavaj, "What Goes Around Comes Around: Knowledge Hiding, Perceived Motivational Climate, and Creativity," *Academy of Management Journal* (forthcoming).

90 **Jonas Salk:** David Oshinsky, *Polio: An American Story* (New York: Oxford University Press, 2005), 205–206 and 208.

92 **"evil father figure":** Douglas Heuck, "A Talk with Salk Sheds Wisdom," *Pittsburgh Quarterly*, Winter 2006.

93 **rare comments about the incident:** Academy of Achievement, "Jonas

Salk Interview," May 16, 1991, accessed March 15, 2012, http://www.
achievement.org/autodoc/page/sal0int-4; and Paul Offit, *The Cutter
Incident: How America's First Polio Vaccine Led to the Growing Vaccine
Crisis* (New Haven: Yale University Press, 2005), 57.

93 **Peter Salk:** Luis Fábregas, "Salk's Son Extends Olive Branch to Polio
Team," *Pittsburgh Tribune*, April 13, 2005.

94 *responsibility bias:* Michael Ross and Fiore Sicoly, "Egocentric Biases in
Availability and Attribution," *Journal of Personality and Social Psychology*
37 (1979): 322–336.

95 **top words:** Mark Peters and Daniel O'Brien, "From Cromulent to Crap-
tacular: The Top 12 *Simpsons* Created Words," Cracked.com, July 23,
2007; and Ben Zimmer, "The 'Meh' Generation: How an Expression of
Apathy Invaded America," *Boston Globe*, February 26, 2012.

97 **reflect on each member's contributions:** Eugene M. Caruso, Nicholas
Epley, and Max H. Bazerman, "The Costs and Benefits of Undoing
Egocentric Responsibility Assessments in Groups," *Journal of Person-
ality and Social Psychology* 91 (2006): 857–871.

97 **recognize what other people contribute:** Michael McCall, "Orientation, Outcome, and Other-Serving Attributions," *Basic and Applied
Social Psychology* 17 (1995): 49–64.

98 *psychological safety:* Amy Edmondson, "Learning from Mistakes is
Easier Said Than Done: Group and Organizational Influences on the
Detection and Correction of Human Error," *Journal of Applied Behav-
ioral Science* 32 (1996): 5–28; and "Psychological Safety and Learning
Behavior in Work Teams," *Administrative Science Quarterly* 44 (1999):
350–383.

99 **major role in innovation:** David Obstfeld, "Social Networks, the Ter-
tius Iungens Orientation, and Involvement in Innovation," *Administrative Science Quarterly* 50 (2005): 100–130.

100 **perspective gap:** Loran F. Nordgren, Mary-Hunter Morris McDon-
nell, and George Loewenstein, "What Constitutes Torture? Psychological Impediments to an Objective Evaluation of Enhanced
Interrogation Tactics," *Psychological Science* 22 (2011): 689–694.

101 **San Francisco hospital:** Robert Burton, "Pathological Certitude," in
Pathological Altruism, ed. Barbara Oakley et al. (New York: Oxford Uni-
versity Press, 2011), 131–137; Natalie Angier, "The Pathological Altruist
Gives Till Someone Hurts," *New York Times*, October 3, 2011; and

personal interview with Burton (February 23, 2012).

102 **put themselves in other people's shoes:** Adam M. Grant and James Berry, "The Necessity of Others Is the Mother of Invention: Intrinsic and Prosocial Motivations, Perspective-Taking, and Creativity," *Academy of Management Journal* 54 (2011): 73–96.

103 **registry gifts and unique gifts:** Francesca Gino and Francis J. Flynn, "Give Them What They Want: The Benefits of Explicitness in Gift Exchange," *Journal of Experimental Social Psychology* 47 (2011): 915–922.

103 **tend to stay within our own frames of reference:** C. Daniel Batson, Shannon Early, and Giovanni Salvarani, "Perspective Taking: Imagining How Another Feels Versus Imagining How You Would Feel," *Personality and Social Psychology Bulletin* 23 (1997): 751–758.

104 **goldfish crackers over broccoli:** Betty Repacholi and Alison Gopnik, "Early Reasoning about Desires: Evidence from 14- and 18-Month-Olds," *Developmental Psychology* 33 (1997): 12–21.

104–105n **younger siblings:** Beatrice Whiting and John Whiting, *Children of Six Cultures: A Psycho-Cultural Analysis* (Cambridge, MA: Harvard University Press, 1975), David Winter, "The Power Motive in Women—and Men," *Journal of Personality and Social Psychology* 54 (1988): 510–519; Frank J. Sulloway, *Born to Rebel: Birth Order, Family Dynamics, and Creative Lives* (New York: Vintage Books, 1997); and Paul A. M. Van Lange, Wilma Otten, Ellen M. N. De Bruin, and Jeffrey A. Joireman, "Development of Prosocial, Individualistic, and Competitive Orientations: Theory and Preliminary Evidence," *Journal of Personality and Social Psychology* 73 (1997): 733–746.

104–105n **"female family members—even infants—might tilt us in the giver direction":** Adam M. Grant, "Why Men Need Women," *New York Times*, July 20, 2013, www.nytimes.com/2013/07/21/opinions/sunday/why-men-need-women.html

106 **"It is amazing":** de St. Aubin, 405.

Chapter 4: Finding the Diamond in the Rough

109 **Reggie Love:** Personal interview (May 28, 2012); and Peter Baker, "Education of a President," *New York Times*, October 12, 2010; David Picker, "Amazing Ride Nears End for 'First Brother' Reggie Love," *ABC News*, November 22, 2011; Jodi Kantor, "Leaving Obama's Shadow, to

Cast One of His Own," *New York Times*, November 10, 2011; and Noreen Malone, "Obama Still Hasn't Replaced Reggie Love," *New York Magazine*, February 16, 2012.

111 **C. J. Skender:** Personal interviews with Skender (January 16 and April 30, 2012), Beth Traynham (May 4, 2012), Marie Arcuri (May 5, 2012), and David Moltz (May 10, 2012); see also Megan Tucker, "By the Book, Sort of . . ." *BusinessWeek*, September 20, 2006; Kim Nielsen, "The Last Word: C. J. Skender, CPA," *Journal of Accountancy*, April 2008; Patrick Adams, "The Entertainer," *Duke Magazine*, March 4, 2004; and Nicki Jhabvala, "Road Trip: UNC," *Sports Illustrated*, November 8, 2006.

113 **Israel Defense Forces:** Dov Eden, "Pygmalion without Interpersonal Contrast Effects: Whole Groups Gain from Raising Manager Expectations," *Journal of Applied Psychology* 75 (1990): 394–398; and "Self-Fulfilling Prophecies in Organizations," in *Organizational Behavior: State of the Science*, ed. J. Greenberg (Mahwah, NJ: Erlbaum, 2003), 91–122.

114 **intellectual blooming:** Robert Rosenthal and Lenore Jacobson, "Teachers' Expectancies: Determinants of Pupils' IQ Gains," *Psychological Reports* 19 (1966): 115–118; and *Pygmalion in the Classroom: Teacher Expectation and Pupils' Intellectual Development* (New York: Crown, 2003).

116 **"Self-fulfilling prophecies":** Lee Jussim and Kent Harber, "Teacher Expectations and Self-Fulfilling Prophecies: Knowns and Unknowns, Resolved and Unresolved Controversies," *Personality and Social Psychology Review* 9 (2005): 131–155.

117 **employees bloomed:** D. Brian McNatt, "Ancient Pygmalion Joins Contemporary Management: A Meta-Analysis of the Result," *Journal of Applied Psychology* 85 (2000): 314–322.

117 **low expectations trigger a vicious cycle:** Jennifer Carson Marr, Stefan Thau, Karl Aquino, and Laurie J. Barclay, "Do I Want to Know? How the Motivation to Acquire Relationship-Threatening Information in Groups Contributes to Paranoid Thought, Suspicion Behavior, and Social Rejection," *Organizational Behavior and Human Decision Processes* 117 (2012): 285–297; and Detlef Fetchenhauer and David Dunning, "Why So Cynical? Asymmetric Feedback Underlies Misguided Skepticism Regarding the Trustworthiness of Others," *Psychological Science* 21 (2010): 189–193; see also Fabrizio Ferraro, Jeffrey Pfeffer, and Robert I. Sutton, "Economics Language and Assumptions: How Theories Can

Become Self-Fulfilling," *Academy of Management Review* 30 (2005): 8–24.

118 **new auditors:** D. Brian McNatt and Timothy A. Judge, "Boundary Conditions of the Galatea Effect: A Field Experiment and Constructive Replication," *Academy of Management Journal* 47 (2004): 550–565.

120 **investment theory of intelligence:** Raymond Cattell, *Abilities: Their Structure, Growth, and Action* (New York: Houghton Mifflin, 1971), and *Intelligence: Its Structure, Growth, and Action* (New York: Elsevier, 1987); see also Frank Schmidt, "A Theory of Sex Differences in Technical Aptitude and Some Supporting Evidence," *Perspectives on Psychological Science* 6 (2011): 560–573.

120 **landmark study of world-class musicians, scientists, and athletes:** Benjamin Bloom, *Developing Talent in Young People* (New York: Ballantine Books, 1985), 173.

121 **"traced the lineage of the world's most beautiful swans":** Daniel Coyle, *The Talent Code: Greatness Isn't Born. It's Grown. Here's How* (New York: Bantam, 2009), 173.

121 **ten thousand hours of deliberate practice:** Malcolm Gladwell, *Outliers: The Story of Success* (New York: Little, Brown and Company, 2008); and K. Anders Ericsson and Neil Charness, "Expert Performance: Its Structure and Acquisition," *American Psychologist* 49 (1994), 725–747.

122 *grit:* Angela L. Duckworth, Christopher Peterson, Michael D. Matthews, and Dennis R. Kelly, "Grit: Perseverance and Passion for Long-Term Goals," *Journal of Personality and Social Psychology* 92 (2007): 1087–1101.

123 **"you can't take motivation for granted":** George Anders, *The Rare Find: Spotting Exceptional Talent Before Everyone Else* (New York: Portfolio, 2011), 212.

126 **Stu Inman:** Wayne Thompson, *Blazermania: This Is Our Story—The Official History of the Portland Trail Blazers* (San Rafael, CA: Insight Editions, 2010); and "My Memories of Stu Inman," NBA.com, 2007, accessed May 14, 2012, http://www.nba.com/blazers/news/My_memories_of_Stu_Inman-208239-1218.html; Jack Ramsay, "Stu Inman was an Old-School Pro," ESPN, 2007, accessed May 14, 2012, https://m.espn.go.com/nba/story?storyId=2750878; Steve Duin, "Stu Inman: The Ultimate Class Act," *The Oregonian*, January 30, 2007; Mandy Major, "Dr. Ogilvie Was an Acclaimed Pioneer in Sports Psychology," *Los Gatos Weekly Times*, July 23, 2003; Chris Tomasson, "LaRue Martin's

Story Proves One of Redemption, Success," AOL News, January 25, 2011, accessed May 14, 2012, http://www.aolnews.com/2011/01/25/larue-martins-story-proves-one-of-redemption-success/; and "Ultimate Rebound: Draft Bust LaRue Martin Lands NBA Gig," AOL News, February 21, 2011, accessed May 14, 2012, http://www.aolnews.com/2011/02/21/ultimate-rebounddraft-bust-larue-martin-lands-nba-gig/; Jerry Sullivan, "NBA Scouts Are Learning to Think Small," *Los Angeles Times*, March 11, 1989; Stats LLC, "Stu Inman, Architect of Trail Blazers' Title Team, Dies at 80," *Associated Press*, January 31, 2007; Rob Kremer, "Stu Inman, RIP" Blogspot, January 31, 2007, accessed May 14, 2012, http://robkremer.blogspot.com/2007/01/stu-inman-rip.html; Dwight Jaynes, "Pioneer Blazer Won with Character," *Portland Tribune*, February 2, 2007; Tommie Smith and David Steele, *Silent Gesture: The Autobiography of Tommie Smith* (Philadelphia: Temple University Press, 2007), 84; Filip Bondy, *Tip-off: How the 1984 NBA Draft Changed Basketball Forever* (Cambridge, MA: Da Capo Press, 2007), 114; Frank Coffey, *The Pride of Portland: The Story of the Trail Blazers* (New York: Everest House, 1980); Chris Ballard, Chuck Wielgus, Clark Kellogg, and Alexander Wolff, *Hoops Nation: A Guide to America's Best Pickup Basketball* (Lincoln: University of Nebraska Press, 2004); and a personal interview with Thompson (May 14, 2012).

130 **teams couldn't let go of their big bets:** Barry M. Staw and Ha Hoang, "Sunk Costs in the NBA: Why Draft Order Affects Playing Time and Survival in Professional Basketball," *Administrative Science Quarterly* 40 (1995): 474–494; see also Colin F. Camerer and Roberto A. Weber, "The Econometrics and Behavioral Economics of Escalation of Commitment in NBA Draft Choices," *Journal of Economic Behavior and Organization* 39 (1999): 59–82.

131 **why and when escalation of commitment happens:** Dustin J. Sleesman, Donald E. Conlon, Gerry McNamara, and Jonathan E. Miles, "Cleaning Up the Big Muddy: A Meta-Analytic Review of the Determinants of Escalation of Commitment," *Academy of Management Journal* 55 (2012): 541–562.

131 **California bank customers defaulted on loans:** Barry M. Staw, Sigal G. Barsade, and Kenneth W. Koput, "Escalation at the Credit Window: A Longitudinal Study of Bank Executives' Recognition and Write-off of Problem Loans," *Journal of Applied Psychology* 82 (1997): 130–142.

132 **invest $1 million in a plane:** Henry Moon, "The Two Faces of Consci-
entiousness: Duty and Achievement Striving in Escalation of Commitment Dilemmas," *Journal of Applied Psychology* 86 (2001): 533–540.

132 **"keep the prospect of failure hidden":** Bruce M. Meglino and M.
Audrey Korsgaard, "Considering Rational Self-Interest as a Disposi-
tion: Organizational Implications of Other Orientation," *Journal of
Applied Psychology* 89 (2004): 946–959; and M. Audrey Korsgaard, Bruce
M. Meglino, and Scott W. Lester, "Beyond Helping: Do Other-Oriented
Values Have Broader Implications in Organizations?" *Journal of Applied
Psychology* 82 (1997): 160–177.

133 **choosing on behalf of others:** Laura Kray and Richard Gonzalez,
"Differential Weighting in Choice Versus Advice: I'll Do This, You Do
That," *Journal of Behavioral Decision Making* 12 (1999): 207–217; Laura
Kray, "Contingent Weighting in Self-Other Decision Making," *Organi-
zational Behavior and Human Decision Processes* 83 (2000): 82–106; and
Evan Polman and Kyle J. Emich, "Decisions for Others Are More Cre-
ative than Decisions for the Self," *Personality and Social Psychology Bul-
letin* 37 (2011): 492–501.

137 **Bob Gross:** Wayne Thompson, "Bob Gross: Moving Without the Ball,"
NBA.com, accessed May 14, 2012, http://www.nba.com/blazers/
news/Bob_Gross_Moving_Without_The_-292398-1218.html; Kyle
Laggner, "Former Blazers' Forward Bobby Gross Leaves a Lasting
Impression," *Oregonian*, December 17, 2008; and Jews in Sports profile,
accessed May 14, 2012, www.jewsinsports.org/profile.asp?sport=basket
ball&ID=358.

138 **givers are willing to work harder and longer:** Adam M. Grant, "Does
Intrinsic Motivation Fuel the Prosocial Fire? Motivational Synergy in
Predicting Persistence, Performance, and Productivity," *Journal of
Applied Psychology* 93 (2008): 48–58.

138–139 **Def Jam Records:** Personal interview with Russell Simmons (June
26, 2012), and Russell Simmons and Chris Morrow, *Do You: 12 Laws to
Access the Power in You to Achieve Happiness and Success* (New York: Penguin, 2008), 156–157.

140 **Clyde Drexler:** Clyde Drexler and Kerry Eggers, *Clyde the Glide: My Life
in Basketball* (New York: Skyhorse Publishing, 2011), 109–114.

142 **Michael Jordan:** Michael Leahy, *When Nothing Else Matters: Michael Jordan's Last Comeback* (New York: Simon & Schuster, 2005); Sam Smith,

The Jordan Rules (New York: Mass Market, 1993); Jack McCallum, *Dream Team: How Michael, Magic, Larry, Charles, and the Greatest Team of All Time Conquered the World and Changed the Game of Basketball Forever* (New York: Ballantine Books, 2012); ESPN Chicago, "Charles Barkley Critical of Jordan," March 1, 2012, accessed May 28, 2012, http://espn.go.com/chicago/nba/story/_/id/7634685/charles-barkley-michael-jordan-executive-not-done-good-job; and Rick Reilly, "Be Like Michael Jordan? No Thanks," ESPN, September 19, 2009, accessed May 28, 2012, http://sports.espn.go.com/espn/columns/story?columnist=reilly_rick&id=4477759.

142n **"making his team members more successful":** Stephen Roulac, "Review of Give and Take," *New York Journal of Books*, accessed on June 3, 2013 at www.nyjournalofbooks.com/review/give-and-take-revolutionary-approach-success

142–143n **Dean Smith:** Bondy, *Tip-off*, 3.

142–143n **"Talented people are attracted to those who care about them":** Personal interview with Chris Granger (June 26, 2012).

145 **"champion great talent":** Anders, 246–247.

Chapter 5: The Power of Powerless Communication

146 **Opening quote:** Theodore Roosevelt, "Letter to Henry R. Sprague," *American Treasures of the Library of Congress*, January 26, 1900.

146 **Dave Walton:** Hayes Hunt, "The King's Speech: A Trial Lawyer's Stutter," *From the Sidebar*, March 3, 2011, and personal interviews with Walton (September 6 and December 15, 2011, and March 9, 2012).

150 **success depends heavily on influence skills:** Daniel Pink, *To Sell Is Human: The Surprising Truth About Moving Others* (New York: Riverhead, 2012).

150 **dominance and prestige:** Nir Halevy, Eileen Y. Chou, Taya R. Cohen, and Robert W. Livingston, "Status Conferral in Intergroup Social Dilemmas: Behavioral Antecedents and Consequences of Prestige and Dominance," *Journal of Personality and Social Psychology* 102 (2012): 351–366.

151 **people expect us to communicate powerfully:** Susan Cain, *Quiet: The Power of Introverts in a World That Can't Stop Talking* (New York: Crown, 2012).

154 **comfortable expressing vulnerability:** see M. Audrey Korsgaard, Bruce M. Meglino, and W. Scott Lester, "Beyond Helping: Do Other-Oriented Values Have Broader Implications in Organizations?" *Journal of Applied Psychology* 82 (1997): 160–177; and Michael C. Ashton and Kibeom Lee, "Empirical, Theoretical, and Practical Advantages of the HEXACO Model of Personality Structure," *Personality and Social Psychology Review* 11 (2007): 150–166.

155 *pratfall effect:* Elliot Aronson, Ben Willerman, and Joanne Floyd, "The Effect of a Pratfall on Increasing Interpersonal Attractiveness," *Psychonomic Science* 4 (1966): 227–228; and Robert Helmreich, Elliot Aronson, and James LeFan, "To Err Is Humanizing—Sometimes: Effects of Self-Esteem, Competence, and a Pratfall on Interpersonal Attraction," *Journal of Personality and Social Psychology* 16 (1970): 259–264.

156 **bottom of the social responsibility list:** Robert H. Frank, "What Price the Moral High Ground?" *Southern Economic Journal* 63 (1996): 1–17.

157 **Bill Grumbles:** Personal interview (October 4, 2011).

157 **joy of talking:** James Pennebaker, *Opening Up: The Healing Power of Expressing Emotions* (New York: Guilford Press, 1997), 3.

160 **top-selling optician:** Personal interviews with Kildare Escoto (August 23 and 28, 2011) and Nancy Phelps (August 23, 2011).

160 **hundreds of opticians:** Adam M. Grant and Dane Barnes, "Predicting Sales Revenue" (working paper, 2011).

161 **expert negotiators:** Neil Rackham, "The Behavior of Successful Negotiators," in *Negotiation: Readings, Exercises, and Cases*, ed. R. Lewicki, B. Barry, and D. M. Saunders (New York: McGraw-Hill, 2007).

162 **insurance salespeople:** Philip M. Podsakoff , Scott B. MacKenzie, Julie B. Paine, and Daniel G. Bachrach, "Organizational Citizenship Behaviors: A Critical Review of the Theoretical and Empirical Literature and Suggestions for Future Research," *Journal of Management* 26 (2000): 513–563.

162 **pharmaceutical salespeople:** Carl J. Thoresen, Jill C. Bradley, Paul D. Bliese, and Joseph D. Thoresen, "The Big Five Personality Traits and Individual Job Performance Growth Trajectories in Maintenance and Transitional Job Stages," *Journal of Applied Psychology* 89 (2004): 835–853.

162–163n **salespeople responsible for women's products:** Fernando

Jaramillo and Douglas B. Grisaffe, "Does Customer Orientation Impact Objective Sales Performance? Insights from a Longitudinal Model in Direct Selling," *Journal of Personal Selling & Sales Management* XXIX (2009): 167–178.

163 **planning to vote:** Anthony G. Greenwald, Catherine G. Carnot, Rebecca Beach, and Barbara Young, "Increasing Voting Behavior by Asking People if They Expect to Vote," *Journal of Applied Psychology* 72 (1987): 315–318.

163 **we get suspicious:** Marian Friestad and Peter Wright, "The Persuasion Knowledge Model: How People Cope with Persuasion Attempts," *Journal of Consumer Research* 21 (1994): 1–31; Jack Brehm, *A Theory of Psychological Reactance* (New York: Academic Press, 1966); and John Biondo and A. P. MacDonald Jr., "Internal-External Locus of Control and Response to Influence Attempts," *Journal of Personality* 39 (1971): 407–419.

164 **self-persuasion:** Elliot Aronson, "The Power of Self-Persuasion," *American Psychologist* 54 (1999): 875–884.

164n **intention questions:** Patti Williams, Gavan Fitzsimons, and Lauren Block, "When Consumers Do Not Recognize 'Benign' Intention Questions and Persuasion Attempts," *Journal of Consumer Research* 31 (2004): 540–550.

165 **Don Lane:** Personal interviews (December 16, 2011, and March 30, 2012).

167 **talking tentatively:** Alison R. Fragale, "The Power of Powerless Speech: The Effects of Speech Style and Task Interdependence on Status Conferral," *Organizational Behavior and Human Decision Processes* 101 (2006): 243–261; see also Uma R. Karmarkar and Zakary L. Tormala, "Believe Me, I Have No Idea What I'm Talking About: The Effects of Source Certainty on Consumer Involvement and Persuasion," *Journal of Consumer Research* 36 (2010): 1033–1049.

168n **Disclaimer:** Amani El-Alayli, Christoffer J. Myers, Tamara L. Petersen, and Amy L. Lystad, "I Don't Mean to Sound Arrogant, But . . . The Effects of Using Disclaimers on Person Perception," *Personality and Social Psychology Bulletin* 34 (2008): 130–143.

169 **Barton Hill:** Personal interview (March 19, 2012).

170 **psychologists in California:** Cameron Anderson and Gavin J. Kilduff, "Why Do Dominant Personalities Attain Influence in Face-to-Face

Groups? The Competence-Signaling Effects of Trait Dominance," *Journal of Personality and Social Psychology* 96 (2009): 491–503.

170 **Psychologists in Amsterdam:** Barbora Nevicka, Femke S. Ten Velden, Annebel H. B. de Hoogh, and Annelies E. M. Van Vianen, "Reality at Odds with Perception: Narcissistic Leaders and Group Performance," *Psychological Science* 22 (2011): 1259–1264.

170 **pizza franchises:** Adam M. Grant, Francesca Gino, and David A. Hofmann, "Reversing the Extraverted Leadership Advantage: The Role of Employee Proactivity," *Academy of Management Journal* 54 (2011): 528–550.

172 **research scientist:** Personal interview with Annie (June 13, 2012).

173 **exercising influence when we lack authority:** Katie A. Liljenquist, "Resolving the Impression Management Dilemma: The Strategic Benefits of Soliciting Others for Advice" (PhD diss., Northwestern University, 2010); and Katie A. Liljenquist and Adam Galinsky, "Turn Your Adversary into Your Advocate," *Negotiation* (2007): 4–6.

173 **effective ways to influence:** Gary Yukl and J. Bruce Tracey, "Consequences of Influence Tactics Used with Subordinates, Peers, and the Boss," *Journal of Applied Psychology* 77 (1992): 525–535; and Gary Yukl, Helen Kim, and Cecilia M. Falbe, "Antecedents of Influence Outcomes," *Journal of Applied Psychology* 81 (1996): 309–317.

174 **Board seats:** Ithai Stern and James D. Westphal, "Stealthy Footsteps to the Boardroom: Executives' Backgrounds, Sophisticated Interpersonal Influence Behavior, and Board Appointments," *Administrative Science Quarterly* 55 (2010): 278–319.

174 **regularly seek advice and help:** Arie Nadler, Shmuel Ellis, and Iris Bar, "To Seek or Not to Seek: The Relationship between Help Seeking and Job Performance Evaluations as Moderated by Task-Relevant Expertise," *Journal of Applied Social Psychology* 33 (2003): 91–109.

176 **"As a favor to me":** Jon Jecker and David Landy, "Liking a Person as a Function of Doing Him a Favour," *Human Relations* 22 (1969): 371–378.

176 **"He that has once done you a kindness":** Benjamin Franklin, *The Autobiography of Benjamin Franklin* (New York: Dover, 1868/1996), 80.

176 **"fundamental rule for winning friends":** Walter Isaacson, "Poor Richard's Flattery," *New York Times*, July 14, 2003.

Chapter 6: The Art of Motivation Maintenance

179 **Opening quote:** Herbert Simon, "Altruism and Economics," *American Economic Review* 83 (1993): 157.

180 **what motivates highly successful givers:** Jeremy A. Frimer, Lawrence J. Walker, William L. Dunlop, Brenda H. Lee, and Amanda Riches, "The Integration of Agency and Communion in Moral Personality: Evidence of Enlightened Self-Interest," *Journal of Personality and Social Psychology* 101 (2011): 149–163.

181 **pathological altruism:** Barbara Oakley, Ariel Knafo, and Michael McGrath, eds., *Pathological Altruism* (New York: Oxford University Press, 2011).

182 **"failing to study":** Vicki S. Helgeson and Heidi L. Fritz, "The Implications of Unmitigated Agency and Unmitigated Communion for Domains of Problem Behavior," *Journal of Personality* 68 (2000): 1031–1057.

182 **completely independent motivations:** Adam M. Grant and David M. Mayer, "Good Soldiers and Good Actors: Prosocial and Impression Management Motives as Interactive Predictors of Affiliative Citizenship Behaviors," *Journal of Applied Psychology* 94 (2009): 900–912; Adam M. Grant and James Berry, "The Necessity of Others Is the Mother of Invention: Intrinsic and Prosocial Motivations, Perspective-Taking, and Creativity," *Academy of Management Journal* 54 (2011): 73–96; and Carsten K. W. De Dreu and Aukje Nauta, "Self-Interest and Other-Orientation in Organizational Behavior: Implications for Job Performance, Prosocial Behavior, and Personal Initiative," *Journal of Applied Psychology* 94 (2009): 913–926.

182 **"two great forces of human nature":** Bill Gates, "Creative Capitalism," World Economic Forum, January 24, 2008.

183 **Overbrook:** Steve Volk, "Top 10 Drug Corners," *Philadelphia Weekly*, May 2, 2007, and Ledyard King, "Program to Identify Most Dangerous Schools Misses Mark," *USA Today*, January 18, 2007.

184 **Conrey Callahan:** Personal interview (January 26, 2012).

185 **job burnout:** Christina Maslach, Wilmar Schaufeli, and Michael Leiter, "Job Burnout," *Annual Review of Psychology* 52 (2001): 397–422.

187 **call center:** Adam M. Grant, Elizabeth M. Campbell, Grace Chen, Keenan Cottone, David Lapedis, and Karen Lee, "Impact and the Art

of Motivation Maintenance: The Effects of Contact with Beneficiaries on Persistence Behavior," *Organizational Behavior and Human Decision Processes* 103 (2007): 53–67; Adam M. Grant, "The Significance of Task Significance: Job Performance Effects, Relational Mechanisms, and Boundary Conditions," *Journal of Applied Psychology* 93 (2008): 108–124; Adam M. Grant, "Employees Without a Cause: The Motivational Effects of Prosocial Impact in Public Service," *International Public Management Journal* 11 (2008): 48–66; and Adam M. Grant and Francesca Gino, "A Little Thanks Goes a Long Way: Explaining Why Gratitude Expressions Motivate Prosocial Behavior," *Journal of Personality and Social Psychology* 98 (2010): 946–955.

189 **"greatest untapped source of motivation":** Susan Dominus, "Is Giving the Secret to Getting Ahead?" *New York Times*, March 31, 2013, www.nytimes.com/2013/03/31/magazine/is-giving-the-secret-to-getting-ahead.html?pagewanted=all

190 **compassion fatigue:** Olga Klimecki and Tania Singer, "Empathic Distress Fatigue Rather Than Compassion Fatigue? Integrating Findings from Empathy Research in Psychology and Social Neuroscience," in *Pathological Altruism*, ed. Barbara Oakley et al. (New York: Oxford University Press, 2011), 368–384; and Richard Shultz et al., "Patient Suffering and Caregiver Compassion: New Opportunities for Research, Practice, and Policy," *Gerontologist* 47 (2007): 4–13.

190n **outsourcing inspiration:** Adam M. Grant and David A. Hofmann, "Outsourcing Inspiration: The Performance Effects of Ideological Messages from Leaders and Beneficiaries," *Organizational Behavior and Human Decision Processes* 116 (2011): 173–187.

192 **buffer against stress:** Adam M. Grant and Elizabeth M. Campbell, "Doing Good, Doing Harm, Being Well and Burning Out: The Interactions of Perceived Prosocial and Antisocial Impact in Service Work," *Journal of Occupational and Organizational Psychology* 80 (2007): 665–691; Adam M. Grant and Sabine Sonnentag, "Doing Good Buffers Against Feeling Bad: Prosocial Impact Compensates for Negative Task and Self-Evaluations," *Organizational Behavior and Human Decision Processes* 111 (2010): 13–22.

192 **radiologists:** Yehonatan Turner, Shuli Silberman, Sandor Joffe, and Irith Hadas-Halpern, "The Effect of Adding a Patient's Photograph to the Radiographic Examination," Annual Meeting of the Radiolog-

ical Society of North America (2008).

193 **Italian nurses:** Nicola Bellé, "Experimental Evidence on the Relationship between Public Service Motivation and Job Performance," *Public Administration Review* (forthcoming).

194 **Wells Fargo and Medtronic:** Personal interviews with Ben Soccorsy (January 10, 2012) and Bill George (March 9, 2010).

194 **Anitra Karsten:** see Ellen J. Langer, *Mindfulness* (Reading, MA: Addison-Wesley, 1989), 136.

196 **give continually without concern for their own well-being:** Vicki S. Helgeson, "Relation of Agency and Communion to Well-Being: Evidence and Potential Explanations," *Psychological Bulletin* 116 (1994): 412–428; Heidi L. Fritz and Vicki S. Helgeson, "Distinctions of Unmitigated Communion from Communion: Self-Neglect and Overinvolvement with Others," *Journal of Personality and Social Psychology* 75 (1998): 121–140; and Vicki S. Helgeson and Heidi L. Fritz, "Unmitigated Agency and Unmitigated Communion: Distinctions from Agency and Communion," *Journal of Research in Personality* 33 (1999): 131–158.

196n **overloaded and stressed:** Mark C. Bolino and William H. Turnley, "The Personal Costs of Citizenship Behavior: The Relationship between Individual Initiative and Role Overload, Job Stress, and Work-Family Conflict," *Journal of Applied Psychology* 90 (2005): 740–748.

196n **equilibrium:** Madoka Kumashiro, Caryl E. Rusbult, and Eli J. Finkel, "Navigating Personal and Relational Concerns: The Quest for Equilibrium," *Journal of Personality and Social Psychology* 95 (2008): 94–110.

196–197n **visible in our writing:** James Pennebaker, *The Secret Life of Pronouns: What Our Words Say About Us* (New York: Bloomsbury Press, 2011), 13.

197 **random acts of kindness:** Sonja Lyubomirsky, Kennon Sheldon, and David Schkade, "Pursuing Happiness: The Architecture of Sustainable Change," *Review of General Psychology* 9 (2005): 111–131.

198 **software engineers:** Leslie A. Perlow, "The Time Famine: Toward a Sociology of Work Time," *Administrative Science Quarterly* 44 (1999): 57–81.

200 **Sean Hagerty:** Personal interview (April 26, 2012).

200 **Australian adults:** Timothy D. Windsor, Kaarin J. Anstey, and Bryan Rodgers, "Volunteering and Psychological Well-Being among Young-Old Adults: How Much Is Too Much?" *Gerontologist* 48 (2008): 59–70.

200 **American adults:** Ming-Ching Luoh and A. Regula Herzog, "Individual Consequences of Volunteer and Paid Work in Old Age: Health and Mortality," *Journal of Health and Social Behavior* 43 (2002): 490–509; see also Terry Y. Lum and Elizabeth Lightfoot, "The Effects of Volunteering on the Physical and Mental Health of Older People," *Research on Aging* 27 (2005): 31–55.

201 **diminishing returns:** Jonathan E. Booth, Kyoung Won Park, and Theresa M. Glomb, "Employer-Supported Volunteering Benefits: Gift Exchange Among Employers, Employees, and Volunteer Organizations," *Human Resource Management* 48 (2009): 227–249.

202 **giving has an energizing effect:** Netta Weinstein and Richard M. Ryan, "When Helping Helps: Autonomous Motivation for Prosocial Behavior and Its Influence on Well-Being for the Helper and Recipient," *Journal of Personality and Social Psychology* 98 (2010): 222–244.

203n **emotional boost from giving doesn't always kick in right away:** Sabine Sonnentag and Adam M. Grant, "Doing Good at Work Feels Good at Home, But Not Right Away: When and Why Perceived Prosocial Impact Predicts Positive Affect," *Personnel Psychology* 65 (2012): 495–530.

203 **firefighters and fund-raising callers:** Adam M. Grant, "Does Intrinsic Motivation Fuel the Prosocial Fire? Motivational Synergy in Predicting Persistence, Performance, and Productivity," *Journal of Applied Psychology* 93 (2008): 48–58.

205 **robust antidote to burnout:** Jonathon R. B. Halbesleben, "Sources of Social Support and Burnout: A Meta-Analytic Test of the Conservation of Resources Model," *Journal of Applied Psychology* 91 (2006): 1134–1145.

205 **started to burn out:** Jonathon R. B. Halbesleben and Wm. Matthew Bowler, "Emotional Exhaustion and Job Performance: The Mediating Role of Motivation," *Journal of Applied Psychology* 92 (2007): 93–106.

205 *tend and befriend:* Shelley E. Taylor, "Tend and Befriend: Biobehavioral Bases of Affiliation Under Stress," *Current Directions in Psychological Science* 15 (2006): 273–277; see also Bernadette von Dawans, Urs Fischbacher, Clemens Kirschbaum, Ernst Fehr, and Markus Henrichs, "The Social Dimension of Stress Reactivity: Acute Stress Increases Prosocial Behavior in Humans," *Psychological Science* 23 (2012): 651–660.

206 **health professionals:** Dirk van Dierendonck, Wilmar B. Schaufeli, and Bram P. Buunk, "Burnout and Inequity Among Human Service

Professionals: A Longitudinal Study," *Journal of Occupational Health Psychology* 6 (2001): 43–52; and Nico W. Van Yperen, Bram P. Buunk, and Wilmar B. Schaufeli, "Communal Orientation and the Burnout Syndrome Among Nurses," *Journal of Applied Social Psychology* 22 (1992): 173–189.

207 **willpower:** Elizabeth Seeley and Wendi Gardner, "The 'Selfless' and Self-Regulation: The Role of Chronic Other-Orientation in Averting Self-Regulatory Depletion," *Self and Identity* 2 (2003): 103–117.

208 **Utah:** Jon Huntsman, *Winners Never Cheat* (Upper Saddle River, NJ: Prentice Hall, 2008); and Steve Eaton, "Huntsmans Urge Strong Work Ethic," *KSL*, May 8, 2011.

210 **income and charitable giving:** Arthur C. Brooks, *Who Really Cares* (New York: Basic Books, 2006), "Does Giving Make Us Prosperous?" *Journal of Economics and Finance* 31 (2007): 403–411; and *Gross National Happiness* (New York: Basic Books, 2008).

211n **as people get richer:** Paul K. Piff, Michael W. Kraus, Stéphane Côté, Bonnie Hayden Cheng, and Dacher Keltner, "Having Less, Giving More: The Influence of Social Class on Prosocial Behavior," *Journal of Personality and Social Psychology* 99 (2010): 771–784.

212 **spend the money on others:** Elizabeth W. Dunn, Lara B. Aknin, and Michael I. Norton, "Spending Money on Others Promotes Happiness," *Science* 319 (2008): 1687–1688.

212 **warm glow:** James Andreoni, William T. Harbaugh, and Lise Vesterlund, "Altruism in Experiments," in *New Palgrave Dictionary of Economics*, 2nd edn, ed. Steven N. Durlauf and Lawrence E. Blume (New York: Palgrave MacMillan, 2008).

212 **neuroscience evidence:** William T. Harbaugh, Ulrich Mayr, and Daniel R. Burghart, "Neural Responses to Taxation and Voluntary Giving Reveal Motives for Charitable Donations," *Science* 316 (2007): 1622–1625; and Jorge Moll, Frank Krueger, Roland Zahn, Matteo Pardini, Ricardo de Oliveira-Souza, and Jordan Grafman, "Human Fronto-Mesolimbic Networks Guide Decisions about Charitable Donations," *PNAS* 103 (2006): 15623–15628.

212 **Americans over age twenty-four:** Peggy A. Thoits and Lyndi N. Hewitt, "Volunteer Work and Well-being," *Journal of Health and Social Behavior* 42 (2001): 115–131.

212 **drop in depression:** Yunqing Li and Kenneth F. Ferraro, "Volunteering

and Depression in Later Life: Social Benefit or Selection Processes?" *Journal of Health and Social Behavior* 46 (2005): 68–84.

212 **actually live longer:** Marc A. Musick, A. Regula Herzog, and James S. House, "Volunteering and Mortality Among Older Adults: Findings from a National Sample," *Journal of Gerontology: Social Sciences* 54B (1999): S173–S180; and Stephanie L. Brown, Randolph M. Nesse, Amiram D. Vinokur, and Dylan M. Smith, "Providing Social Support May Be More Beneficial Than Receiving It: Results from a Prospective Study of Mortality," *Psychological Science* 14 (2003): 320–327.

212 **massages:** Tiffany M. Field, Maria Hernandez-Reif, Olga Quintino, Saul Schanberg, and Cynthia Kuhn, "Elder Retired Volunteers Benefit from Giving Massage Therapy to Infants," *Journal of Applied Gerontology* 17 (1998): 229–239.

212 **national survey of Americans:** Roy F. Baumeister, Kathleen D. Vohs, Jennifer L. Aaker, and Emily N. Garbinsky, "Some Key Differences between a Happy Life and a Meaningful Life," *Journal of Positive Psychology* (forthcoming).

212 **happiness can motivate people:** see Sigal G. Barsade and Donald E. Gibson, "Why Does Affect Matter in Organizations?" *Academy of Management Perspectives* 21 (2007): 36–59; Sonja Lyubomirsky, Laura King, and Ed Diener, "The Benefits of Frequent Positive Affect: Does Happiness Lead to Success?" *Psychological Bulletin* 131 (6): 803–855; and Timothy A. Judge, Carl J. Thoresen, Joyce E. Bono, and Gregory K. Patton, "The Job Satisfaction—Job Performance Relationship: A Qualitative and Quantitative Review," *Psychological Bulletin* 127 (2001): 376–407.

212 **faster and more accurate diagnoses:** Carlos A. Estrada, Alice M. Isen, and Mark J. Young, "Positive Affect Facilitates Integration of Information and Decreases Anchoring in Reasoning Among Physicians," *Organizational Behavior and Human Decision Processes* 72 (1997): 117–135.

213 **Virgin mogul:** Richard Branson, *Losing My Virginity: How I've Survived, Had Fun, and Made a Fortune Doing Business My Way* (New York: Crown Business, 1999), 56; and *Business Stripped Bare: Adventures of a Global Entrepreneur* (New York: Penguin, 2011), 327.

214 **more sustainable contributions:** Adam M. Grant and David M. Mayer, "Good Soldiers and Good Actors: Prosocial and Impression Management Motives as Interactive Predictors of Affiliative Citizenship Behaviors," *Journal of Applied Psychology* 94 (2009): 900–912.

Chapter 7: Chump Change

215 **Opening stories:** Personal interviews with Jason Geller (December 14, 2011), "Lillian Bauer" (January 15, 2012), and Peter Audet (December 12, 2011, and January 19, 2012).

216 **consultants in a large professional services firm:** Diane M. Bergeron, Abbie J. Shipp, Benson Rosen, and Stacie A. Furst, "Organizational Citizenship Behavior and Career Outcomes: The Cost of Being a Good Citizen," *Journal of Management* (forthcoming).

220 **victims of crimes:** Robert Homant, "Risky Altruism as a Predictor of Criminal Victimization," *Criminal Justice and Behavior* 37 (2010): 1195–1216.

220 **thin slicing:** Malcolm Gladwell, *Blink: The Power of Thinking Without Thinking* (New York: Back Bay Books, 2007); and Nalini Ambady and Robert Rosenthal, "Half a Minute: Predicting Teacher Evaluations from Thin Slices of Nonverbal Behavior and Physical Attractiveness," *Journal of Personality and Social Psychology* 64 (1993): 431–441.

221 **close friends:** Stephen Leider, Markus M. Mobius, Tanya Rosenblat, and Quoc-Anh Do, "What Do We Expect from Our Friends?" *Journal of the European Economic Association* 8 (2010): 120–138.

221 **agreeableness:** Lauri A. Jensen-Campbell, Jennifer M. Knack, and Haylie L. Gomez, "The Psychology of Nice People," *Social and Personality Psychology Compass* 4 (2010): 1042–1056.

221n **scan the brains:** Colin G. DeYoung, Jacob B. Hirsh, Matthew S. Shane, Xenophon Papademetris, Nallakkandi Rajeevan, and Jeremy R. Gray, "Testing Predictions from Personality Neuroscience: Brain Structure and the Big Five," *Psychological Science* 21 (2010): 820–828.

222 **regardless of whether our personalities trend agreeable or disagreeable:** on the distinction between compassion and politeness, see Colin G. DeYoung, Lena C. Quilty, and Jordan B. Peterson, "Between Facets and Domains: 10 Aspects of the Big Five," *Journal of Personality and Social Psychology* 93 (2007): 880–896; on compassion connecting more strongly to honesty and humility than agreeableness, see Michael C. Ashton and Kibeom Lee, "Empirical, Theoretical, and Practical Advantages of the HEXACO Model of Personality Structure," *Personality and Social Psychology Review* 11 (2007): 150–166; on distinguishing agreeableness from giver values, see Sonia Roccas, Lilach Sagiv, Shalom H. Schwartz, and

Ariel Knafo, "The Big Five Personality Factors and Personal Values," *Personality and Social Psychology Bulletin* 28 (2002): 789–801.

222 **Mike Homer:** Personal interviews with Danny Shader (February 13, 2012), Greg Sands (March 5, 2012), and an anonymous mentee (February 28, 2012).

223 **givers are more accurate:** Dawne S. Vogt and C. Randall Colvin, "Interpersonal Orientation and the Accuracy of Personality Judgments," *Journal of Personality* 71 (2003): 267–295.

223 **givers become sensitive to individual differences:** Harold H. Kelley and Anthony J. Stahelski, "The Inference of Intentions from Moves in the Prisoner's Dilemma Game," *Journal of Experimental Social Psychology* 6 (1970): 401–419; see also Nancy L. Carter and J. Mark Weber, "Not Pollyannas: Higher Generalized Trust Predicts Lie Detection Ability," *Social Psychological and Personality Science* 1 (2010): 274–279.

226 **Strangers and dating couples:** William R. Fry, Ira J. Firestone, and David L. Williams, "Negotiation Process and Outcome of Stranger Dyads and Dating Couples: Do Lovers Lose?" *Basic and Applied Social Psychology* 4 (1983): 1–16.

227 **appeal to Rich's self-interest:** see E. Gil Clary, Mark Snyder, Robert D. Ridge, Peter K. Miene, and Julie A. Haugen, "Matching Messages to Motives in Persuasion: A Functional Approach to Promoting Volunteerism," *Journal of Applied Social Psychology* 24 (1994): 1129–1149.

227 **empathize at the bargaining table:** Adam D. Galinsky, William W. Maddux, Debra Gilin, and Judith B. White, "Why It Pays to Get Inside the Head of Your Opponent: The Differential Effects of Perspective Taking and Empathy on Negotiation," *Psychological Science* 19 (2008): 378–384.

227–228n **"veterinarians who empathized with their customers charged them lower prices":** William L. Cron, Mary C. Gilly, John L. Graham, and John W. Slocum Jr., "Gender Differences in the Pricing of Professional Services: Implications for Income and Customer Relationships," *Organizational Behavior and Human Decision Processes* 109 (2009): 93–105.

229 **cooperative when working with cooperative partners:** Paul A. M. Van Lange, "The Pursuit of Joint Outcomes and Equality in Outcomes: An Integrative Model of Social Value Orientation," *Journal of Personality and Social Psychology* 77 (1999): 337–349; see also Jennifer Chatman and Sigal Barsade, "Personality, Organizational Culture, and Cooperation: Evidence from a Business Simulation," *Administrative Science Quarterly*

40 (1995): 423–443.

229 *tit for tat:* Martin A. Nowak and Roger Highfield, *SuperCooperators: Altruism, Evolution, and Why We Need Each Other to Succeed* (New York: Free Press, 2011), 36.

230 **optimistic belief:** Randy Pausch and Jeffrey Zaslow, *The Last Lecture* (New York: Hyperion, 2008), 145.

230 **Abraham Lincoln:** Doris Kearns Goodwin, *Team of Rivals: The Political Genius of Abraham Lincoln* (New York: Simon & Schuster, 2006), 104.

233 **men were earning substantially more money:** Linda Babcock and Sara Laschever, *Women Don't Ask: The High Cost of Avoiding Negotiation—and Positive Strategies for Change* (New York: Bantam, 2007); Deborah A. Small, Michele Gelfand, Linda Babcock, and Hilary Gettman, "Who Goes to the Bargaining Table? The Influence of Gender and Framing on the Initiation of Negotiation," *Journal of Personality and Social Psychology* 93 (2007): 600–613.

234n **are women more likely to be givers than men?:** Alice H. Eagly and Maureen Crowley, "Gender and Helping Behavior: A Meta-Analytic Review of the Social Psychological Literature," *Psychological Bulletin* 100 (1986): 283–308.

234–235n **"but only when told that their empathy was being tested":** William Ickes, Paul R. Gesn, and Tiffany Graham, "Gender Differences in Empathic Accuracy: Differential Ability or Differential Motivation?" *Personal Relationships* 7 (2000): 95–109.

235 **large concessions:** Emily T. Amanatullah, Michael W. Morris, and Jared R. Curhan, "Negotiators Who Give Too Much: Unmitigated Communion, Relational Anxieties, and Economic Costs in Distributive and Integrative Bargaining," *Journal of Personality and Social Psychology* 95 (2008): 723–738.

235 **income penalty:** Timothy A. Judge, Beth A. Livingston, and Charlice Hurst, "Do Nice Guys—and Gals—Really Finish Last? The Joint Effects of Sex and Agreeableness on Income," *Journal of Personality and Social Psychology* 102 (2012): 390–407.

235n **"giving is sometimes more rewarding for men than women":** Madeline E. Heilman and Julie J. Chen, "Same Behavior, Different Consequences: Reactions to Men's and Women's Altruistic Citizenship Behavior," *Journal of Applied Psychology* 90 (2005): 431–441.

235n **"gender may be an amplifier of giver success and failure":** Adam M.

Grant, "Do Women Civilize Men?" *LinkedIn Influencers*, Jul 23, 2013, www.linkedin.com/today/post/article/20130723030236-69244073-do-women-really-civilize-men

236 **Studies in more controlled settings:** Bruce Barry and Raymond A. Friedman, "Bargainer Characteristics in Distributive and Integrative Negotiation," *Journal of Personality and Social Psychology* 74 (1998): 345–359.

236n **second factor at play:** see Lilach Sagiv, "Vocational Interests and Basic Values," *Journal of Career Assessment* 10 (2002): 233–257; Idit Ben-Shem and Tamara E. Avi-Itzhak, "On Work Values and Career Choice in Freshmen Students: The Case of Helping vs. Other Professions," *Journal of Vocational Behavior* 39 (1991): 369–379; Jeylan T. Mortimer and Jon Lorence, "Work Experience and Occupational Value Socialization: A Longitudinal Study," *American Journal of Sociology* 84 (1979): 1361–1385; and Robert H. Frank, "What Price the Moral High Ground?" *Southern Economic Journal* 63 (1996): 1–17.

236 **Sameer Jain:** Personal interview (December 16, 2011).

237 **176 senior executives:** Hannah Riley Bowles, Linda Babcock, and Kathleen L. McGinn, "Constraints and Triggers: Situational Mechanics of Gender in Negotiation," *Journal of Personality and Social Psychology* 89 (2005): 951–965.

238 **negotiated on behalf of a friend:** Emily T. Amanatullah and Michael W. Morris, "Negotiating Gender Roles: Gender Differences in Assertive Negotiating Are Mediated by Women's Fear of Backlash and Attenuated When Negotiating on Behalf of Others," *Journal of Personality and Social Psychology* 98 (2010): 256–267.

241 *relational account:* Hannah Riley Bowles and Linda Babcock, "Relational Accounts: A Strategy for Women Negotiating for Higher Compensation" (working paper, 2011).

247 **twenty-eight different studies:** Carsten K. W. De Dreu, Laurie R. Weingart, and Seungwoo Kwon, "Influence of Social Motives on Integrative Negotiation: A Meta-Analytic Review and Test of Two Theories," *Journal of Personality and Social Psychology* 78 (2000): 889–905.

248–249 **becomes second nature:** Brian R. Little, "Free Traits, Personal Projects and Idio-Tapes: Three Tiers for Personality Research," *Psychological Inquiry* 7 (1996): 340–344; and "Free Traits and Personal Contexts: Expanding a Social Ecological Model of Well-Being," in

Person-Environment Psychology, 2nd edn, ed. W. Bruce Walsh, Kenneth H. Craik, and Richard H. Price (New York: Guilford Press, 2000): 87–116.

Chapter 8: The Scrooge Shift

250 **Opening quote:** Adam Smith, *The Theory of Moral Sentiments* (Kila, MT: Kessinger Publishing, 1759/2004), 3.

250 **Craigslist:** Jenna Lloyd and Sherry K. Gunter, *craigslist 4 Everyone* (New York: Pearson Education, 2008).

251 **Freecycle:** Personal interview with Deron Beal (June 19, 2012); Richard Jerome, "Free for All," *People*, May 10, 2004; Deron Beal and S. James Snyder, "Power of One," *Time*, November 30, 2009; and Carol Brennan, "Deron Beal," *Encyclopedia of World Biography*, 2005.

252 **what drives people to participate in exchange systems:** Robb Willer, Francis J. Flynn, and Sonya Zak, "Structure, Identity, and Solidarity: A Comparative Field Study of Generalized and Direct Exchange," *Administrative Science Quarterly* 57 (2012): 119–155.

255 **defendant of pure altruism:** C. Daniel Batson, "How Social an Animal? The Human Capacity for Caring," *American Psychologist* 45 (1990): 336–346; and C. Daniel Batson, Karen Sager, Eric Garst, Misook Kang, Kostia Rubchinsky, and Karen Dawson, "Is Empathy-Induced Helping Due to Self-Other Merging?" *Journal of Personality and Social Psychology* 73 (1997): 495–509.

255 **devil's advocate:** Robert B. Cialdini, Stephanie L. Brown, Brian P. Lewis, Carol Luce, and Steven L. Neuberg, "Reinterpreting the Empathy-Altruism Relationship: When One into One Equals Oneness," *Journal of Personality and Social Psychology* 73 (1997): 481–494; and Jon K. Maner, Carol L. Luce, Steven L. Neuberg, Robert B. Cialdini, Stephanie L. Brown, and Brad J. Sagarin, "The Effects of Perspective Taking on Motivations for Helping: Still No Evidence for Altruism," *Personality and Social Psychology Bulletin* 28 (2002): 1601–1610.

258 **red herring:** Frans de Waal, *The Age of Empathy* (New York: Crown, 2009), 75.

259 **writing Wikipedia entries:** Oded Nov, "What Motivates Wikipedians?" *Communications of the ACM* 50 (2007): 60–64; see also Joachim Schroer and Guido Hertel, "Voluntary Engagement in an Open

Web-Based Encyclopedia: Wikipedians and Why They Do It," *Media Psychology* 12 (2009): 96–120.

260 **lead partner:** Personal interview with "Phillippe" (January 24, 2012).

261 **Common ground:** Mark Levine, Amy Prosser, David Evans, and Stephen Reicher, "Identity and Emergency Intervention: How Social Group Membership and Inclusiveness of Group Boundaries Shape Helping Behavior," *Personality and Social Psychology Bulletin* 31 (2005): 443–453.

261 **"common identity":** John F. Dovidio, Samuel L. Gaertner, Ana Validzic, Kimberly Matoka, Brenda Johnson, and Stacy Frazier, "Extending the Benefits of Recategorization: Evaluations, Self-Disclosure, and Helping," *Journal of Experimental Social Psychology* 33 (1997): 401–420.

264 **"when people received help from one peer, they were more likely to give help to another peer":** Leonard Berkowitz and Louise R. Daniels, "Responsibility and Dependency," *Journal of Abnormal and Social Psychology* 66 (1963): 429–436.

264 **another man named Adam Rifkin:** Personal interviews with Panda Adam Rifkin (January 28, 2012) and Hollywood Adam Rifkin (February 2, 2012). For the full story of how the two Adam Rifkins met, see www.ifindkarma.com/attic/local/realadam.html and www.ifindkarma.com/attic/local/denial.html.

266 **remind us of ourselves:** Brett W. Pelham, Matthew C. Mirenberg, and John T. Jones, "Why Susie Sells Seashells by the Seashore: Implicit Egotism and Major Life Decisions," *Journal of Personality and Social Psychology* 82 (2002): 469–487; John T. Jones, Brett W. Pelham, Matthew C. Mirenberg, and John J. Hetts, "Name Letter Preferences Are Not Merely Mere Exposure: Implicit Egotism as Self-Regulation," *Journal of Experimental Social Psychology* 38 (2002): 170–177; Brett W. Pelham, Mauricio Carvallo, and John T. Jones, "Implicit Egotism," *Current Directions in Psychological Science* 14 (2006): 106–110; and Ernest L. Abel, "Influence of Names on Career Choices in Medicine," *Names* 58 (2010): 65–74.

267 **attracted to potential dates:** John T. Jones, Brett W. Pelham, Mauricio Carvallo, and Matthew C. Mirenberg, "How Do I Love Thee? Let Me Count the Js: Implicit Egotism and Interpersonal Attraction," *Journal of Personality and Social Psychology* 87 (2004): 665–683.

267 **Kiva:** Jeff Galak, Deborah Small, and Andrew T. Stephen,

"Microfinance Decision Making: A Field Study of Prosocial Lending," *Journal of Marketing Research* XLVIII (2011): S130–S137.

267n **alternative explanations:** Uri Simonsohn, "Spurious? Name Similarity Effects (Implicit Egotism) in Marriage, Job, and Moving Decisions," *Journal of Personality and Social Psychology* 101 (2011): 1–24; Leif D. Nelson and Joseph P. Simmons, "Moniker Maladies: When Names Sabotage Success," *Psychological Science* 18 (2007): 1106–1112; Ernest L. Abel and Michael L. Kruger, "Symbolic Significance of Initials on Longevity," *Perceptual and Motor Skills* 104 (2007): 179–182; "Athletes, Doctors, and Lawyers with First Names Beginning with 'D' Die Sooner," *Death Studies* 34 (2010): 71–81; and Nicholas Christenfeld, David P. Phillips, and Laura M. Glynn, "What's in a Name: Mortality and the Power of Symbols," *Journal of Psychosomatic Research* 47 (1999): 241–254.

268 **"Googlegangers":** Stephanie Rosenbloom, "Names That Match Forge a Bond on the Internet," New York Times, April 10, 2008, accessed June 26, 2013, www.nytimes.com/2008/04/10/us/10names.html?_r=1&

269 **fingerprints:** Jerry M. Burger, Nicole Messian, Shebani Patel, Alicia del Prado, and Carmen Anderson, "What a Coincidence! The Effects of Incidental Similarity on Compliance," *Personality and Social Psychology Bulletin* 30 (2004): 35–43.

270 *optimal distinctiveness*: Marilynn B. Brewer, "The Importance of Being *We*: Human Nature and Intergroup Relations," *American Psychologist* 62 (2007): 728–738; and Kennon M. Sheldon and B. Ann Bettencourt, "Psychological Need-Satisfaction and Subjective Well-Being within Social Groups," *British Journal of Social Psychology* 41 (2002): 25–38.

271 *elevation*: Jonathan Haidt, "Elevation and the Positive Psychology of Morality," in *Flourishing: Positive Psychology and the Life Well-Lived*, ed. Corey L. M. Keyes and Jonathan Haidt (Washington, DC: American Psychological Association, 2003), 275–289; and Sara B. Algoe and Jonathan Haidt, "Witnessing Excellence in Action: The 'Other-Praising' Emotions of Elevation, Gratitude, and Admiration," *Journal of Positive Psychology* 4 (2009): 105–127.

272 **ten features of Superman:** Leif D. Nelson and Michael I. Norton, "From Student to Superhero: Situational Primes Shape Future Helping," *Journal of Experimental Social Psychology* 41 (2005): 423–430.

273 **"even a penny will help":** Robert B. Cialdini and David A. Schroeder, "Increasing Compliance by Legitimizing Paltry Contributions: When Even a Penny Helps," *Journal of Personality and Social Psychology* 34 (1976): 599–604; for a recent extension, see Sachiyo M. Shearman and Jina H. Yoo, "Even a Penny Will Help! Legitimization of Paltry Donation and Social Proof in Soliciting Donation to a Charitable Organization," *Communication Research Reports* 24 (2007): 271–282.

273 **energy consumption:** Jessica M. Nolan, P. Wesley Schultz, Robert B. Cialdini, Noah J. Goldstein, and Vladas Griskevicius, "Normative Social Influence Is Underdetected," *Personality and Social Psychology Bulletin* 34 (2008): 913–923; P. Wesley Schultz, Jessica M. Nolan, Robert B. Cialdini, Noah J. Goldstein, and Vladas Griskevicius, "The Constructive, Destructive, and Reconstructive Power of Social Norms," *Psychological Science* 18 (2007): 429–434; and Hunt Alcott, "Social Norms and Energy Conservation," MIT Center for Energy and Environmental Policy Research (working paper, 2009).

277 **"ready to aid one another":** Charles Darwin, *The Descent of Man and Selection in Relation to Sex* (London: Murray, 1871).

279 **underestimating the givers:** Francis J. Flynn and Vanessa K. B. Lake (now Bohns), "If You Need Help, Just Ask: Underestimating Compliance with Direct Requests for Help," *Journal of Personality and Social Psychology* 95 (2008): 128–143.

280 **only natural to assume:** Dale T. Miller, "The Norm of Self-Interest," *American Psychologist* 54 (1999): 1053–1060.

280 **"explaining almost every act of their lives on the principle of self-interest":** Alexis de Tocqueville, *Democracy in America* (Garden City, NY: Anchor Press, 1835/1969), 526.

281 **"social norms against sounding too charitable":** Robert Wuthnow, *Acts of Compassion* (Princeton, NJ: Princeton University Press, 1993).

281 **"no one believes":** David Krech and Richard S. Crutchfield, *Theory and Problems of Social Psychology* (New York: McGraw-Hill, 1948).

281 **Harvard freshmen:** Stephanie Garlock and Hana Rouse, "Harvard Most Values Success, 2014 Says," *Harvard Crimson*, September 2, 2011; "Harvard College Introduces Pledge for Freshmen to Affirm Values," *Harvard Crimson*, September 1, 2011; and Hana Rouse, "College to Remove Signatures from Freshman Kindness Pledge," *Harvard Crimson*, September 7, 2011.

281 **"Ideas can have profound effects":** Barry Schwartz, "Psychology, Idea Technology, and Ideology," *Psychological Science* 8 (1997): 21–27.

283 **Reciprocity Ring:** Wayne Baker and Adam M. Grant, "Values and Contributions in the Reciprocity Ring" (working paper, 2007).

283 **reputational benefits:** Dan Ariely, Anat Bracha, and Stephan Meier, "Doing Good or Doing Well? Image Motivation and Monetary Incentives in Behaving Prosocially," *American Economic Review* 99 (2009): 544–555.

284 **brainstorming:** Harry M. Wallace and Roy F. Baumeister, "The Performance of Narcissists Rises and Falls with Perceived Opportunity for Glory," *Journal of Personality and Social Psychology* 82 (2002): 819–834.

284 **go green to be seen:** Vladas Griskevicius, Joshua M. Tybur, and Bram Van den Bergh, "Going Green to Be Seen: Status, Reputation, and Conspicuous Conservation," *Journal of Personality and Social Psychology* 98 (2010): 392–404.

284 **bank tellers:** Chun Hui, Simon S. K. Lam, and Kenneth K. S. Law, "Instrumental Values of Organizational Citizenship Behavior for Promotion: A Field Quasi-Experiment," *Journal of Applied Psychology* 85 (2000): 822–828.

285 **"sets a terrible precedent":** Harry Lewis, "The Freshman Pledge," Blogspot, August 20, 2011, http://harry-lewis.blogspot.com/2011/08/freshman-pledge.html.

286 **people made their identity plans known to others:** Peter M. Gollwitzer, Paschal Sheeran, Verena Michalski, and Andrea E. Seifert, "When Intentions Go Public: Does Social Reality Widen the Intention-Behavior Gap?" *Psychological Science* 20 (2009): 612–618.

286 **might backfire:** Sonya Sachdeva, Rumen Iliev, and Douglas L. Medin, "Sinning Saints and Saintly Sinners: The Paradox of Moral Self-Regulation," *Psychological Science* 20 (2009): 523–528.

287 **attribute it to an external reason:** C. Daniel Batson, Jay S. Coke, M. L. Jasnoski, and Michael Hanson, "Buying Kindness: Effect of an Extrinsic Incentive for Helping on Perceived Altruism," *Personality and Social Psychology Bulletin* 4 (1978): 86–91; and Ziva Kunda and Shalom H. Schwartz, "Undermining Intrinsic Moral Motivation: External Reward and Self-Presentation," *Journal of Personality and Social Psychology* 45 (1983): 763–771.

287 **To paraphrase the writer:** E. M. Forster, *Aspects of the Novel* (New York: Penguin Classics, 1927/2005).

287 **important aspect of their identities:** Marcia A. Finkelstein, Louis A. Penner, and Michael T. Brannick, "Motive, Role Identity, and Prosocial Personality as Predictors of Volunteer Activity," *Social Behavior and Personality* 33 (2005): 403–418; Adam M. Grant and Jane E. Dutton, "Beneficiary or Benefactor: Are People More Prosocial When They Reflect on Receiving or Giving?" *Psychological Science* 23 (2012): 1033–1039; and Adam M. Grant, "Giving Time, Time After Time: Work Design and Sustained Employee Participation in Corporate Volunteering," *Academy of Management Review* 37 (2012): 589–615.

287–288n *Fortune* **500 retail company:** Adam M. Grant, Jane E. Dutton, and Brent D. Rosso, "Giving Commitment: Employee Support Programs and the Prosocial Sensemaking Process," *Academy of Management Journal* 51 (2008): 898–918.

Chapter 9: Out of the Shadows

289 **Opening quote:** Marcus Aurelius, *Meditations* (New York: Random House, 2002), trans. Gregory Hays, 55.

289 **Derek Sorenson:** Personal interview (January 11, 2012).

291 **sharper negotiators:** Bruce Barry and Raymond A. Friedman, "Bargainer Characteristics in Distributive and Integrative Negotiation," *Journal of Personality and Social Psychology* 74 (1998): 345–359.

294 **Sherryann Plesse:** Personal interview (April 13, 2012).

296 **Peter Audet:** Personal correspondence (July 1, 2012).

297 **"making significant, lasting contributions to a broad range of people":** Adam M. Grant, "Relational Job Design and the Motivation to Make a Prosocial Difference," *Academy of Management Review* 32 (2007): 393–417.

298 **"Givers advance the world":** Simon Sinek (https://twitter.com/simonsinek/status/262949144870649857)

Actions for Impact

302 **top-secret mission:** Personal interviews with Jay (April 19 and May 10, 2012) and his assistant (May 3, 2012).

303 **job crafting:** Amy Wrzesniewski, Justin M. Berg, Adam M. Grant, Jennifer Kurkoski, and Brian Welle, "Job Crafting in Motion: Achieving Sustainable Gains in Happiness and Performance" (working paper, 2012).

304 **Mercer study:** Corporate Executive Board, "Creating an Effective Reward and Recognition Program," March 2006, accessed May 12, 2012, www.performancesolutions.nc.gov/motivationInitiatives/ RewardsandRecognition/docs/CLC-Rewards&Recognition.pdf.

304 **Love Machine:** Personal interview with Chris Colosi (March 20, 2012).

305–306 **"One of my objectives is listening":** Personal interview with Jim Quigley (August 23, 2011).

306 **GetRaised:** Personal interview with Matt Wallaert (February 8, 2012).

306 **ServiceSpace:** Personal interview with Nipun Mehta (March 23, 2012).

307 **aggressively helpful:** The interviews about The Kindness Offensive were conducted by Laurence Lemaire and Matt Stevens with founders David Goodfellow, Benny Crane, James Hunter, and Rob Williams (March 3, 2012); and the interview with Ryan Garcia was conducted by Valentino Kim (March 20, 2012).

308 **BNI:** Personal interview with Ivan Misner (January 31, 2012).

309 **Start the spark:** Wayne Baker and Cheryl Baker, "Paying It Forward: How Reciprocity Really Works and How You Can Create It in Your Organization," University of Michigan, winter 2011, accessed May 14, 2012, http://www.bus.umich.edu/Positive/News/newsletter/2-23-11/ baker-paying.html

INDEX